GARDNER'S *guide to*

Creating
2D Animation

in a Small Studio

Bill Davis

GARTH GARDNER COMPANY

GGC publishing

Washington DC, USA · London, UK

D1287509

Acquisition Editor: Bonney Ford
Editor: Chris Edwards
Editorial Assistant: Benesia Babb
Layout: Rachelle Painchaud-Nash
Cover Design: Nic Banks
Publisher: Garth Gardner, Ph.D.

Editorial inquiries concerning this book should be mailed to: The Editor, Garth Gardner Company emailed to: info@ggcinc.com. http://www.GoGardner.com

Printed in Canada

Library of Congress Cataloging-in-Publication Data

Davis, Bill.
  Gardner's guide to creating 2D animation in a small studio / Bill Davis.
    p. cm. — (Gardner's guide series)
  Includes bibliographical references and index.
  ISBN 1-58965-007-7 (pbk.)
  1. Animation (Cinematography) I. Title: Guide to creating 2D animation in a small studio. II. Title. III. Series.
  TR897.5.D38 2006
  778.5'347—dc22
                        2004001747

This book is dedicated to anyone and everyone who cannot imagine a day without drawing.

ACKNOWLEDGEMENT

I'm not sure if there's a specific order to an acknowledgement page. Chronological or by importance? When you stop and think about a 34-year career and all of the people you've met, shared information with, and learned from, it can be overwhelming. All of them are important, though not all of them are remembered. Should I go back as far as the age of ten when my uncle, Harley Brown, showed me some sketches that he had done? Or only as far back as Louise James from San Fernando Junior High, or Mrs. Garcia from San Fernando High School, or Mrs. Lake and Mr. Torek from Dorsey High School? I learned that Art (with a capital 'A') exists from these folks.

Vitally important to getting the career started was/were the Bill Tara (the late), Bill Pajaud, Marv Rubin, Gene Holtan, Archie Boston, Don Weller, John Miyauchi, Bill Brown, Chris Jenkins, Charles White the third (the black one), Dave Brain, Dave Bhang, and all of the guest instructors from the Tutor Arts Program Saturday classes in the basement of the Old Otis Art Institute. I learned that Art (with a capital 'A') can be an achievable career goal from these folks.

Sam Weiss and Nick Bosustow deserve great thanks for giving me my very first job. Bob Johnson, Tony Rivetti, Lou Melendez, too. Thanks also to Dan Bessie and Ben Norman, from this particular patch of the past.

Corny Cole has to receive a very special thank you, because, he is probably the most responsible for me being an animator, and for tenaciously holding on to the capital 'A' of Art when others were merely whizzing it out. Corny's mention should have been one of those 'last but not least' things, but I couldn't be certain that he would read all the way to the end.

The actual 'last, but not least' goes to Sam Kirson, Fine Artist and occasional maniac, who served as a model for Artistic Tenacity, and who introduced me to Colleen, my wife and Vital Chunk.

So there,
Bill Davis

FOREWORD

Every year I run into animators who don't know what to do with themselves. Fuelled by a tendency to polarize the world, they seem to believe that their road in animation is paved only two ways: studio or starvation. Working for 'the man' (i.e., Disney or Warner) would pay pretty well, they argue, but it wouldn't offer much in the way of creative satisfaction. Conversely, doing an independent project would fill the creative void, but not the bank account. It doesn't have to be this way and in most cases, it isn't.

First of all, many animators find the big studio environment to be creatively rewarding. They like the team atmosphere and value the chance to provide input into the production. Secondly, I don't know of a single independent animator who has starved to death. Yuri Norstein, Priit Pärn, Igor Kovalyov, Jerzy Kucia, George Griffin, Piotr Dumala, Caroline Leaf, Wendy Tilby, Frederick Back—to name some of the giants of independent animation—have all worked on a variety of commissioned jobs ranging from commercials and TV Shows to feature animation.

It's not like they have a choice, though. Despite an invasion of TV channels and multi-media outlets, distribution and exhibition of independent animation remains severely limited. Unless you're Bill Plympton (the single most successful independent animator around) your chances of seeing anything close to a profit for your personal work is less than minimal. No one is immune from food and that's why many animators have struck a deal somewhere in the middle by creating their own small (or 'boutique') studios. Bolex Brothers (U.K.), Filmtecknarna (Sweden), Cuppa Coffee (Canada), Eesti Joonisfilm (Estonia), Folimage (France), and Wild Brain (U.S.A.) are just a few examples of small studios that have successfully straddled the line between commissioned and non-commissioned work. Let's not forget that both Aardman Animation and Pixar (not to mention Walt Disney)—now big time studios—were once fledgling studios whose output consisted primarily of independently produced short films.

The key to success for these small studios has been economic, structural, aesthetic flexibility, and, ultimately, faith in their own creative skills. All of the studios above have done their share of 'hired gun' jobs, but they've also attracted clients because of their unique styles and visions. Paul Fierlinger, for example, hasn't made a non-commissioned film and yet no matter the client, his work—featuring his sketchy, minimal style—always seems like an independent production. For that matter, every time you see those Charmin ads featuring a big brown bear, you're also looking at the very familiar drawing of U.K. indie animator, Joanna Quinn *(Body Beautiful).*

Of course, none of these success stories happened overnight. Even with improvements in technology, starting your own studio can be a pretty daunting task, especially if you're a young animator fresh out of school. Unfortunately, while many animation schools do a great job preparing and nurturing students creatively, rarely do they provide them with the tools needed to survive on their own. It's almost as if schools don't see starting your own studio as an option. I've grumbled many times during school visits or Ottawa Animation Festivals about this void because it's one thing to prattle on and on about success stories to animators, but quite another to give them the cold, hard facts needed to start their own studio.

Clearly someone was listening to my mumbling moans because Bill Davis' book is the very thing animators—whether student or veteran—need. In a lucid and lighthearted manner, Davis covers all the basics you need to get out there and pave your own road.

Now there can be no more excuses.

Use this book well my friends.

Chris Robinson
Artistic Director
Ottawa International Animation Festival

CONTENTS

INTRODUCTION

Creating 2D Animation in a Small Studio is written primarily for artists who would like to produce animation in a small studio or as a freelance artist. If you're a student with very little or no professional experience, you will also be able to benefit from this book. If you're already an established professional or company, you may find it interesting or helpful to see how another company approaches their work, perhaps adding alternate techniques to your own per-

sonal methods, and coming out in the end with an even better system.

Terms of Enlightenment

Let's begin with some of the terms you will see throughout this book. Animation that is drawn on paper is referred to as **Traditional Animation.** Of course, you can also draw directly on acetate cels, even tin foil or gum wrappers. Any surface that accepts an image can be aligned with other images and then played back for viewing. You can also use cutouts or collages or even objects to employ the principles of animation. These alternate methods mentioned are really more experimental, but they all produce a sequence of images that can be shown in rapid succession to produce the illusion of motion. The overall approach in this book is based on this basic form of animation—drawn animation.

Traditional Cel on Film Production is the phrase used to describe the methods, tools, and steps used to add color and environment (backgrounds) to a project and the path to the project's final delivery form. In Traditional Cel on Film Production, the animation drawings are transferred to acetate cels and painted on the back of the cel, behind the image. The painted cels are placed on top of backgrounds and shot onto film using an animation camera. The film is then developed and used as the basis for the project's final delivery form. The fact that an animation project is produced using traditional techniques doesn't restrict its final delivery form. The film elements can be mixed with audio and delivered as a film, transferred to video, or digitized for further manipulation or digital usage. Traditional methods can be more time consuming, costly, and labor intensive with fewer options, though, and should be considered seriously.

Digital Production is the term used to describe the methods, tools, and steps used to add color and environment to a project and the path taken to the project's final delivery form using digital methods.

Both methods start with the same animation drawings. Using digital methods, the artwork is **scanned** into the computer where they are 'painted' using the tools in an animation or paint program, then **composited** in an animation or compositing program's digital exposure sheets or timeline (compiled, composed, and combined with the background or other visual or even audio elements), then output to the final delivery form—video, digital file, or even film. Digital production can also be entirely **CGI (C**omputer **G**enerated **I**mages).

The skills and steps involved in traditional animation will be first explained in terms of traditional cel on film production, then explained and expanded in terms of digital production, the prevailing, if not default, mode. Explaining in terms of traditional cel first gives a better foundation of knowledge and understanding, even a touch of historical context. There are digital terms and concepts that are based on traditional terms and concepts: Digital 'layers' are based on the animation concept of 'cel levels.' 'Paint Behind the Line' modes of digital painting are based on the fact that transparent animation cels are flipped over and painted on the reverse side 'behind' the drawn lines (there's more on that step in the Ink & Paint chapter and in the Appendix).

About the Author: Bill Davis

For some reason, I can remember all the way back to when I was about three- or four-years-old. In my mind's eye, I can vividly see the old television set, and on that television is animation. Mickey Mouse, Mighty Mouse, Heckle and Jeckle, (my Dad's favorite), and Mr. Magoo. I thought the animated characters might have been life forms unto themselves (actually the 'life form' concept didn't happen until

the mid-1960s when Star Trek came on, but you get the idea).

I loved animation. I didn't know how it was done, but I was constantly commandeering my mother's ball-point pens and using them to profusely produce artwork on brown paper bags and the classifieds section of the news-paper. Drawing and animation have nearly always been a part of my life. I was probably born to be an animator.

My original career goal in life was to be an illustrator and drawer of funny pictures like my heroes Mort Drucker and Jack Davis in Mad magazine. In high school, I was fortunate enough to receive a scholarship to what was called the Tutor Art Program and went to Otis Art Institute on Saturdays. Advertising, Illustration, and Life Drawing were the main topics. I was on my way to Illustration Land. At the beginning of the second year something new was added: ANIMATION! I had finally actually found out how cartoons were made. What a revelation! But at first I was not

impressed. All those drawings of essentially the same thing. All those other people involved? The artistic compromises? Drawing characters that had to be simplified so that other people could 'follow-up' and assist you? Make a deal with a camera service?

About My Partner: Colleen Davis

Colleen Davis, my wife and partner, started her professional career with the desire to be an art teacher. Since the majority of the work that Artbear Pigmation produces is educational in nature, she is still somewhat of a teacher. Colleen is actually more of a fine arts and crafts person than a commercial animation type artist. In spite of having worked in graphic design at Lehn and Fink in the 1960s, she is primarily a painter who stumbled into a job doing animation painting and wasn't able to free herself because she picked up 200 pounds of animator husband (me), and the realization that this animation thing is a profitable outlet for her ability to do repeatable creativity. In other words, that was nice—now do it 500 more times. By tomorrow afternoon.

Colleen and I spent two decades producing traditional animation on cel before incorporating and finally switching over completely to producing our work on computer. We started in Los Angeles in the 1970s, later moved to South Nyack, New York (about 20 miles north of NYC), and finally, to our present location in Ithaca, New York. To give you an indication of where we are now, one of the popular local T-Shirts has the inscription "Ithaca, NY: Centrally Isolated." Later, we found out just how true that statement is.

Each move has taken us further away from vital services related to our work. We either had to purchase an animation camera and a laboratory or find another solution to the problem. The need and desire for, along with a willingness to try something new, electric, and self-contained arose, and we bit the bullet and bought a computer.

I had gained a bit of computer experience while working as an illustrator on staff at the Water Resources Institute at Cornell University (one of those slow periods, post-move that a small company/freelance folks go through). The experience was exhilarating and led to the purchase of a Hewlett Packard 286 from Sears. It was

occasionally fun, but wasn't really up to the challenge. Fortunately, we were lead to digital wonderland by graphic designer Jeff Speiser (of OffBeat Design), who at that point in time was a Cornell University student and our intern. He had been working with computers since he was a kid and helped us make some good choices. We decided on the

Macintosh platform and purchased an IIfx. That particular computer is still in use, hooked up to the Betacam SP for the occasional non-digital output.

We were on our way and thrilled with the capability of producing digital art and combining it with our scanned traditional animation. But output was still a problem. Our second purchase was a Sony BVW-75 Betacam SP recorder. Our studio now had the elements we needed to produce traditional animation in the digital world from script to broadcast quality video.

Over the years, we have learned to produce a high-quality product in an efficient and cost-effective way, using methods and shortcuts gained through experience that we feel add to, not subtract, from the product. Something vital to the survival of a small studio. We're passing along this information in the form of this book, feeling justified, perhaps, because as we move forward into a more computerized world, we've noticed certain things:

- The rising demand for animated content.
- The rising number of people doing it.
- The rising number of people doing it rather poorly.
- Clients expecting more for less and getting it because of the abundance of suppliers.

The Goal of This Book

The goal of this book is to impart the information learned from 30 years of experience doing animation in a small studio. The approach will be traditional, using the basic steps: script, storyboard, design, and drawing. And of course, the role of the computer will be dealt with at every opportunity.

The information and approaches in this book represent the way we at ArtBear happen to work. These techniques work for us, but they are not the only way to do things.

There is one final thing to mention. Books of this helpful, how-to nature tend to have icons that guide or denote specific types of information being given; hints, shortcuts, warnings, and the like. It seemed logical to me that the icons should represent the various functions and departments in the animation studio that the information most relates to. The icons take the form of bears because:

- I couldn't resist drawing caricatures of people I have worked with, and if I do, they might see this book and get upset or something and I wouldn't want that. And,

- A bear is a part of the company name and logo and I'm feeling shameless tonight.

It is possible for the skills and functions in the icon descriptions to be contained in fewer people. Even one person. In a small studio, this compression of skills and functions is the norm. In a student, the default. The job descriptions, explained briefly, and in their simplest primal forms are:

Producer: The person at the top of the whole hierarchy that controls and coordinates everything, dealing with the finances, the clients, and the talent. This is the person that has the final word and gets the credit or the blame for the project's success. Ideally, the Producer is the visionary behind the whole operation.

Director: The person that guides, oversees, directs, and 'times' the animation to set the pace and flow of the action. The Director makes sure that the original concepts are correctly translated to the final animated form. This person controls all aspects of the production down in 'the trenches' where the actual work is done.

Storyboard Artist: The person that translates the written ideas and descriptions of the script into the visualized sequence of images that guide the production: the storyboard.

Designer: The special creative lifeform that sets the 'look' of the piece, designing the characters, backgrounds, and all the necessary visual bits.

Layout Artist: The person who translates the storyboard into drawings that the animator and background artist use as guides.

Animator: The person responsible for doing the drawings that convey the basic timing and motion.

Assistant Animator: The person who produces the inbetween drawings that fill in the timing and action.

Ink & Paint Person: The one who adds color to the artwork.

Camera Person: The one that records the animation artwork and backgrounds to film in a traditionally produced piece.

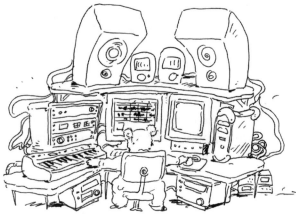

Audio Person or Sound Designer: Refers to the person or department concerned with recording, voices, music, sound effects, track readings, and all things audio.

Editor: The person that coordinates, organizes, and cuts together film or video and audio elements in a traditionally produced film. The Editor is the person that 'reads' the audio tracks and gives the Animators the timings and phonetic break-downs of the dialogue for lip syncing.

Compositor: The person that coordinates, organizes, and digitally combines the animation elements for output in a digital setting.

These will suffice for the purposes of this book, though there are more categories, of course, depending upon the size and complexity of your 'operation.' For example, in the animation department, there are artists who specialize in special effects like mechanical actions or water ripples and other natural phenomena as opposed to character animation. The ink & paint department has a category for a checker, a person that makes sure that all of the elements exist and work together correctly and another category for a person that cleans and polishes cels. The category of Producer also has many sub-categories: Executive Producer, Associate Producer, Assistant Producer, Line Producer, Ample-Mammaried Girlfriend, and Nephew to name a few. See why I chose bears?

That's about all of the introductory material that you'll need to begin making use of this book. Anything that has been forgotten or left out will be injected as we move along.

Let's get started with *Chapter 1: An Introduction to Animation.*

CHAPTER 1
AN INTRODUCTION TO ANIMATION

In the Beginning...

Several thousand years ago, the real "back-in-the-day," there was this dejected, rejected, bored, and zitty little cave dweller. A bit of a loner, a bit of an outcast, still living at home with Mama and Daddy, he sat cold and alone on his stony sofa. Perhaps through some pre-historic divine inspiration, or a bit of dislodged ceiling, he was struck by an idea. Rushing to his room and grabbing a piece of charred vine he had rescued from the cooking fire for just this sort

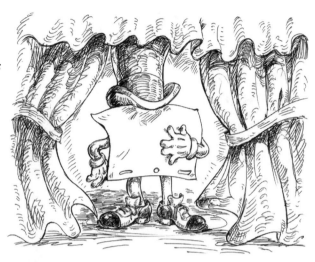

of occasion, he proceeds to pictorially pour out his heart on the cavern walls. As he sits in the glow of the flickering nightlight, his imagination takes hold and he sees the images move. This animated reverie is interrupted by the slam of the rock door of the cave entrance.

Mom and Dad are home and, of course, pitch a pterodactyl about the unauthorized cave decorations. The artist's punishment is to re-draw the decorations a thousand times. Off to the quarry he goes to chisel his 'canvases' from the rock. Canvases cut, the artist begins to draw, but each copy is altered slightly just for inspiration. With the task finished, and the stack of drawings

leaning against the side of the quarry, the artist climbs downhill and heads for home. There is a rumble. The artist looks over his shoulder to discover the cause. It seems the pterodactyl that Mom and Dad pitched has just landed on and dislodged the stack of stone art, sending the drawings tumbling down the hill toward the artist. As they tumble toward him, he is treated to the drawings in motion. Animation is invented, or perhaps discovered. The artist is unfortunately crushed, and personkind is forced to wait until the early part of the 20th century and the films of Emile Cohl, James Stuart Blackton, and the great Winsor McKay.

That little artificial history of animation appearing above wasn't just a spontaneous writing exercise. We will be using it as the subject of a few tutorials in the book, illustrating some of the various steps of animation production like storyboard, layout, audio, and character animation. By the end of the book, you will have some 'hands on' experience, perhaps a few new resources, and, hopefully, the ability to move forward on your own. And now let's learn the real history of animation, however brief it may be.

A Brief History of Animation

There is a long, rich history of discovery and invention in the field of optics and visual effects that led up to the traditional animation that we know today. It began with the work of Athanusius Kircher, a German priest and mathematician, and his invention of the first (rather crude) slide projector back in 1644. He also worked extensively on those antique light projecting devices known as "magic lanterns." The next time you're stuck watching someone's boring vacation slide presentation, thank Kircher.

Next, came Claude Milliet de Chales' work with lenses, the eye, and optics in general. He developed a two-lens system for the existing magic-lantern designs. This enabled the lantern to project a more focused image for a greater distance. He also discovered that the eye really perceives color and light not objects and motion.

The work of scientist and teacher William Molyneux in the 1690s came next. He further refined the magic lantern by developing lenses with adjustable focus. These were the foundation of today's projectors.

There was also the development of the kinetograph, the kinetoscope, an early motion picture camera and the viewer that went along with it, developed at Thomas Edison's laboratory. It was Edison along with one of his assistants, William Dickson, who discovered that film stock was the best way to reproduce and display moving pictures.

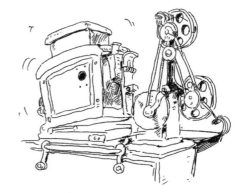

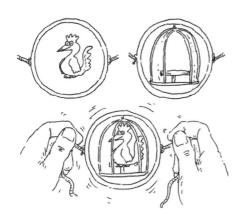

The development of frame-by-frame stop motion photography by George Melies and others is also noteworthy. They worked with puppets and other 3D photographic items, not 2D images. It was a form of animation, but not the traditional animation that we're focusing on in this book. The first device that produced animation in a sequence of 2D images was a machine called the thaumatrope.

The thaumatrope was a disc about the size of a half-dollar (approximately 1.25–1.50 inches in diameter) with a bird rendered on one side and an empty bird cage on the other. A string was attached to either side of the disc. The strings were twisted and twirled, spinning the disc rapidly and causing the images to appear combined into a single image; a bird in a cage. The human eye can blend a sequence of images into a single moving image if they are moving rapidly, well lit, and interrupted at a regular interval. Basically and crudely explained (reflecting my essential nature), this allows the eye to take a series of rapid fire snapshots of the action. The brain blends these snapshots into continuous motion and Voila! You're entertained. This is also known as the **persistence of vision** phenomenon. You may, in fact, have made one of these neat little devices at some point in your early life because they are one of those elementary school rainy day projects.

There were other 'tropes and 'scopes following the thaumatrope, all making use of the persistence of vision phenomenon. The most notable was the zoetrope, a drum with slits cut into it and a strip of paper with a sequence of images placed inside. Looking through the slits of the spinning drum allowed you to see the moving images. A toy that was the most like the traditional animation that we recognize today, the kineography. Today, we know this item as the flipbook, a sequence of animated images bound at one edge like a book (keeping the artwork properly aligned or registered to one another). When the pages of the kineography are thumbed, they flip past in 'rapid succession' (they go by fast, man) and create the illusion of motion. We'll deal with, and even make, flipbooks later on in the Animation chapter. Edison put together a device called a mutoscope, a more complex mechanism based on the kineography concept. Emile Reynaud developed the praxinoscope, a machine similar in principle to the kineograph, but one that incorporated a projector and used long strips of paper and eventually celluloid as the surface that the animation was drawn upon.

The science and the tools were coming into focus and beginning to be used by artists like Emile Cohl, a French cartoonist who made an animated film using drawn stick figures that were photographed frame-by-frame onto film, pretty much the same way it's done today.

In 1906, James S. Blackton produced an animated film of faces drawn on a chalkboard. The faces were animated by shooting a frame of film, erasing a part of the face, and redrawing it slightly altered, then shooting another frame. This process was repeated until the project was done. It was smudgy, but animated. Blackton later became one of the founders of Vitagraph, a pioneering film studio.

James Blackton is considered to be the very first American animator, though that title is often incorrectly given to the guy that he and Emile Cohl paved the way for, Winsor McCay.

Winsor McCay was a fantastic artist. A genius even. He was a former newspaper artist/cartoonist who was inspired to try frame-by-frame, hand-drawn animation by a flipbook that his son showed him. He produced an entire animated film after seeing animation produced by a friend and fellow cartoonist named George MacManus (the creator of the comic strip, 'Jiggs and Maggie'). Four thousand drawings later, McCay had his first 3-minute animated film, "Little Nemo in Slumberland," produced with the aid of Vitagraph and James S. Blackton. The film was shown in 1911. "Gertie the Dinosaur," McCay's third film, was his most famous. He developed a vaudeville stage act with Gertie where he, working from a script, would stand on stage and interact with the projected animated images. "Gertie the Dinosaur" was a great success and paved the way for the work of Disney, Fleischer, the Warner Brothers animation department, and all the other greats.

Today's Animator

Today, animation is an art form that can be done by anyone with the desire to bring images and artwork to life. The ability to draw is important for most forms of animation but, though it pains me to say because I'm a drawing kind of guy, you can get around the drawing part of the equation. However, if you're interested in doing animation that centers on characters and their personalities, actions and reactions, you should have some bit of drawing skill and be prepared to do a lot of drawings. Actually, any moving pictorial element is technically animation, and there are some beautiful examples of that kind of animation. But for the main part of this book, let's pretend that we're all old school draughts-persons.

Even if you're doing some 'Monty Python-esque' collage animation, or some sort of experimental animation that doesn't even involve or contain drawings, the basic principles of motion and timing that will be explained later on in this book still apply.

The steps involved in traditional animation are simple and straightforward; they haven't really changed much over the years, even though some of the methods and tools have.

Traditional animation starts with a **concept,** that initial idea. That concept is given life and a direction by writing a **script.** That concept is then visualized when the **storyboard** is drawn and receives its visual style and flair when it goes through the **design** phase. The concept is given its sound characteristics at the **audio recording.** If the characters are going to speak or the action is based on the audio, audio **track reading** is done to determine the location of the audio events. Now the concept is ready to be put into an animatable form by translating the storyboard into **layouts.** The layouts are used as the basis of the animation. Once the animation is done, it is filled in by the assistant animator's **inbetweens.** In order to see the motion of the animation, a **pencil test** of the animation is shot. The task of adding color is added in during the **ink & paint** step.

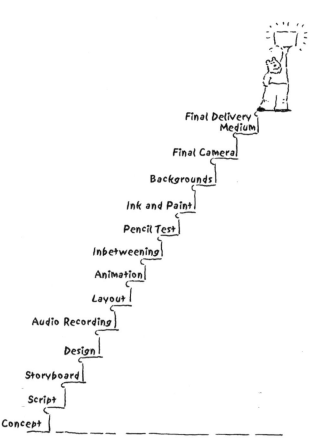

Final Delivery Medium

Final Camera

Backgrounds

Ink and Paint

Pencil Test

Inbetweening

Animation

Layout

Audio Recording

Design

Storyboard

Script

Concept

Backgrounds, though originating in the design phase, are generally worked on and completed at this phase. Once the elements of the animation are prepared, they are gathered and taken to **final camera** where they are shot onto film or video. That film or video is transferred or converted to its final delivery format. Executing these steps connects you to the time-honored tradition of animation.

Traditional and Digital Animation

Animation that is drawn on paper is referred to as **traditional animation.** Animation that is created on a computer is called **digital animation** or **CGI** (**C**omputer **G**enerated **I**mages). Animation production also comes in two flavors: Traditional and Digital. Two projects, both with the same desired end, may start with the same 'traditionally animated images on paper' ingredients, but are 'cooked' differently.

Traditional production means that the animated paper 'ingredients' will use the traditional production methods of transferring the artwork to acetate, painting it with acrylic paints, and shooting it over a rendered artwork background on an animation or rostrum (the British term) camera set-up onto film or videotape. **Digital production** refers to the modern method of scanning or digitizing the traditionally animated images on paper ingredients into a computer, digitally coloring or manipulating the images, compositing (combining) them with a background, and rendering a digital file that can be viewed or output in a wide variety of formats.

Regardless of the production method, you still need a concept, an idea, and the desire to bring something come to life.

Getting Ready to Begin

If you are operating your own studio, then you are the person, acting in the role of Producer, who will interact with the client. You'll help in or guide the decision-making and be involved in the creation of graphic variations until the right design solution is found. If you are working in a larger studio, or have a particular job function, your involvement in the design or any decision-making function regarding the look of the film will be based on your job description. One of the goals of this book is to give knowledge of the entire process of traditional animation, making the assumption that you, the reader, will want to know and perform all of the functions, and 'wear all the hats' at one time or other.

The following is a fast, rough primer briefly explaining and expanding the previously mentioned steps involved in the process of animation. In short, how an animated film is put together (it's really more of a composite of some jobs that we here at Artbear Pigmation have produced). We will assume that you will be doing a lot of the work yourself or will at least 'have a hand in' most if not all of the process. Brief job descriptions based on the icons will be added and enhanced with each step (*to let you know just how overworked you really are*).

This primer outlines a job that will be animated traditionally, scanned into and completed in the computer, then output to Betacam SP or Digi-Beta for dubs and delivery, the way a lot animation work is done today. Let's also say that the client has a pre-written script and a pre-designed character and overall style based on a series of books she had published that you need to match and bring to life in animation.

Step 1: Storyboard

Concepts, scripts, songs, ideas, and the like are visualized and drawn in a series of drawings called a **storyboard.** The camera angles and visual style of the film are set at this stage. Where and when actions take place in relation to the script's descriptions are also determined here. The storyboard, as mentioned in the icon descriptions in the Introduction, is done by the Storyboard Artist.

The **Storyboard Artist** translates, interprets, and visualizes the written creativity of the script. The storyboard artist needs to be a versatile artist that can draw in a variety of styles. This artist should also have some directorial knowledge in order to draw the shots and angles needed to convey the action and set up the drama of the script. The storyboard

artist can be anyone with the required abilities, though directors and animators tend to be the most likely candidates.

At this early stage of production, if it isn't pre-designed by the client, character, and background designer, the overall look and style of the piece, can be set, in a series of drawings called **Color Models.** This style setting work is done by the **Designer.**

There are a wide range of designer options (almost sounds like buying a car). There are artists who specialize in designing characters. There are animation artists that are versatile enough to design an entire production. There are artists that specialize in imitating other people's styles, a situation that arises when a producer wants the style of a particular artist, but doesn't have or want to pay the price the artist demands. There are artists who, like Illustrators and Graphic Designers, have their own unique and sought after styles. Popular Illustrators and Graphic Designers are often called upon to design animated commercials and the like.

PRODUCER'S NOTE:

Often a client will have their own designs that they need animated. Along with their own designs, they will have very strong opinions on how it should be done. They know exactly what they want, in spite of the fact that they know little or nothing about the process of animation. As a producer, it's important to have people available who can follow the designs of others. The really fulfilling and fun spots, though, are the ones where the clients are relying on you, the animation studio, for the design and style of their spot.

Step 2: Audio

The basic audio track for the spot is usually done at this point in the production. Audio recording is done by the **Audio Person** or **Sound Designer**. Sound Designer has a nicer ring to it, eh? The Sound Designer is your audio expert, able to cast talent for your production in a pinch, record voices, search for, find, and line up sound effects and music for your production. An ideal Sound Designer is also a musician, giving you the option of using original music. An ideal Sound Designer can 'read tracks.' During the recording, the actors doing the voices can use the storyboard as a visual guide to the actions of the characters as they record the text from the script. If there are specific things needed in the voice work, the correct voice inflections are easier to achieve when there are drawings of the characters and their expressions as a guide. Once the audio track has been recorded, the audio information is translated phonetically and written out on forms that have lines representing frames of film or video called exposure sheets. This activity is called **track reading** and is a very vital part of the whole animation

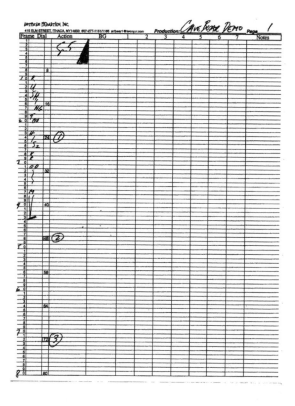

process. This is how you determine the timing of the action and the syncing of the voices and other audio elements. In the case of film or animation, the correct lining up or corresponding of the audio and the visual elements is called **syncing.** Ever see a film or video where the motion of the actors' (or your favorite Boy Band, perhaps?) lips do not match the audio that you are hearing? That is a problem with sync. The elements are 'out of sync.'

At this point, the Director, working with the storyboard, audio track, and exposure sheets, can indicate screen directions, scene lengths, timings of actions, and make notes to the layout artist and animator regarding specific things that need to be done or seen.

Step 3: Layout

The scenes from the storyboard are analyzed and broken down into layered animation elements (characters, backgrounds, foregrounds, etc.) and re-drawn in the style that the film is going to be animated in. Additional poses are added to the storyboard's visualization and the panning and zooming movements of the camera in each scene are worked out. If a soundtrack and exposure sheet exists or if the overall length of the piece is known, the accurate timing can be used to draw and 'pose' the character's interactions. Where do

the characters move, how are they posed, and what do they use as props? What do the characters walk behind or interact with? These things are determined and set up for the animator at this point. Background drawings are also made as guides for the animator. The background artist receives copies of the layouts to use as the basis of the final background renderings. Though an accurately drawn storyboard drawing can occasionally be enlarged and used as a layout, most scenes will require some additional set up work by a competent and versatile **Layout Artist**.

The Layout Artist needs to have a general knowledge of the mechanics of animation, how elements need to be layered in order to be available for a character's interaction, and how to draw background layouts with the needed perspective and accuracy. The Layout Artist needs to have a good knowledge of camera mechanics in order to set up any mechanical moves in a scene. Like nearly all of the drawing-related categories in animation, the ability to draw in a variety of styles is important. Well-drawn character layouts can be a big help to the Animator. Directors often work directly with the Layout Artist during the Layout phase of a production.

Step 4: Animation

This is what it's all about. The actual timing and drawing of the action, *the acting,* is done by the Animator on drawings called **Extremes.** For design control or to save time, the layout drawings can be used as extremes, but additional artwork is done by the Animator to represent the desired action. To smooth out and fill in the action and produce the artwork for the actual final timing, drawings called **Breakdowns** and **In-betweens** are inserted between the extremes. The breakdowns are done by the **Assistant Animator** and the in-betweens are done by the In-betweener, depending on the studio set-up. In some instances, the animator does the animation in a rough and loose fashion, concentrating only on the action of the character. The assistant cleans up the extremes and some of the key breakdowns and the In-betweener has the task of cleaning up the remainder of the drawings in preparation for the Ink & Paint process.

Animators need to have an understanding of acting and drama because they are essentially envisioning the actions of the characters even though it is behind the

scenes. Rhythm and timing are key elements in animation. Knowledge of anatomy, human and animal, can help an Animator produce realistic action. An animator has to produce lots of drawings. The words lazy and animator don't belong in the same sentence. The same goes for Assistant Animators and In-betweeners. These are the folks that do the bulk of the drawing.

Step 5: Pencil Test

Regardless of the production mode used, traditional or digital, in order to accurately see the action, the animation drawings need to be shot frame-by-frame and played back for the animation team and client. This is called the Pencil Test. The animation drawings can be shot on film or video using an animation camera, or even a home movie camera with stop motion capabilities. A pencil test can also be produced by shooting the animation on a video animation system like a Lightfoot Ltd. set-up or an old Lyon and Lamb Video Animation set-up. If the production is being done digitally, the animation drawings can be scanned into a computer animation system, placed in correct order in an animation program, and played back or output to videotape or other viewing medium. (You can also send Quicktime movies via the Internet to your client.)

Adjustments and corrections to the action and timing are made at this phase and re-tested until the desired end is achieved. This work is done by the **camera** person in a traditional cel to film project. The camera person needs to have a complete knowledge of the camera equipment. Not only the 'how to use it' part but the 'how to fix it' part as well. Usually the animation production company produces the artwork until the very last second, which means that it doesn't arrive at the camera service until late in the day, which means that the camera work is done at night. Any breakdowns or repairs need to be done by the camera person because the repair folks are at home asleep like all of other sane people. The camera person needs to have a strong knowledge of the entire process of animation because the camera person is, and should be, called upon to give advice on how best to set up the animation production for fast and easy recording onto film or video. In a digital production, the work that was once entirely done by the camera person is now done by others. The artwork needs to be scanned, an Ink & Paint function, then digitally put in order, a function of the compositor, or someone acting in that role. In digital, anyone with the knowledge (or the manual) can cover these multiple functions.

If music or sound effects are being done for the spot, the person doing the sound work should receive a copy of the final and most current pencil test. This allows the Sound Design person to begin lining up the audio tracks to the animated picture instead of waiting until the final color product is available.

Step 6: Ink & Paint

During the Ink & Paint phase of production, color is added to the animation drawings. This is the point where the project's production department starts to come into play, determining how color is added to the animation drawings. If traditionally produced, the artwork is copied onto acetate sheets called 'cels' and water-based acrylic paint is applied to the back of the cel for color. The animation drawings can be hand-inked or photocopied

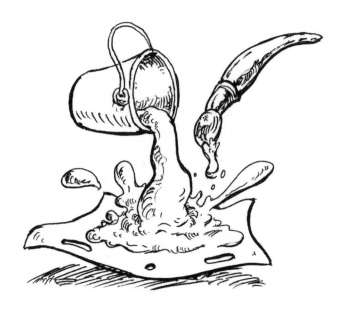

onto the cels. In some cases, as mentioned earlier, the animator might animate directly onto acetate or the animation drawings can be cut out and carefully pasted onto the cels, then colored. Cels are traditionally .005 mil thick, and in fact are not absolutely crystal clear. They have a slight tint to them, which affects the painted color applied to the back. If too many of them are used, stacked on top of each other during the animation camera phase when the artwork is shot frame-by-frame onto film, they can cast a cel shadow over the background. This is really noticeable the closer the camera is to the artwork.

If the animation is being produced digitally, the artwork is scanned into the computer system and color is applied in the animation program being used, an image editing program like Photoshop, or a paint program like Painter.

All of this color work is done by the Ink & Paint person(s). Traditionally, an inker or a painter needs a skillfully controlled hand. The inker's contribution to the character, the quality of the line, be it thick or thin and technical, or thick and thin 'feathered' or squiggly... all come from the skillfully controlled hand. There are times, however, when the animation department will produce artwork that is correct as far as the motion is concerned, but not correct as far as the style is concerned. This is when an Inker with a high level of drawing skill is needed. Working with a set of accurate character models, a really good Inker will be able to render the animation artwork onto acetate in the correct and accurate style.

Animation Painters fill in the colors of the animated drawings, following the color model produced earlier in the production by the designer. Painters, like inkers, need that skillful, controlled hand, along with common sense and a keen eye. These skills are needed for traditional cel work and for digital work. In a traditional cel production, the painter needs to have enough control to paint the areas of the cel flat and thin so the stack of cels or levels that the  camera person shoots remain as flat as possible. If the cels are rippled or uneven in thickness, the cels can produce unwanted cel shadows or highlights that will ruin the frames of film shot and require a costly re-shoot. In a digital production, the keen eye and steady hand are required to accurately outline areas to be filled with color. If there are gaps or open spots in the lines that enclose areas of a drawing, the color will flow through the gap and fill other areas. Even if you're working in a program like Flash where the gaps can be filled automatically, a keen eye and the ability to recognize the potential problem area will enable you to choose the correct, 'gap filling' paint mode.

At the end of the Ink & Paint phase of the production, the elements of the design are gathered and checked. Ideally, the backgrounds are finished before the animation is completely colored in order to check the animation over the finished backgrounds and make sure that everything registers (matches) and works correctly. Whether traditionally or digitally produced, the backgrounds still need to match the layouts in order to interact correctly with the animated characters. In traditional times and productions, the background artist was a person who was skilled and comfortable in a wide variety of paint media: watercolor, gouache, pastels, acrylics, inks, etc. Background artwork can still be produced in traditional ways, then scanned into the computer system and used in the production. In addition to traditional drawing and painting skills, knowledge of image editing and paint programs (Photoshop, ImageReady, Illustrator, Freehand, Painter, etc. and even 3D (Studio Max, Maya, Electricimage, Strata StudioPro, etc.) is vital.

Step 6: Final Compositing and Output

The background and animation elements are brought together and combined into a series of moving images during the Final Shoot, if you're doing a traditional production, or the Final Compositing and Output step, if you're doing a digital production. If it is a traditional animation production shot on film variety, the art elements are taken to an animation camera service (or down the hall to the camera department, if the studio has one), where the animation cels are laid down on top of the background and shot frame-  by-frame onto film. The film is developed and viewed by the animation team and client. There really shouldn't be any changes at this stage. If there are, the studio is within their rights to charge extra for them.

If the production is being done digitally, the compositor person is doing essentially the same thing that was done at the pencil test stage, only this time, with the completed color elements. The scanned and colored animation artwork and backgrounds are combined in the animation program being used, or a program designed for this purpose in a process called 'compositing.' The resulting combination is output in the computer to a video format such as Quicktime that can be viewed on the computer in real time, then output to videotape, film, or digital media.

By now, the soundtrack is completed. If the production was done on film, the final film is transferred to videotape and the audio person can combine the audio elements with the video. This process is called **laying back.** If the production was done digitally, there are a couple of options. The final computer composition can be output to videotape and have the audio layed back, just like a traditional film production. Generally, though, the audio is lined up with the visual elements and is part of the compositing phase of production. That way, you come out of the compositing step with the completed project. A copy of the final production will be sent to the client for final approval.

Conclusion

That is essentially the process of doing an animated film. Not nearly as complicated as you may have heard, but not necessarily a walk in the park. There is work involved. And in digital production for a small studio, steps that were once handed over to someone else, like animation camera or editing chores can be, and often are, done by *you*.

Traditional Animation has always offered a lot of creative possibilities, but modern day traditional animation has been given a wonderful boost by the developments and use of computers and the wide variety of programs available. The ability to work easily with 3D images, collage, and live action gives you a nearly endless number of possibilities. In fact, you can create an animation spot and deliver it to a client without having to leave the house. Of course, working at home isn't for everyone.

Each step in the process of creating Traditional animation will be explained and expanded in the following chapters in order to give you the complete picture. Onward to *Chapter Two: Preparing for Production.*

Chapter 2

Preparing for Production

The best first step in the process of preparing for production is to sit down with all of the available information you have related to the job—things like the script, the storyboard if one has been created, and any notes you may have from conversations you've had with the client—and ask some questions. There are many questions to ask and answer when setting up an animation production. For example:

What technique is being used to produce the animation: Digital or Traditional?

What is the style of the project? If you are a designer, can you design it or will you have to hire someone? Is the client providing the design? Does the client have a designer in mind? **What** will the animation be used for? Is it commercial? Is it educational? Broadcast television? Internet? **Who's** going to pay? **Where** is this film going to be produced? Can the project be produced in your present studio set-up? **Who** is going to produce the animation artwork? **How** much will they be paid?

What materials are going to be needed?

Where are you going to get them? Mail order? Retail? **How** much do the materials cost? And the big question: **How** much is the budget? Questions related to the budget can be the most difficult for an artist. Inspiration can often override logic when it comes to money. There are and will always be intensely low-budget projects that seem absolutely perfect and you may feel that the opportunity will never ever come again. So you take the project on and end up pouring your talent, time, effort, and personal resources into it, giving it the same quality of production that you would a higher-budget job. And when the project is completed, you find that it isn't as gratifying as you thought it would be because you haven't been properly compensated and may even be 'in the hole' for a substantial amount. To catch up, you will need to take on more jobs, some with lower budgets. Before you know it, you're in a spiral that is very difficult to get out of. So remember that there will be times when no matter how much you might want to do a particular project, you have to ask yourself if can you afford to produce it on the budget proposed. If the answer is 'no,' refuse it, move forward, and don't look back.

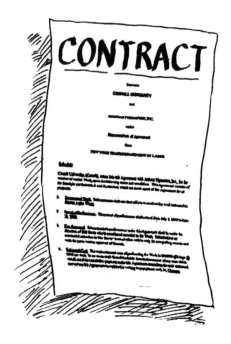

These are the primary pieces of information you need to know before you can settle into the warm gooey joy of making artwork. This is the **budget and administration phase** of preparing for production. The answers to these questions go into the written, protective, and binding agreement signed by the Supplier or Producer (you) and the Client (them): The Contract.

The important production-related items that should be covered and contained in a contract are:

1. *Who Supplies What....* (Which party is responsible for supplying what elements of the production?)
2. *...And For How Much Money?* (What is the budget?)
3. *Cost of Changes Beyond the Agreed Amount.* (Which party is responsible for additional charges?)
4. *The Payment Schedule.* (When are payments to be made and for how much?)
5. *A Timeline.* (The schedule of approvals and delivery.)
6. *The Kill Fee.* (What happens if the job is cancelled?)
7. *Ownership.* (Who owns the rights to the work produced?)

While the knowledge and expertise of the animation production process will come from you, you should have your contracts drawn up and reviewed by an attorney. An attorney will have knowledge of the range of additional items that should be included in the contract for your legal and fiscal protection. Let's review each necessary part of the contract.

1. Who Supplies What...

The client will usually supply the script or some written form of their concept to you. They may also supply the storyboard and basic audio track as well, but for the sake of this example, let's assume that the client is only supplying the script. If you and your studio are supplying the script,

you should have your client give their approval of the final version of the script, *in writing,* before recording the soundtrack. This process of getting the client's approval is called **signing off**—the client "signs off" on the script or any element that they are approving.

After receiving the script approval, you and your studio will then supply a storyboard. A black and white thumbnail storyboard (a small and roughly drawn variation of a storyboard) is a good place to start.

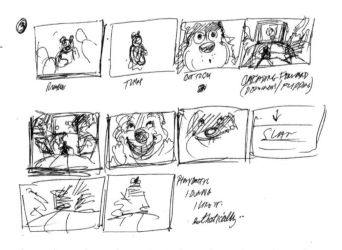

The rough thumbnail storyboard will give you an opportunity to work out your ideas and decide which direction you want to take the project. When the client signs off on the thumbnail storyboard, you can follow up by drawing a more complete storyboard and a set of color models showing the final look of the project.

After the concept, content, and style have been approved, they become **bill-able.** This means you can invoice the client for an additional amount of money above and beyond the budget for any **changes** that they make after giving their written, "signed off" approval. The possibility of having to spend additional amounts of money for their indecision often acts as a deterrent and keeps the client from making lots of unnecessary changes.

This next step brings the production closer to a tangible, motion-filled reality. You supply the **layouts.** The layouts, simply put, are the drawings that the animator bases the action on. They are drawn in the actual animated style of the production, occasionally even incorporated into the production as extremes. If you feel it's prudent, as a final pre-animation approval point, you can show the layouts to the client. Again, get them to sign off.

The next item that you supply, also an approval step, is the **pencil test.** The pencil test is an action test of the animation shot on film or video, usually in black and white if you're producing traditionally, but should be shot or output in color to show the set of color models. If you're producing digitally, the artwork is scanned and output as Quicktimes or other digital formats of output to video. At this stage, you and the client will view the animation on film, video, or whatever medium the animated spot is going to be delivered in. The client can make comments and request changes in the action at this first pencil test and not be billed for it. A second version of the pencil test will be produced that incorporates any of the client's changes. If there are further changes, they are generally, if not arguably, billable.

Producer's Note:

Billing can be a touchy issue. Clients tend to think that they have unlimited opportunities to make changes until you have successfully produced the exact series of images that they have in their heads. This is fine if you

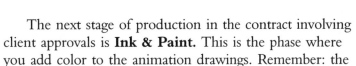

think you can afford to do it, but it is not a good path to follow. Chances are, the

client will not respect you as a professional and it will not guarantee that they will be coming back to you in the future with more work. Get the approval in the form of a sign off and you'll be protected.

The next stage of production in the contract involving client approvals is **Ink & Paint.** This is the phase where you add color to the animation drawings. Remember: the client was provided a set of color models showing the final look, in color, early in the whole process. Ink & paint commits the animation to its final form, whether you're producing in a

---

traditional cel method or digital method. Any changes from the ink & paint phase forward are billable and expensive. Make sure the client knows this up front. Their original ideas look much better if they realize they have to dig deeper into their pockets to pay for changes at this point. Final delivery of the full-color animation follows.

2. ...And For How Much Money (The Budget)

As mentioned earlier in the chapter, the budget can be the most difficult part of preparing for production. The financial end of things is a vital part of producing animation. Animation is art, but it is also a business, and you have to be compensated appropriately. Here's a checklist of things to list on a budget and who's responsible for them. Even if you are not going to be responsible for a particular category in your production, this checklist will give you the opportunity to note what items are being provided and paid for by you and what items the client will be handling.

Items Supplied By You: (These categories are all part of the animation studio's outlay.)

- Producer
- Designer/Storyboard
- Layout
- Assistant Animator
- Backgrounds
- Computer Equipment
- Scanning/Digitizing
- Hand inking/Xerox *(traditional production)*
- Still Photo Rights (if applicable)
- Administrative Staff
- Office Supplies
- Accounting
- Contingency
- Insurance

- Director
- Track Reading
- Animation
- Pencil Test
- Ink & Paint
- Computer Program Upgrades and Updates
- Final Camera/Lab or Digital Output
- Supplies and Disposables
- Studio Rent
- Telephone and Utilities
- Agent/Commission
- Taxes & Benefits

The Either/ORs: (These categories are items that can be provided and paid for by the client or you, the studio.)

- Script and story rights
- Sound Editor
- Music Rights
- Final Sound Mix and Layback
- Dubbing

- Talent
- Rough sound layback
- Film to tape transfer
- Final Output to delivery medium

PRODUCER'S NOTE:

If you are producing animation for another production company (an example being an animated character in a live action commercial), then the live action company will more than likely make and pay for the audio work and video transfers. If, however, you are providing the audio and video work, make sure you make a backup, high-quality (Digital or Betacam SP) dub of the master video for your company's archive and reel.

Payroll

Deciding how much to pay the people working on the production can be figured out in a number of ways. Ask yourself some of these questions:

- How much money is in the budget? Will the people involved in the production be willing to equally share the amount of money in the production budget? Will everyone be contributing equally?

- Does the person you would like to hire to perform a particular function in the production have experience and therefore an expected rate? Can you afford it?

- What is the local rate for the type of work required? Are you in a location that has other people that produce animation or artwork and therefore 'compete' with you? You don't want to budget too high and lose the job and you don't want to budget too low and get a reputation for being 'low budget, cheap, and easy.'

- What is the current minimum wage? The minimum wage or some multiple of it can be used as a basis for payment, but should be the last resort, usually.

- What is the accepted hourly rate or daily rate for the desired service? This is the most professional approach to the question and leads to the next and most practical solution.

Whether they are members or not, most people in art-related fields use union rates as a guide to pricing their services. Whether you are a 'Union house' or not, Union pay scales are generally the gauge of what markets will bear. Below their rates and you're approaching 'low budget.' Above their rates and you're approaching 'high budget.' Union rates mainly apply to commercial and broadcast animation. Rarely are the funds available in educational or industrial market budgets to pay union rates. You just can't recoup your outlay when producing animation in those markets. But big bucks can be made off of cereal, cookie, chocolate milk, automobile, and telephone service commercials.

Remember, pay and wage scales change often. Today's published current pay scale is tomorrow's obsolete pay scale. The most practical approach to getting actual numbers is accessing the information directly. The following contact information should help:

The Motion Picture Screen Cartoonists-Local 839 (http://mpsc.org). Their web site is very informative and should be the first stop when looking for current animation related price and wage scales. They provide information for computer-generated animation as well as traditional cel animation. Union rates for staff are minimums used at large production and commercial animation union studios. For current contract information, contact a union studio or the union itself.

Another source of pricing information is the *Graphic Artists Guild Handbook: Pricing & Ethical Guidelines.* This handbook is published yearly. Their website is: http//www.gag.org. This handbook contains a lot of important information on art related fields from textile design to cartooning, web design to greeting cards. There are sample contracts, invoices, and other legal and financial information. It really should be a part of every artist's library.

Below are some of the primary categories covered by guilds and unions that a small studio works with. The list is certainly not comprehensive, and though it's not meant to be current to the moment you are reading this book, it can serve as a reference point. The rates are 'rounded off,' hourly, and are relative to a standard 40 hour work week.

CATEGORY	HOURLY RATE
Director	$33 - $38
Storyboard Artist	$35 - $37
Designer	$30 - $32
Layout Artist	$35 - $37
Animator	$35 - $37
Assistant Animator	$25 - $27
Animation In-betweener	$21 - $22
Background Artist	$35 - $37
Inker	$20 - $22
Painter	$20 - $22
Digital Painter	$20 - $22
Checker	$21 - $24

Categories in a Typical Animation Budget

Where the money goes:

- **Pre-production**
  - Script
  - Design
  - Storyboard
- **Production Staff**
  - Producer
  - Director
  - Consultation
  - Co-Producer
  - Production Assistant

- **Production**
  - Actors
  - Track Reading
  - Animation
  - Background
  - Checking
  - Voice Recording
  - Layout
  - Assistant Animation
  - Ink & Paint
  - Compositing/Camera
- **Materials and Supplies Post Production**
  - Music & Efx
  - Sound Mix
  - Editing
  - Transfer to Video
- **Insurance**
  - Liability, E&O, Media Coverage, Worker's Comp.
- **Other**
  - Travel & Shipping
  - Rent
  - Phone
  - Overhead
  - Utilities
  - Maintenance
- **Profit**
  - We all wish. The point of it all.

The budget approach explained above is based on hourly rates. This is the most basic, detailed, and comprehensive way to do it. But there are other ways of calculating budgets. These include: budgeting by footage rates, per minute rates, and per second rates.

Footage Rates: Animation is calculated in 35mm film footage. The basic unit of film is the frame. The next basic unit is the foot. There are 16 frames in a foot of film. There are one and a half feet in one second of film, therefore 24 frames for each second of film. There. That's the technical knowledge. Animation falls into categories of difficulty, complexity, and quality and has a corresponding approximate price for each category.

- Limited is the least expensive. It involves doing a minimal amount of work on the least number of characters per scene. Shortcuts abound, like separating mouths from faces to make it easier to do lip sync and using as many separate, easier to animate layer as possible.

- Full is the most expensive. It involves multiple characters, fuller, more involved, traditional high-quality type animation. Lots of lip sync and full, excellent acting. Uses fewer layers because the entire characters are animated, not just separated arms or heads or mouths.
- Medium footage splits the difference. A combination of nice full acting with shortcuts to lighten the load. This is the category that is used most often by small studios in the educational field.

Per Minute Rates: This is a budget calculating system used for productions that are one minute or longer. Often based on previous experience and productions, the cost of producing the animation is added up and averaged into a price per minute.

Per Second Rates: This is a budget calculating system for productions that are less than a minute long. Commercials fall into this category.

3. Cost of Changes Beyond the Agreed Amount

The charge for any specific change can be based on your hourly fees. This amount can also be pro-rated based on the original fee schedule or budget. At the risk of sounding redundant, it is important to decide who is responsible for providing what elements in the production. You must let the client know when changes and redoes cross over into the 'billable' zone.

The Cost of 'Unintentionals'

An unintentional is an amount over and beyond the original agreement. Your contract needs to have a clause that covers you for overages such as these. In live action, you shoot a 10:1 time or footage ratio in order to edit it down to a one minute spot. This means that you would still have plenty of existing footage left over to make a 1:15 video. In animation, that extra 15 seconds is an extra 25% more work that wasn't planned for and doesn't exist without 25% more labor and time. Overages can be based on the time or footage (90 feet = one minute) beyond the original agreement. The client needs to have this intended charge in writing to approve it. If they don't want to pay then it is their responsibility to adjust the length of the track.

4. Payment Schedule

Amounts are usually payable in thirds. The 1st third is due upon the signing of the contract. This is working capital or **hand-out money.** The money that will be used to acquire supplies, equipment, or retain the services of workers. The 2nd third is customarily due at the approval of the pencil test. This should be used to pay for services contracted on the outside. The final third cleans up the remainder of your financial outlay and pays you, your taxes, and other expenses. Anything left over is considered profit.

5. Timeline

When preparing for production, you will need to write up a schedule or **timeline** that includes delivery and approval dates for each stage. The amount of time that the client has in order to respond with comments or changes has to be defined at this point. For example, if the client takes seven business days instead of three to get back to you with comments, then you have the right to extend your time of production. Please note that Saturday and Sunday should not count as available production time, as they are not considered "business" days. The weekends should be yours to use for catching up if you happen to fall behind schedule. Make sure this is indicated in the contract.

Here is another important bit of required scheduling information, possibly second in difficulty only to the 'wage' question. How long will it take **you** to produce this animation? In order to accurately calculate your budget, you need to know how much time you're budgeting for in each category of the budget. Five hours of layout at $30.00 per hour? Ten hours? How do you know? Some approaches:

The client's deadline. Often, a client will already have a definite date that they need to have the finished production 'in hand.'

The time of production on previous jobs of a similar complexity. If you have previously produced animation or just have a decent amount of experience drawing and animating, you may already have an idea of how long it should take you to produce the job. Add a five to ten percent lump of time on top of your estimate in order to be 'safe.'

Calculate the time by doing a sample. Producing the color model can be a useful tool for calculating the basic unit of time needed to draw a character. Though it's a sacrifice of time, especially if the budget you're putting together is a bid and not a budget for a job you have actually been commissioned to do, animating a one-second piece of animation can be very useful. Not only will you learn how long it takes the character and style of art, but you can use it as a example to show the client how you envision the character in motion. This may also help you get the job.

6. The Kill Fee

If the client cancels the job at any point before the storyboard is completed, there is usually a 10-20% payment called a **kill fee.** If the project is cancelled after the completion of the storyboard, the client is responsible for all expenses and costs for work done up to cancellation. This can include the balances on rental contracts or leases that are not refundable and materials that are not returnable.

7. Ownership

Most work for clients is **work for hire.** This means that you do the work and they own the rights to it. If it looks like the job might turn into a series or larger production, try to include a clause in the contract called a **Right of First Refusal.** Basically, this means that should the job actually turn into something lucrative, they are required to offer the production to you and your company first. If you choose not to follow through on the production, they are then free to find another production company. If you have proposed, and it has been accepted by the client, that you will be using characters that you have previously designed and own the rights to, make sure that you do indeed own the rights. You do this by copyrighting the characters with the United States Copyright Office (www.copyright.gov). There will be more on this copyrighting stuff later in the chapter.

If the client supplies the contract, get an attorney to look it over and advise you. Make sure you understand what you are signing. If you write the contract, have your attorney make sure you didn't give everything away for nothing.

Planning a Production

A lot of information was laid on the table in the previous sections regarding contracts and budgets. Let's take a look at a couple of examples of how to put that information to use.

Scenario 1: Your own thing, the muse-inspired, self-financed mode.

You are an animation person. Perhaps a student or a small company owner. Not destitute, but not involved in lighting your cigars or Cherries Jubilee with high-denomination greenbacks. You have an idea for an animated film. You have a mini-budget, using your own precious resources. You've designed some characters and want to feature them in your production. Now what? First thing. Get copyright forms (VA for visual arts) and copyright your characters. These forms are available from:

Library of Congress
Copyright Office
101 Independence Avenue. S.E.
Washington, D.C. 20559-6000
Phone: 202-707-3000
You can also download the forms from: http:/
/www.copyright.gov

This will protect your characters or other creative work from blatant theft (it happens). If they serve as an 'inspiration' for someone else's characters and you want to pursue them legally, you have proof of your creative ownership and a date to go with it. Once the artwork has been copyrighted, anyone who comes along and just **loves** the characters and wants to use them has to pay you a licensing fee or use fee. The cost of copyrighting your work is minimal and well worth the cost.

Assess and Analyze the Project

There are Who, What, Where, When, Why, and How questions in any production. The chief question is what is the mode of production: traditional or digital? What supplies are you going to need? Who is going to help? How much will they need to be paid? Where is the production going to be done? What is the schedule—in other words, when will it start and end? Like budgeting, you gather the available elements and as much information as you have about the project and plan your approach.

Back to the scenario. This is your own concept and design, so storyboard, animation, and assistant animation will probably be executed by your hand, depending upon your range of skills or desire to expand that range of skills. Since you have a mini-budget, the more you are able to do yourself, the less you will have to *hand out* (outlay, lay on the line, out of pocket expend, shell out).

The actual animation of the concept or characters is done pretty much the same, whether you're going to xerox or ink the artwork onto acetate cel or scan it into an animation program and produce the project digitally. There are things that are unique to each production method, some better than others. The big differences happen after the animation is drawn.

For instance, if you're producing traditional cel animation and shooting on film, you'll need things like acetate cels, paint, a variety of brushes, and enough space in your studio for racks or shelves to dry the cels on. You'll need to get the artwork to an animation camera service to record it onto film, then send the film to lab for processing, and then video transfer. And you'll need the time for all of these steps.

If you're producing in a digital mode, working with computer-generated images or scanning traditionally animated images into a computer program, you may already have everything you need in order to produce an animated project. A scanner, an animation program to compile, compose, and color your digital animation drawings, plenty of memory and hard disk space, and a way of getting the animated production from the hard drive to the final viewing medium are the major digital needs. There are also services that can take your digital files and output them to film or tape.

Breaking it Down:

- You'll need art materials and supplies, whether you're producing in digital or traditional film output. So out of your mini-budget you will need to buy paper to animate on, cels, pencils, pens, paint, and brushes. Paper can be purchased through Cartoon Colour or other animation supply companies. Cels are considerably more expensive and sold by the 100, 250, or 500 packs. The more you buy at one time the less they are per cel. It is best to contact the suppliers directly for the most current prices and availability of supplies. Depending on the size of the project you are working on, you may decide to purchase an animation cel punch. This will enable you to use either traditional 10.5" x 12.5" paper or 8.5" x 11" paper for scanning into a computer. In order to get the drawn animation onto cel if working in a traditional cel mode, you will need access to a copy machine that will handle up to 11" x 17" inch paper and not melt cels. If that is not accessible or you can't afford to send the cels to a xerox service, you will need to use hand-inking techniques to trace the artwork onto cel.

- In order to get the animation artwork onto your hard drive and work with it in your animation, paint, or compositing program, you'll need to scan or somehow digitize the artwork in register.

- Your characters have voices so you'll need voice talent, an audio person for recording the voice tracks, and putting the 'sound design' together. There's also music and sound effects. There are services that will edit and read your soundtrack, putting the audio phonetically onto animation sheets. This goes for music beats also. This is needed for both digital and traditional production.

- Access to a frame-by-frame video set-up like a Lightfoot Ltd. or an old Lyon & Lamb Pencil Test System would get you through the pencil test phase. Check local colleges or universities and see if they have one and if you can gain access to it. Any available single frame video recording system is a good pencil testing solution whether you're producing traditional or digital. It is more immediate than sending artwork to a camera service and lab or scanning and outputting a Quicktime. You just shoot, rewind, and view. If a dedicated single frame video animation system isn't available, a set-up using a tripod, a video camera, and your animation disk can be used (more on that in the Experimental Animation chapter).

- You'll need an Ink & Painter, a person to add color to the artwork (unless you do that stage yourself). This is needed for digital or traditional film production.

- The animation environment needs to be rendered, regardless of the production mode, so you'll need a Background artist (you again?) with a digital or traditional production.

- You will need a camera service or, at least, access to an animation camera for the final shoot in color on film or video. If shot on film, you will also need to process the film at a lab and transfer it to video. This is needed in a traditional film production.

- There's editing; lining up the visual and audio elements if you're doing a traditional film production. If you're doing digital, you can easily do your own editing.

- At the end of a traditional or digital production, the animation drawings, cels, background artwork, or any other physical forms or artwork can be dropped (carefully, of course) in a box and placed on a shelf. But what about the digital files? You will need some sort of storing solution like DVDs, or even a hard drive that has been set aside to hold old jobs.

Animation Equipment

To get the animation artwork done, you will need some basic equipment. Traditionally drawn animation can be labor intensive work. Depending on the complexity of the project, you may need to produce hundreds or even thousands of drawings. Because of that, it's good to have a comfortable drawing set-up to work with: a sturdy table, comfy chair, and ample lighting.

Animation also requires some special equipment. The most important piece of animation-related equipment in your set-up is the animation disk.

The most common variety of animation disk is a metal disk with a rectangle cut in the center. The opening is fitted with a pane of translucent glass or plastic. Attached to the disk is a set of pegs used for registration. If the disk is part of a special animation set-up, it will fit into a hole that has been cut into the accompanying table. The hole contains a light unit to enable you to trace through multiple layers of paper when animating.

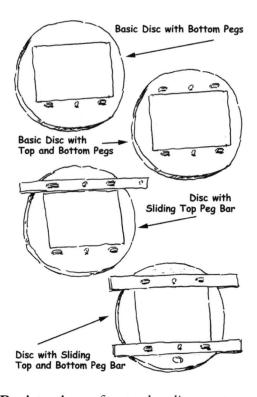

Basic Disc with Bottom Pegs

Basic Disc with Top and Bottom Pegs

Disc with Sliding Top Peg Bar

Disc with Sliding Top and Bottom Peg Bar

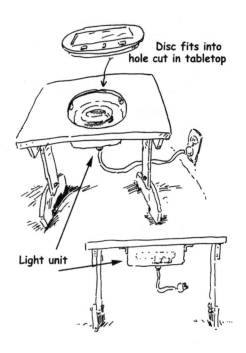

Disc fits into hole cut in tabletop

Light unit

Registration refers to the alignment of all the animation drawings, backgrounds, and other elements in the scenes. Registration keeps the images lined up in the same position relative to each other so that the sequence of separately drawn images will appear to move smoothly when projected, played back, flipped, or otherwise viewed. If the images are not in alignment or register, the action will be very erratic and jerky. For example, a scene in a movie shot by a camera mount on a sturdy and steady tripod is smooth and would represent correctly registered animation. A scene in a movie shot from the window of a vehicle moving down a rough, rocky road would be jerky, bumpy, and difficult to view, representing poorly registered animation.

The layout process, explained in a later chapter, is the first stage of production where registration becomes important. The positions of the background elements and the various positions of the characters are set at this stage and there has to be a method to guarantee that each element 'lines up' and maintains a correct relative position. The system used in animation to achieve this alignment is a peg system. The peg system consists of three metal pegs attached to the surface that the animation artwork is being drawn upon. Holes that match the pegs are punched into the paper or cels used for all of the animation art. The entire production, animation, ink & paint, scanning, camera, etc. use the same system. There are many different types of animations set-ups you

MATERIALS NEEDED
TOOLS NEEDED

can use and you can even make your own. Search the web to find out how to make an animation set-up at home.

The two primary commercially available standard types of animation pegs are Acme and Oxberry. The pegs are named after the companies that manufacture them, along with other animation equipment.

OXBERRY   **ACME**

The center peg in the cnfiguration is cylindrical and the two outer pegs are flat. The primary differences between the two peg systems is the size of the pegs. A system based on the standard three hole punch found in everyday three ring school binders can also be used in animation.

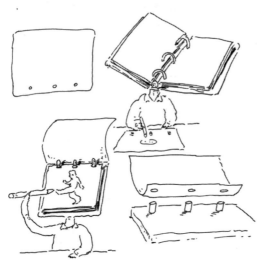

The Disney studios, being huge and self-contained, have their own personal peg configuration. The type of pegs that you choose, Acme or Oxberry, isn't really important because they perform the same task—keeping the artwork in register. What is important is that everyone involved in the production has and uses the same system. They are not like jpegs or tifs. They are not cross platform. If you decide to invest hundreds of dollars in a paper punch, the type of peg system that you choose for that punch is the type of peg system that you will be using for all of your productions.

Another important piece of equipment is a cel punch. This device is used to punch the peg holes into paper, cel, art papers for background work, or anything else you might need registered. Once the animation artwork is done, additional equipment will be needed to complete the project in the chosen production mode, traditional or digital.

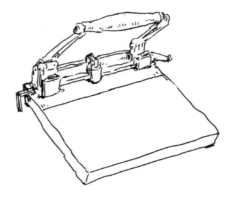

Traditional: You will need cels, paint, polycons, brushes, pens, an inking board (if you're using a different set-up than your animation set-up), a lightstick, racks or shelves to hold painted cels, shelves to hold paint, access to a Xerox machine, and artwork to produce backgrounds. Your animation set-up can double as your ink & paint set-up, unless you are a two-person studio sharing the table.

Digital: You will need a computer and monitor, pressure sensitive pen and tablet, storage media (hard drives and portable), scanner, animation programs, output device, and media.

Those are the needs. Now for a few solutions. In order to get an idea of how much you'll need of an item, say paper for example, it's a good idea to know the length of the film you want to produce and how that time is broken down. No matter what format or medium your film is going to be delivered in, animation is always counted in film footage.

The basic unit of film is the frame. The next basic unit is the foot. There are 16 frames in a foot of film. There are one and a half feet in one second of film, therefore 24 frames for each second of film. Film travels through a projector at a rate of 90 feet per minute (1,440 frames, a lot of drawings). Animation is done at 24 frames per second but each drawing

is held for two frames, or shot on 2s. (Don't worry, "2s" will be explained in more depth later on.) That's a minimum of 12 pieces of paper and 12 cels per second for animation alone. You have to add on about 25% to cover layout, background layouts, mistakes, throwaways, and other random uses of the paper. Most supplies are usually sold in multiples of 50 or 100, so 1 minute of animation, straight ahead on 2s will require 2 reams of paper and 750 cels.

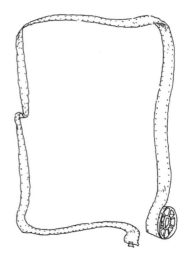

A solution to the expense of buying animation paper is to use some sort of 8.5" by 11" paper that is widely available at office supply stores. It can be punched for animation usage on a regular animation punch available through animation supply companies. It comes in a wide variety of qualities, colors, textures, and prices.

For simple animation, using a small number of drawings and repeating them can fill time with a minimum amount of effort or materials. These repeating bits are called **cycles**. Animating with cycles does help in the amount of drawings needed and time spent animating, but if there are a lot of these cycles (multiple levels or layers), you are still looking at similar numbers in materials.

Finishing Up: Traditionally

Moving forward in the scenario, let's say the project has been produced, traditionally, on cel. The animation has been drawn, xeroxed, or hand inked onto cel, the cels have been painted, and the backgrounds have been completed. To complete the project, the character and background elements have to be combined and transferred into a form that enables you to see your animated masterpiece. So it's off to camera, lab, and/or video transfer. Camera services run from $150–$250 per hour for shooting your animation onto film or video. If, in the animation stage, you combined characters or even backgrounds on a very few layers, you will have a short, inexpensive animation camera shoot. If you took shortcuts to eliminate work by separating the elements into several layers, you will have a longer, more expensive shoot. It takes much longer to shoot multiple layers and cycles. There is also more opportunity for mistakes to happen.

When the animation has been shot onto film, the film has to be processed at a film laboratory. **Lab**, as it is called, is billed to the camera service and tacked on to the shooting charge. For a video transfer, things are a little different. A simple, unsupervised (often overnight) transfer is much less expensive than a supervised transfer session, but you have no real control in the unsupervised transfer. In a supervised transfer, you should bring along samples of the animation artwork in color in order to accurately match it. Sometimes, supplying a piece of the original art for the unsupervised transfer will help you achieve a more accurate color match, if the video transfer facility is willing to be flexible and work with you. Attitude can be everything— a batch of homemade cookies for midnight snacking may just get you a really great unsupervised transfer—no savings on the cost, but a great-looking video. The next step depends on the final intended usage of the animation. Where is it going to be seen? Video for broadcast television or a digitally for Internet use? Both? Can your video facility handle the task of getting your project into its final form?

Finishing Up: Digitally

Let's say the project has been produced digitally. The animation has been drawn, scanned, and colored and the backgrounds are completed. To complete the job, the character and background elements have to be combined and transferred into a form that enables you to see your animated masterpiece. Instead of a camera person laying down each animation cel on top of the background and clicking off frames of film until the animation is shot, in a digital production, you, or someone there in the studio, does the work. Now you need a digital version of your exposure sheets, the document that shows the order, position, and timing of your animation (among other things). Depending on your animation program, you will be working with a digital version of your regular exposure sheets or a timeline, either of which need to have your animation and background files entered into them. Like traditional camera shooting, if you took shortcuts like breaking the character down into separate parts to have less to draw and animate and used a lot of layers, it will take more time to build your scene for output than it would if you had animated fuller with fewer shortcuts. A shortcut in one area can bloat another area.

Once the digital exposure sheets are done, you can render or output a Quicktime movie or some form of video that will enable you to see your animation in motion. The final output medium has to be dealt with next. If you have the right computer set-up, you may be able to output your project directly to its final form. Or, you may need to take the digital output files to a video or film facility to get your animation project to its final form.

Retaining Quality but Cutting Corners: Some General Approaches

- **Instead of renting studio space, make a home studio.** This makes for more flexible hours, more available hours, and no travel time.

- **Do you have an art school nearby with an animation department?** Students are always looking for an internship that actually allows them to learn more than just how to fetch coffee. It might be possible to work with a professor and have the student earn credit for working as an intern on a project. If credit is not available the student might be willing to work for minimum wage and lunch and credit on the film. Know that if you take on a intern you will be working around the academic schedule. Interview each student and have them show you a portfolio. It is good to get a feel for how committed to learning the animation business he/she is and what areas are of most interest. You may find you will take on someone for animation and someone else for ink & paint.

- **Assume more duties.** You are the storyboard person, layout, animator, assistant, and whatever other position needs filled. Hopefully, you will get help on ink & paint and sound. Remember, you do have some real out-of-pocket expenses: supplies, camera, video transfers, and upgrades to your computer software or hardware.

- **Pay on a footage rate instead of hourly.** You're better off paying for work actually done than you are paying for someone to draw part of a picture, get up for a cup of coffee, chat, linger about a bit, then return to their work area in time for lunch. Limited, Medium, and Full are the categories. The more complicated the action and the more characters, the higher the rate. Simple characters with limited animation is the low end of the scale (Limited). Again, books like the Graphic Artists Guild Ethical Pricing Guide or a visit to the Motion Picture Screen Cartoonists Local 839 web site can be helpful for finding the current rates.

- **Keep accurate records of all expenses.** Be aware that the Federal and State government will expect their share of your remaining pie in the form of Medicare, Social Security, FICA, and income taxes. Figure on stashing 20–25% for April 15th. You may have to pay quarterly if you have a relatively regular freelance income. Keeping accurate records, invoices, receipts, bills, and checking account registers allows you to declare all legitimate deductions before you report what you paid yourself. If you've collected enough receipts and kept good records, you may be in good shape, and April 15th may not be totally traumatic.

Keeping records can be done in a ledger book or you can use a computer program like Quicken to keep track of income and assign categories to each expense.

In conclusion, experience can be the best teacher. A couple of 'pizza favor' endeavors will help you develop your 'producing muscles.' You will at least have a good idea of your own capabilities and ability to deliver on time.

The next chapter, *Storyboarding,* gets us back to creativity.

CHAPTER 3

STORYBOARDING AND DESIGN

Now that you've gotten the business side of things out of the way, the next step in the production is to prepare the storyboards. Though the script is the initial vital piece in any production, it is the **storyboard** that acts as the real guide. The old adage, "A picture is worth a thousand words" is especially true here. At this stage in the production, everyone can be brought on to 'the same page' regarding the direction the project takes. The actual meaning of the writer's words are visualized here, understood, and agreed upon. Once the storyboard is 'signed off' on, you're ready to get down to the business of making an animated film.

Storyboarding is the process of taking the perceived, written, or spoken word and giving it a visual and sequential form. Storyboards can be simple black and white line drawings or elaborate and colorful. When drawing a storyboard for a project using collage, the process of finding the right images for the film can be combined with the storyboard phase. Photocopies of the images can be cut out and pasted, giving the artist and client a better feel for the final result.

Storyboards are often started as a series of numbered, sequential thumbnail-sized drawings, sometimes in the margins of the script itself.

Once the story or idea has been 'seen' in your mind as a sequence, these tiny rough drawings can be expanded into story sketches. (I should note that some studios and artists have a different order of doing things. Some skip the thumbnail phase, do some quick story sketches, then go right to the storyboard. Some do thumbnails and skip the story sketches, preferring to find and flesh things out as they draw the storyboard.)

Story sketches are broad stroke drawings. You draw the key parts or points of the story, usually feeling out the design and flow of the piece. Seeing as much of the environments as possible. Where the furniture is placed. Where the entrances and exits are. Where's the closet and what's been hiding in it? This is an opportunity to expand and enrich the visuals and concept of the story.

Storyboards can be done on pre-printed forms available from art supply stores that are available in a variety of sizes and styles, or they can be custom-made yourself with a copier or output from your computer. There are single frame per page and multiple frames per page forms, both large and small. Storyboards can also be done on those nice, cheap unlined writing tablets that you get in grocery stores.

Having suggested the nice, cheap writing tablets, I should mention that it is a good idea to do your storyboard in correct proportion to the medium you are working in because your storyboard drawings can sometimes be used as layouts for backgrounds.

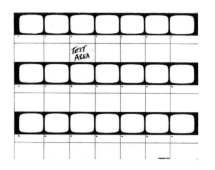

The screen that the final animated film is going to be seen on has a specific proportion called the aspect ratio. 4:3 for TV and video (technically, it's 1.33:1), 1:85 for wide screen film, and 16:9 for high definition TV.

If you happen to use those nice cheap pads, be aware that they are wider than normal for TV and a bit too tall for wide screen, so compose your drawings with that in mind. If you make your own storyboard forms, use a **field guide** (the field guide will be discussed in the layout portion of the book) to draw the frame to the right proportion. Or, if you're making them on a computer, use the measurements from the field guide and make your document that size and proportion.

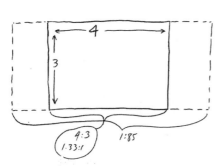

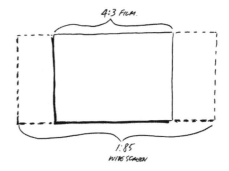

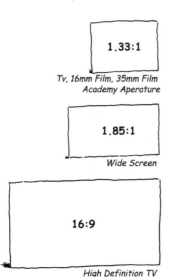

Storyboards can also be drawn large enough to be used as layouts, the next step in the production of an animated film, where the visualized script of the storyboard is redrawn at the size and proportion needed for the final production. This method of tracing information directly from the storyboard can save a lot of time if you're in a bind or just want to save a step or two.

Director's Note:

Stories are told and storyboards are drawn in relation to the audience or viewer. The audience is represented by the camera. This is true whether you are producing in traditional or digital mode. It is just basic storytelling or filmmaking. Since the camera is not just the device used to record the action, but is an actual 'entity,' it needs to be referred to in a special way. In this book, when the camera is being referred to it will be capitalized (Camera). Sometimes the entire word is written in uppercase letters (CAMERA), depending on the personal style or taste of whoever is writing the storyboard descriptions. It's a personal choice, really. Camera directions and terms, however, are always written in uppercase letters. ZOOM IN to a CLOSE UP of the character's face is an example.

Storyboard Language

There are some standard motion picture terms that are used for storyboarding. The most important and useful, in relation to animation storyboarding, are terms that describe frame compositions, camera movements, and transitions.

The first set of terms are framing terms. **Framing** refers to the subject or subjects that need to be featured in a scene and their size in it. Their size is determined by the distance of the camera from the subjects. The subject being focused on can be anything in the scene. The most common focus is the main person in the scene, so the terms will be described in relation to a human figure walking towards the Camera. There are three primary frame sizes. They are (abbreviations in parentheses):

Wide shots (WS): The whole subject, from head to toe is shown.

Medium Shots (MS): About half of the subject, from head to a little below the waist is shown.

Close Shots (CS): About a quarter to a third of the subject, from head to mid-chest is shown.

Then there are Close Ups, a subspecies of the Close shot. These focus on the facial area of the subject and can be used to reflect and reveal emotions, reactions, or focus on important speech.

Wide Close Up (WS): The subject's head down to the shoulders, approximately, is the area of a Wide Close Up.

Full Close Up (CU): The subject's head and neck is the approximate area of a Full Close Up.

Medium Close Up (MCU): The Medium Close Up generally focuses on the subject's head or face only.

Extreme Close Up (ECU): An Extreme Close Up focuses on the subject's face area at its widest and can focus in as close as desired. Examples include an Extreme Close Up of a subject's eyes reacting to something, or an Extreme Close Up of a subject's sweating brow or drooling mouth.

Wide Shot

Medium Shot

Close Shot

The Full shot and the Medium shot have a sub-species, too, that include the medium wide shot (MWS) and the medium close shot (MCS). There are some additional types of shots that can be used to add variety, drama, and clarity to the storytelling process in storyboarding. These shots or angles can also give the Point of View (POV) of the Camera or subject.

The Over the Shoulder Shot: The camera is positioned behind the subject to allow the viewer to see what the subject sees. The head and shoulder of the subject can be used as a framing device, helping to focus on the background or the reaction of others in the scene. In animation, this kind of shot can be used as a lip-syncing shortcut. You don't show the mouth of the character therefore you don't have to draw the mouth's lip sync mouth action. It saves drawings and time.

Wide Close-up Shot

Full Close-up Shot

Medium Close-up Shot

Extreme Close-up Shot

The Overhead Shot (AKA: TILT DOWN shot): The Camera's POV is positioned above the action in the scene. This kind of shot can be used to establish the location of the action or see the action as it unfolds. Perhaps something is approaching, unseen to the subject. These shots can be quite dramatic and can be used to illustrate the scale of objects in the scene.

The Low Angle Shot (AKA: TILT UP shot): The Camera's POV is from ground level. An insect's eye view, a small pet's eye view, or any other stature challenged eye view. These can also be dramatic shots that show scale.

The Camera action used to achieve an overhead shot or a Low Angle Shot is called **TILTING.** The Camera is **TILTED UP** into a Low Angle type shot or **TILTED DOWN** into an Overhead type shot.

The next couple of terms you'll need are Camera motion terms. These terms describe the camera's motion or the location and angle that the camera is set at to view the scene.

ZOOM IN or ZOOM OUT: Changes the frame size from a wide shot to a Close shot and vice versa. You **ZOOM IN** from a wider shot to a closer shot and **ZOOM OUT** from closer shots to wider shots. Similar to live action **DOLLY** moves where the Camera is physically moved **IN** closer or **OUT** further from the subject.

PAN or PANNING: Camera motion in a vertical or horizontal direction. You can **PAN LEFT**, **PAN RIGHT**, **PAN UP**, or **PAN DOWN**.

Over the Shoulder Shot

Overhead Shot

Low Angle Shot

Medium Wide Shot

Medium Close Shot

Though the above film terms are the primary ones used in animation storyboarding, there are a lot of other terms that can and should be learned. There is a book listed in the Bibliography at the back of the book entitled "Film Directing—Shot by Shot" written by Steven D. Katz that is highly recommended. It is a very straightforward and comprehensive and discusses many important aspects of filmmaking.

Some of these terms, when used in a traditional 2D, flat animation context, refer to an attempt to emulate a live action camera. The animation or rostrum camera cannot do everything that a live action camera can do. Later in the book, we will discuss the animation camera and its use, but a brief introduction right here will be help you understand the storyboarding terms as they relate to the camera used in the production of traditional animation.

An animation camera can physically move down its column, closer to artwork in order to ZOOM IN on it, or move up its column, further away from the artwork to ZOOM OUT. This animation camera action gives the range of frame sizes described earlier: Wide Shots to Close Ups. Otherwise, it is a stationery camera.

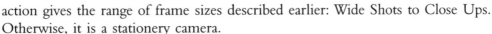

Closer = ZOOM IN   Further = ZOOM OUT

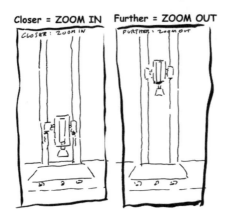

The artwork that is being shot is limited to a certain plane on the tabletop. The artwork can move in the directions of the compass, North, South, East, and West and all points in between. East-West moves are PAN LEFT or PAN RIGHT moves. North-South moves are PAN UP or PAN DOWN moves.

There are also other variations depending on the production mode. In a traditional cel to film production, TILT SHOTS (Overhead or Low Angle shots) have to be drawn in order to illustrate those camera angles. Digital production enables you to actually use a virtual live action camera as opposed to a stationery animation camera. Therefore, terms like TILT or DOLLY can actually be done as camera moves as opposed to drawn backgrounds or a sequence of animated drawings that imitate those moves.

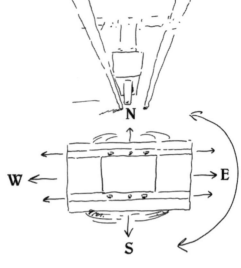

The third category of terms are **Transitions.** These refer to ways of getting from one scene to another. The basic ones include:

CUTS: A simple and sudden change to the next scene.

DISSOLVES or CROSS DISSOLVES: One scene fades out as the next scene is fading in.

FADE INs and FADE OUTs: The present scene fades or dissolves out of view to a screen of black, white, or even a pattern. This transition is usually used as a way of beginning or ending a sequence.

WIPE: The next scene is brought in and replaces the present scene. The new scene can replace the present scene by being revealed on an angle or in a circle or other shape. A variation is to use the incoming scene to push the present scene out of view. There are a wide variety of Wipes and other transitions built in digital editing software.

The Process of Storyboarding

When storyboarding, you're telling a story in a series of pictures. Your mind's eye is the camera. Any and all visual techniques are available to you along with a fantastic array of visual effects. But all the effects in the computer world won't rescue a poorly set up animation. Be creative, but be aware that there are things to pay attention to like continuity.

Continuity refers to the details of the story. The location and number of props from scene to scene is something to be carefully maintained. Excessive zooming in and out should be avoided unless you're illustrating something that specifically requires that Camera action. The use or overuse of transitions and effects is also something to avoid. For example, old-time film iris effects are nice and fun, but if used too often or in the wrong place in the film, the effect just won't work.

These storyboarding considerations also depend upon your personal taste, intent (maybe you're actually doing a parody of an old silent film where those effects were popular), and your audience. If this is a personal or experimental project and YOU are the client, then no problem. It's good practice to view a lot of films, both classic and current ones. Note the different cinematic styles that are out there. Though not quite as glamorous, animation is a filmmaking art form.

Storyboarding also includes setting up the audio part of your film. Alongside or underneath, depending upon the style of storyboard, your audio/dialog and description of the panel or scene has to be included. It is a good practice to write your voice over or character dialog in capital letters with quotation marks to make a distinction between the dialog and screen/camera directions. A storyboard panel can illustrate one word or an entire speech, depending upon the style of the film and the action being shown. A rule of thumb is one panel per second, but it is a very flexible rule. You want to convey the message of the story, but you don't want to do an excessive number of drawings. Leave the excessive amounts of drawing for the animation phase.

There's another item to consider at this stage of production. What is the look/style/design of the film and characters? If it's hard to draw at the storyboard stage, it's going to be hard in every phase to follow. This question may sound silly, but are you going to be making reproductions of the board? Photocopies? If so, then don't use a non-photo blue pencil as the final mark making tool. And red pencils copy as black line, so that really beautiful drawing you just did that was roughed in using a crimson Col-erase and tightened up with the 6B Kohinoor may look like it was drawn with a charcoal briquette after you copy it.

Since art and design are so very subjective, I should say right about here that there really aren't any hard and fast rules in design. One person's trash is another person's treasure or something like that. Some considerations:

Once a storyboard is completed, it is often a good idea to see it on film, video or some digital medium. The storyboard, when combined with a soundtrack, can give a rough, but good idea of how the final film will look or feel. The storyboard and audio track, when put on film, video or digital viewing medium, is called an *animatic*. Another, old fashioned, 'back in the day' type term for shooting the storyboard onto film to get an idea of its flow is a **Leica reel**.

In addition to the storyboard there is the other important thing to be confirmed and set at this early stage of the production. The animated actors or characters.

Character Design

When designing characters or any part of an animated production, keep in mind that what you are doing is graphic problem solving. Do the locations of the characters convey the message of the project? If so, what do they need to look like in order to best accomplish that? Often, an animator will just draw favorite, funny characters that don't really have anything to do with the project. They may animate nicely and give a lot of pleasure to the animator and even to the people who view the animation, but does the character really work in relation to the animated piece? Sometimes, clients will have a pre-designed character that is to be used and whose design is to be strictly adhered to. If you, the production company's designer-director-animator person have been given the responsibility of designing characters, there are a few things to consider before and while designing the characters.

Who is your audience? Simpler shapes and heavier outlines are usually used for animated characters intended for juvenile audiences. Maybe it relates, somehow, to the fact that kids use crayons and those fat soft pencils in school. Thinner lines are more sophisticated and can be used to draw more complex shapes and shadings and are, therefore, considered to be more mature and adult.

What is the message to be conveyed? Serious? Hard sell? Youth oriented? Intended for a mature audience? Public service? Will the message be best conveyed by a human character, a talking animal in a top hat, or an anthropomorphic (definition: giving human form or personality to animals, or normally inanimate objects) version of the client's product?

What is your personal or 'house' style? Quite often, animation artists are asked to work in styles that are not necessarily their own. Versatility is very important when working as an animation artist. One assignment may have you drawing thin, squiggly lines and simple characters, the next may have you drawing an army of robot squirrels in a style reminiscent of old Warner Brothers cartoons from the 1940s. You never know. Be prepared by learning to be as versatile as possible. Practice drawing a variety of styles.

There are animation artists and studios that have their own distinct styles that are highly recognizable and no matter what the style they have been asked to work in, some recognizable element of their personal style manages to shine through. Bob Kurtz of Kurtz and Friends Animation Company in Los Angeles comes to mind, but there are others.

DESIGNER'S NOTE:

Remember that every artist has their own style. It may be inspired by, or even a near direct copy of another artist's work, but it is still uniquely yours. Uniqueness and individuality are the ultimate goals of any artist and should be encouraged. If you can achieve success in animation and never have to emulate someone else's style, you are to be congratulated, admired, and revered, in addition to the thing that you will most certainly be—emulated.

Simple or complex? Whether to go with a simple or complex character can sometimes be determined by the amount of time you have to produce the animation and the size of the budget. Detailed characters with a lot of colors are appealing and grab and hold the interest of your audience quickly, but they take more time to draw and color. And if they take more time, then they cost more to produce. This leads us to our next consideration....

Can the style of the character be drawn easily and quickly by your assistants? This thought is pretty self-explanatory. It is a good idea to know the skill boundaries of the people you are depending on to help you. You don't want to have to spend a lot of time fixing the artwork because the characters turned out to be more complex than your assistants could quickly and efficiently execute.

The length of the film? Will the style of character wear thin after a long period of time? A squiggly, vibration line and loose flashing color may work well for a 30-second commercial or in short segments in a music video or cable TV comedy network-inspired spot, but will all of that graphic activity be distracting in a ten minute industrial or theatrical short?

Model Sheets: A Guide for Accurate Drawing and Re-drawing

Let's say that the little cavebear from the storyboard is our character. No matter how powerfully and phenomenally versatile, talented, and skilled you and your team of artists are, it's difficult to maintain the accurate drawing of a character through an entire production. The more you draw a character, the better and easier you draw them. But then you want the character to evolve, and with total innocence and ignorance you will begin to ever so slightly and subtly change the character. If this goes unchecked for an entire production, the character in the last scene can appear to be related to the character in the first scene only through the recognition of costume color and dental records. Oh, alright...not quite that bad, but there can be unintentional variations in the way a character is drawn through a production. This was a roundabout way of saying that once the characters have been designed, you will need to draw a **model sheet.**

A model sheet is a page of drawings showing your character in a variety of poses, designed to help visualize the entire character from different angles and with different expressions. Think of a virtual reality rotation; a walk around the entire character. Of course, if the character is designed in a 3D program, you can just animate the character around. More on that in the Animation chapter. In 2D or traditionally drawn animation, you will need to draw the character from the front, back, 3/4 view, top, bottom, and both sides. You need to draw both sides because, for example, a wristwatch on one wrist or a badge on a single lapel or an earring in one ear makes each side distinct. It is best to make sure that the character is well-defined.

Poses of the character in action, samples of the character's mouth while talking (lip sync), and any props the character may use should also be defined. If you envision any particular mannerisms that you'd like to see the character have, they can be indicated on the model sheets.

Front   3/4   Side   Rear

If the character is interacting with other characters, size relationships will be important, too. You will need a model sheet with a line up of all the characters to indicate their height relationships.

Further Design: The Animation Environment

The animation environment is another way of saying **backgrounds** or **stage.** At this early stage of the production, you're deciding on the style, not actually beginning to paint or render final, usable artwork. Background style and design is more subjective than character design because it supports the stage where the defining action and storytelling is taking place. The design style of the backgrounds should compliment the characters and help feature the "actors" not compete with them by being too cluttered, bright, or otherwise distracting or overwhelming.

The mode of production can determine the approach to the backgrounds. Traditional and digital methods are 'cross-discipline,' meaning traditional techniques—color media on paper or canvas in a size that matches the animation format—can be rendered and digitized for use in a digital production. Conversely, digital techniques—3D or other CGI—can be printed out in the correct proportion to be used as a background in a traditional production.

The same questions that guide the design of characters can be used to determine the style of the backgrounds.

Who is the audience? Is it a young audience? Would simple child-like artwork best convey the message? Is it a mature, sophisticated audience? Would artwork in a New York magazine style work well?

What is the message? Do you need realistic backgrounds to convey or illustrate the message?

Do you have a personal or 'house' style? Would the project work best if the characters and backgrounds match?

Should the backgrounds be simple or complex? Would a simple plain color background work or would a complex drawing with a lot of bright colors work?

Can the chosen style be done by the available background artist?

Will you have to hire someone from outside of your usual 'crew'? Will they need to be paid more?

Will the style still be interesting and appealing through the project? Will the colors, complexity, or imagery in the backgrounds become tedious or unpleasant by the end of the film?

An investment of time (storyboarding, designing characters, discussing things with the client, etc.) and money (the client has sent your initial payment, you've hired some help, purchased supplies related to the production, etc.) have been made, and now, assuming that all approvals are in, it's time to begin the real production. The next step is to get into the audio process.

CHAPTER 4

AUDIO

In spite of their name, silent movies really weren't that silent. There was always an organist or some keyboard accompanist playing along with the movie. Playing rapidly for dramatic scenes or slowly for sad ones.

Whenever you watch a film and hear a clarinet, you can be pretty sure that something comical is about to happen. And those familiar wah, wah, wah sounds of a trombone usually signal the end of a sequence. Music announces upcoming cinematic possibilities by becoming ominous. Music can convey emotions with sappy, syrupy strings or a happy, bouncy beat.

And speaking of beats, you know that when you hear a heavy beat and an electric guitar with a distorted tone, the corporate client is targeting the wallets of a youthful demographic. Add a wah-wah pedal and a funky bass guitar line and you know the target is a melanin-enriched ethnic minority group.

Preparing for Production

Audio for animation—or the broader category, film—isn't only about music. Sound effects are used to accentuate action. And the vocal characterizations and performances of the actors that supply the animated character's voices are key components in defining characters. It's a fun part of any production, and the decisions that are made and implemented in the final production are important to the success of a project.

Music, like design, is incredibly subjective. Every director or animator or film-maker has some idea of the music he or she likes and feels is appropriate for their film. And there are tons of musicians with synthesizers and home studios that can provide anything you might desire. Knowing or being familiar with the musician can be a plus. Having an idea of the style or approach they might have toward your subject matter can save a lot of time. Of course, sometimes you can receive a pleasant surprise. Knowing or deciding on the bpm (beats per minute), or rhythm early on in the process also helps. While animating, the accents of the action can be aimed at some part of the beat. There are many parts of the beat, therefore, you really don't have to worry about the animation being predictable or repetitious because you're having things happen to a steady beat. Think jazz solo or song stylist. Working in this way also gives the musician and sound effects person more possibilities to hook effects to. It makes it more fun and you can end up with a fuller film if the music/sfx people are having a good time, too.

Visualize the Project

In a single person or small studio setting it is good to be able to do as many things as possible. Not that you are trying to be an absolute control freak; just knowledge-able, informed, aware, and ultimately, profitable. In a small studio, like any other business, you have to keep an eye on budgets. What can you do to help make things go as smoothly, and therefore, as economically as possible. With that in mind and before going too deeply into the audio process, it's a good idea to sit down and visualize your project.

If the music is being recorded before the animation is to be done and will in fact be used as the basis of the animation because you're animating a song or to specific pre-scored music, you'll need to meet with the musician and go over the storyboard with them to show them what your specific needs are. A key item that you'll need at that meeting is a written and timed indication of your needs. These instructions are called **cue** or **dope sheets.** They are closely related to **exposure sheets**, an essential part of the animation process, which will be explained shortly.

Of course, you already visualized the project while storyboarding, but this time you're focusing on audio and not illustrating the written words. In addition, you have an aid in the process this time. Use the storyboard as a guide, go through it imagining the character's voices, the sounds you might hear, the style of music that might work well, and jot down ideas as they come to you. Like the earlier design phase, it can be helpful to ask yourself a few questions about your film and the music that might be used with it. This is, after all, audio design. What is the message of the film? What are the thoughts and feelings that you want to convey? What is the length of the film? What style of music do you feel will best convey the thoughts and feelings that you want to express? Will the style that you're leaning toward sustain through the whole film, or will it grow tedious after a while? Will the music be a distraction, causing the viewers to dance in the aisles instead of watching the visual?

This is a good time and place to try an exercise.

The storyboard panels that have been inserted here are from the cavebear storyboard in the Storyboard and Design chapter. These panels are going to serve as the basis of a demonstration in the Layout chapter, but I thought that they might be able to serve a purpose here, too. Using these storyboard panels as guides, let's take a look at the scene that they represent and jot down some thoughts that occur regarding the sound effects that could be added. And maybe even some musical thoughts as well.

First, the action: The cavebear enters the room, from offscreen, through a doorway. While we ZOOM OUT to reveal the room, the cavebear skids into the room and steps forward to stand in front of a blank wall. He reaches forward and picks up a stick of charcoal and draws on the wall, then steps back and takes a deep breath. Where to start? Well...what sort of music would make this more interesting? Subjective, subjective, subjective. The entire film needs to be looked at, not just one scene (if there is a musical theme for the entire film, then some variation on it might work on a single scene). What is the film about? Should the time period of the film influence the music choice. Since it's a prehistoric cavebear, would a primitive drums track work well? Something punny like 'rock' music? A contrast, using sophisticated classical music to contrast the prehistoric theme?

What sound effects do you need? In panel 18, we could use the sound of approaching footsteps. Specifically, barefoot on dirt. The cavebear's skid to a halt in panel 19 could be the sound effect of a car screeching to a halt instead of something that would more exactly match the visual of bare feet sliding in dirt. If a car screeching to a halt is used, then wouldn't it make sense to have the sound of an approaching car along with or instead of the approaching footsteps? Would it be too much to have a sound effect for panel 21 where the bear picks up the charcoal stick? Maybe a music cue might be better? What kind of sound for the drawing action? Accent the speed by having something 'whooshie,'

or accent the scratching sound that drawing on a cave wall would make. Will you be able to find a deep breath sound effect for panel 23, or will it have to be recorded? Would a music cue work better? There are no hard and fast rules and, therefore, no absolutely correct answers, because audio, like art and design, is very subjective. It boils down to what the person with the final word truly likes. In a commissioned piece of work, it's the client. In a personal piece of work, it's you.

Of course, sometimes the client will select the music and will work actively with you (or sometimes against you) in the selection and placement of music and effects. In this case, you will need to come to some kind of agreement with the client about the appropriate audio.

Composing Your Audio Thoughts

When you have your thoughts and notes about the direction that you think your audio should go, you are ready to have some useful fun in the next step. To begin the next part of the audio process, gather together whatever available audio elements you have that you think will work well with your project and put together an audio sketch. Later in the production, when the animation has been created, the audio sketch can be transferred to the medium used in the production, aligned or synced up with the animation, and used as a rough audio track called a scratch track.

An audio sketch can serve as an inspiration to the animator, or can be a time and money saving effort, supplying audio elements to the sound designer. These rough audio tracks give you an audio background over which you can imagine, plan, and otherwise envision your animation. If you are doing animation with lip sync, an audio sketch can be analyzed or 'read' along with the character's voices, giving you a frame accurate location for animated actions that sound effects or music cues represent.

If the scratch track is done after the animation has been completed, the music and sound effects can be accurately lined up to the animation. If you make the scratch track before the animation is done and the animation doesn't match, the elements can be repositioned and made to match the animation.

Some Suggestions to Get You Started:

- You can find a piece of music from a CD and digitize it. This piece of music can serve as a guide for your sound designer when you go over the project for your real and final audio work.

- If you are hearing a tune or melody in your head and have a synthesizer or other instrument, you can play and record a little melody track to use in a scratch track.

- There are sound effects libraries available on CD at record stores that have a wide variety of effects that can be used in a scratch track (or just for inspiration).

Sound Effects (SFX)

There are many sound effects libraries available on CD. There are also services with libraries like the Hollywood Edge collection or other collections from actual old cartoons. There are, naturally, fees involved. You can record your own with a synthesizer or regular household items and a portable recorder.

Audio Note:

Sound effects can be layered to enhance their effect. For example, in an
industrial film that we produced re-
cently there was a bull character who
was about to be divided into sections.
The bull, naturally, retreated very
quickly from the scene. Instead of only
using rapid hoof beats, our sound
effects person layered hoof beats with
the sound of car tires screeching and
peeling out and a couple of other sounds. It was funny and effective.

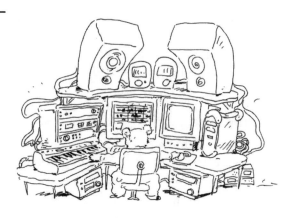

Producer's Note:

Something to remember about using pre-
recorded sound effects or music: the RIGHTS.
Pre-recorded music requires that you pay fees
(hefty, sometimes) if you use a piece of music for
commercial purposes. If you're putting together
a film that's only going to be seen by you and
your amigos in your dorm room, you're OK. If,
however, you're producing a film to be shown
publicly for a price or will receiving any sort of
financial input from the film, you'll need to
acquire rights to the audio piece. The same applies to some sound effects CDs

that are available in record or music stores.
You have to check the label to see if the
audio elements are restricted or available
for usage without additional fees (royalties).

There are huge libraries of prerecorded
music and sound effects available on CD
that are royalty free; the usage fee is built
into the purchase price. These are very
valuable and sound investments, no pun
intended, and also can be very inspiring.

Recording

Sound can be recorded at any good quality sound studio. Where you record depends a lot on your budget, format, and quality needed for delivery. Something that is going to be broadcast nationally needs the highest quality you can muster. A job that is experimental and will never be seen by anyone but you and the goldfish may not really need to be recorded in

that several hundred dollar per hour studio downtown with the carpeted walls and attitude. Sometimes a small, fairly unknown recording studio with reasonable rates can be a real gem. You can even record in a home studio with the right equipment.

The complexity or sophistication of the audio sketch that you make depends on your abilities and equipment.

These audio sketches can be done regardless of the mode you're producing in, traditional or digital. The mode does, however, determine the form that they take and the steps in getting to that final form.

The easiest and most common way to work with audio, regardless of final output and usage, is digitally. It makes sense since most if not all of the elements you'll be gathering and using —music and sound effects—are already in some kind of digital format (CD, DVD, mp3, etc.). An audio sketch that is made with the intention of being used later in the production as a scratch track in sync with the animation needs to have the individual elements in a form that can be easily rearranged in order to accurately sync up with the animation's visual events. This is easier, faster, and more economical in a layered digital form than an audio tape or film form. Deciding on the location of the audio element and clicking the mouse a couple of times to move and align it is easier and faster than finding the location to sync to and physically cutting the tape. There are other easier tape methods that can be used to perform the task, but none of them are as quick, easy, clean, and straightforward as the digital methods. Once you've got the elements you want to use and have arranged them in the order you want, you can proceed according to your production mode. If you're producing in a traditional cel on film mode, your audio sketch needs to be transferred to the film stock used for film audio work—mag stripe. The sound editor will sync up the magstripe with the film visual.

The Next Step

Unless you happen to be an audio expert, your audio will be gathered, supplied, recorded, organized, and otherwise taken care of by a sound designer. Whether you have put together an audio sketch or not, it is a good idea to discuss the audio needs of your project with the person who will be doing the audio work. This is when you can go over your scratch track, character designs, and storyboard with that person and incorporate whatever input they might have. Be open to suggestion. Most, if not all, sound designers work digitally.

Music and sound effects are different than working with a camera or other type of machinery. You're dealing with emotional content and will have different needs. You will also have different discussions with a sound designer than with a camera person. The sound designer is adding to the content of the film, so you should work with someone whose music and work you have actually heard and admired. It's nice if you already know or can get to know the person or can at the very least get along with them. Great reputations or fabulous talents are great, but if you can't agree on anything, it's certainly going to make things more difficult. Of course, the person doesn't have to totally agree with all of your ideas. There will usually be some compromise. But your general direction and desires for your soundtrack should be respected and hope-fully adhered to by the sound designer. Learning to accurately convey your thoughts, concepts, and desires accurately is essential.

If the animation already exists in its final form or as a pencil test, the mode of production comes into play. If you're producing traditional cel on film, the sound designer can be given a videotape of the animation with a voice or scratch track as a sync guide (how the tracks need to be aligned to match your animation's lip sync) along with a version of the animation with audio time code recorded onto it. The audio time code will ensure that the voice, music, and effects tracks will all be, and remain, in sync to the picture. If you're producing the animation digitally, the sound designer can still be supplied a videotape of the animation with timecode for sync.

Getting Into Production

Animated films aren't just about the quality of the animation. They are films, and as such require all the elements of a live action production including well-done audio. A project has three main audio needs: the voice, the music, and the sound effects. The audio augments the visuals. It can make a good film a great one. It can even help a poorly animated film appear to be better. A bad, boring, or inadequate soundtrack, however, can bring even the best animation to its knees.

When you discuss the characters with the voice person, it is always good to have character sketches, preferably in color, available to show them. You can tell right away if the voice will work with the character. Like the sound designer, the voice person will be bringing their own ideas to the table. More than likely the voice person is an actor or actress, so be prepared to be entertained, cajoled, and forced to compromise a bit. The better you actually know your characters, the better you will be able to convey that information to the voice person, and the happier you'll be with the result. Go beyond the physical drawn design of the character and invent a history and a life for it, something the actor can use as motivation.

It is always a good idea to have the storyboard and character models with you at a recording session. The actors need to know 'who they are' in order to match their voice performance to the look and personality of the character. Sometimes, even though the visual of the character is pre-conceived, something in the voice of the actors can inspire subtle nuances and possible improvements. If this happens, give abun-

dant thanks, praise, and acknowledgment to your voice talent person because there's a great opportunity for mutual good fortune.

DIRECTOR'S NOTE:

OK. You've gone over the storyboard with the sound designer, you know what music you want and what effects you want and where they should go. You've gone over the storyboard and shown the characters to the voice folks and everything seems like it's going to work. Its time to record. Here are some helpful tips to keep in mind:

• If you weren't able to discuss the character voices needed with the actor before the recording session, you will need to do it before the session starts. Usually everyone gathers together in the waiting area of the studio a few minutes before the session is scheduled to begin in order to take care of any last

minute business (signing releases, and the like) and go over any basic direction that needs to be understood before beginning the session.

• The actor(s) may have some specific or new ideas about the characters that may fit in with your vision and work very well. Or, the actor may have a particular voice that they really want to use and may even insist upon using. Don't be bullied.

Insist on getting the performance that you feel is best for the project. If there is time, let them get their specific thoughts out of their system at the end of the session.

• Conduct the actors. Think of them as an orchestra. If there are cues that need a particular spark or oomph, gesture, point, or otherwise act out the script.

• Act in response to the actors. If a particular emotion has not been especially well conveyed by the actors, act it out. Show the expression on your face. It becomes an interesting interactive experience that can enhance the session and the performances. You're the director. Assess the situation and act accordingly.

If you hired a competent audio person, they will know their equipment and the technical aspects of recording your session. Let them do their job. Most professionals don't mind if you have a technical question, especially if it will help you set up your future sessions or projects better, making their jobs easier. Remember that you're dealing with a professional, and that you will possibly alienate them if you come on too strong with some insignificant bit of info you picked up in a magazine article.

If you're recording at a good quality recording studio, you'll have a variety of recording media to record onto or transfer to. Reel-to-reel audio tape, audio cassette, a variety of digital audio tape (DAT, ADAT, DA-88) formats, videotape (Betacam SP or digital formats), CD, DVD, or audio files posted on an FTP site that allows you to download the files directly to your computer.

Exposure Sheets

In order to match audio events on the soundtrack, you'll need to know where those audio events are happening. This is where exposure sheets come in. These are written indications of the audio track that are broken down phonetically by the individual word or phrase or by music or sound effect accents. The guide doesn't absolutely HAVE to be traditional exposure sheets, though. If you're in a time bind or just need rough

indications, you can quickly read the track and make indications on your script or storyboard. The main things you need are the frame numbers or time code numbers that the words or effects (audio events) occur.

You can have a soundtrack read by professional track-reading services or by just about any film editor. Even if the editor doesn't do it very often, they at least have the equipment and may be open to teaching you how to read a track. Of course, if you have the time, or are short on budget (a recurring theme in this book), or just want to have as much control as possible, you can do it yourself.

Producer's Note:

You can make your own custom bar sheets with custom increments in the 'layers' section. The Bar Sheet illustrated here has twelve frames corresponding to each bar of music so this set of sheets would work well for a project being animated at 12 frames per second or 24 frames per second on "2s." If you're working on a project that is being animated specifically for video output (30 fps) or Internet output (typically, 10-15 fps) you can make a custom set of sheets in a page layout program like Pagemaker or Quark Express.

Traditional Track Reading

Track reading is the process that takes the recorded audio and breaks it down phonetically so the animator can animate to specific audio events. There are a couple of main ways that this is done, depending on the mode of production. In traditional film animation, the recorded audio track is transferred to a type of film stock called mag stripe. This is a kind of sprocketed film with a pair of magnetic audio tape tracks embedded on one side of it.

If you are doing a traditional production, you will need a couple of pieces of equipment, a synchronizer with a frame counter and a sound head (for picking up the audio from the magnetic stripe) and a 'squawk box' or amplifier. A synchronizer is a device used in the film industry to line up or sync multiple tracks of audio with a picture track. When synching up audio with picture, yet another piece of equipment is used, a viewer.

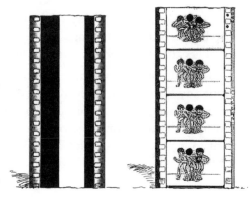

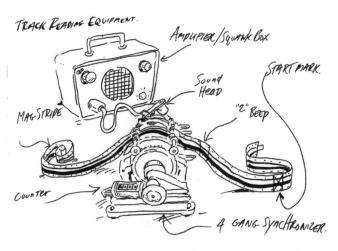

The soundtrack is placed in the synchronizer, a start mark is placed on the mag stripe, the frame counter is set to zero, the sound head is lowered onto the mag stripe, and the audio track is manually run through the synchronizer. The soundtrack is scrubbed or run back and forth to find and decipher the audio. The phonetic breakdown of the audio track is written down on the exposure sheets at the frame that the sound occurs at. Other audio events that require their precise timing, music beats, background sounds, and the like, can be done at this time and written down on the exposure sheets.

A more detailed demonstration of traditional track reading is included in the Appendix.

Digital Track Reading

Digital track reading, regardless of the computer platform, requires less extra equipment than the traditional film method. In order to work with it, your audio track needs to be input into your computer. This can be done by having your audio person make digital audio files of your soundtrack and transferring them to CD,

Jaz, Zip, or whatever form of input media you use. The files can even be posted on an FTP site and downloaded directly into your computer.

Audio files from tape or other external audio source can also be input into your computer through your audio inputs located, usually, on the back of your computer.

Once the audio is digitized and resting comfortably on your hard drive, you can open the files in any audio program with the ability to display the wave form in a timeline relative to the frame rate of your animation's final output; 24 fps (frames per second) for film, 30 fps if non-drop frame video, 29.97 fps if drop-frame video, and 25 fps for PAL, the European standard. Viewing the audio file's waveform as frames is the best and easiest way to work, but the SMPTE timecode display works well, too. In a pinch, or for quick reads, you can just use the basic and default minutes and seconds display. You use your cursor to select an area of audio and play it as many times as necessary to get the needed information and write it down on your exposure sheets.

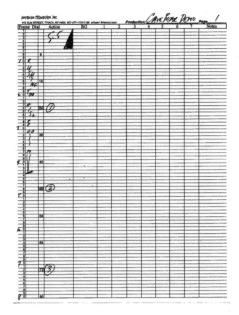

Since track reading is such an integral part of an animation production, this next exercise will show you how to 'read' a little three second, 80 frame (one exposure sheet) bit of audio track. This will show how to read voice over track (where you only need to know the location and timing of individual words or phrases) and lip sync track (where you need to know the phonetic location and timing of the words and syllables in order to make a character appear to speak).

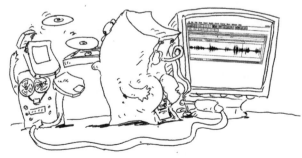

If you have ProTools, Sound Edit 16, Peak, Sonic Foundry, or some other high end audio program you will have a lot of powerful digital audio tools at your disposal to clean up and boost your track and can go much deeper into it than this

---

exercise and book will take you. No matter the program you use, it is always best to start with a clean, clear, strong, audio track whenever possible.

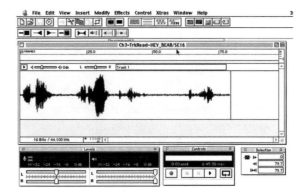

If you record the audio to your own hard drive, you can follow along with this exercise. The numbers probably won't match exactly, but the principle of the whole thing is simple enough for you to follow along.

AUDIO NOTE:

To read an audio track you're going to need:
• A pencil with an eraser.
• Enough exposure sheets to cover the length of the audio track.
• The script, or some legible, written form of the words you're working with.

For this exercise, a tiny script was written as a guide. In a production, you'll need to have a copy of your script handy in order to know exactly what words are being said, in case the vocal performance is somewhat unclear.

Next, a rough storyboard was drawn up to illustrate the script and set up the animation action. In a production, the storyboard can act as a script since it contains the written words that the audio track was made from.

To prepare your exposure sheets, you need to:

- Decide on a frame rate for the production. Your exposure sheets are written in reference to the frame rate.
- Gather enough exposure sheets to cover the length of the audio track to be read.
- Number the exposure sheets sequentially.
- Indicate the seconds on all sheets, starting with the first sheet. You do this by marking off every 10 frames and simply adding the correct sequential number in front of the 0 in the far left column.

When you're done, the exposure sheets should look something like these examples.

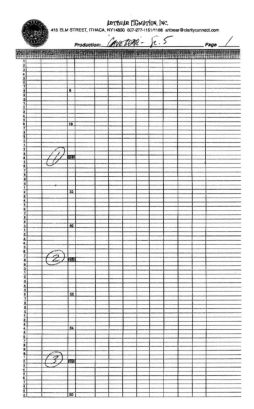

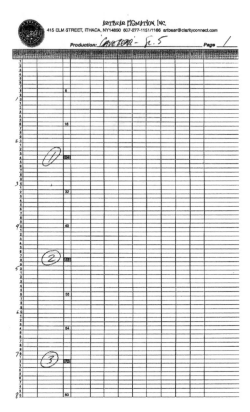

Reading the Track

With your audio on your hard drive and your exposure sheets prepared, open the file in your audio editing program. This exercise is being done in Macromedia's SoundEdit 16, v. 2.

One of the first things you'll need to do is set up the audio output parameters. The track has to be viewed and 'read' at the same frame rate as your final output.

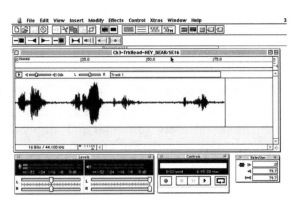

A Short Guide to Frame Rates

- 24 fps for film
- 29.97 fps for video (dropframe) or 30 fps (non-drop frame)
- Internet/Web formats play at a variety of speeds: 4-15 fps.

    Experiment and use the frame rate that will give you an acceptable 'smoothness' for the smallest number of files and smallest overall file size for the completed animated piece.

AUDIO NOTE:

It is also a good idea to set the Preferences to: 'Play from Insertion point.' When playing the short sections of audio you select and analyze, you will want the audio to play from the exact point that the cursor is blinking, not from the default position, the beginning of the entire file.

The Steps

1. Open your sound file and adjust your ruler units to reflect the output parameters you just set. (VIEW>Ruler Units).

2. Adjust your window size. Scale your view down to single frame increments using the horizontal zoom bar located at the bottom left-hand side of the window; 1-10 frame units works well for basic track reading; 1-5 frame units work well if you really need to get crucial.

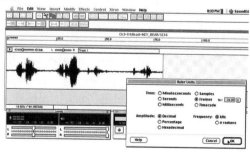

You will need to indicate your track reading onto the pre-numbered exposure sheets you just set up.

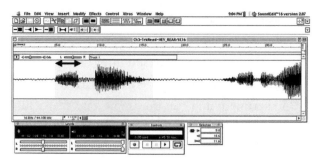

3. Select the area around the first waveform shape, frames 5-8. Press the 'space' bar and play the sample, hearing the word 'hey.'

4. At frame 5 of your exposure sheets, write the word 'hey,' the first frame of the word.

5. On the exposure sheet, draw a vertical line down to frame 8, the end of the word, then make a horizontal line at the bottom of the vertical line (making an upside down "T"). The vertical line indicates the duration or length of the word, the horizontal line indicates that this is the last frame of the word.

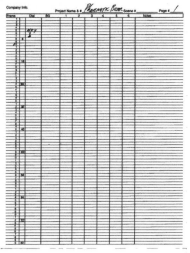

6. Roll forward to frame 10, the beginning of the word 'bear.' Write the word on the frame line in the dialogue column just as you did with the word 'hey.' Draw your duration line to indicate the length of the word down to frame 16.

Continue this technique of locating the beginning of the word, writing it down on the corresponding frame of the exposure sheet in the 'dialogue' column, scrubbing forward to determine the duration of the word and locate the end of the word, then indicating it on the exposure sheet with a line, until you get down to frame 60, in order to track read the remainder of the words that only need to be indicated as complete words. At frame 60 we reach the word that needs to be 'read' for lip sync, the word 'phonetic.'

To read words phonetically for lip sync:

1. Locate the beginning of the word 'phonetic' at frame 60. Write 'Ph' or 'F' (without quotation marks) in the dialogue column of the exposure sheet to indicate the sound. 'F' will work just as well as the correctly spelled 'Ph' if it helps you to accurately indicate the sound.

GARDNER'S guide to Creating 2D Animation in a Small Studio

2. Scrub forward to determine the duration of the 'Ph' sound and the beginning of the next syllable.

3. The next syllable, the 'eh' sound, occurs at frame 63. Write 'eh' in the dialogue column. Unlike word or phrase track reading, you don't really need to draw lines to indicate the duration of the sounds because there are a lot of them and they are usually very close together. It keeps it cleaner, simple, less cluttered, easier to read if you don't draw in duration lines.

4. Scrub forward to frame 66 and the 'n' sound. Indicate it on the exposure sheet as you did with the previous syllables.

5. Scrub forward to frame 69 and the 'eh' sound. Indicate it on the exposure sheet as you did with the previous syllables

6. Scrub forward to frame 72 and the 't' sound. Indicate it on the exposure sheet as you did with the previous syllables.

7. Scrub forward to frame 74 and the 'ih' sound. Indicate it on the exposure sheet as you did with the previous syllables.

8. Scrub forward to frame 75 and the 'k' sound. Indicate it on the exposure sheet as you did with the previous syllables. Since this is the last syllable and end of a complete word, you can draw in a duration line.

This is what the completed exposure sheet looks like.

You have just read a track.

Audio Note:

I'm sitting in the South Boarding Lounge in Chicago's Union Station. I'm trying to read, but it's kind of difficult because of the *ambient sound*. Ambient sound is basically the background sound or noise that exists everywhere. If you were standing on the shores of a quiet lake you would hear the lapping of the waves on the shore, the rustling of the wind through the leaves of nearby trees, the chirping of birds. Ambient. Natural. Add a jet flying past, or the impatient honking of a car in the parking lot or shrieks and squeals from the kids over at the concession stand and you're adding effects. Specific sound events that are not a natural part of the environment. Sitting here in Union Station, I'm hearing, 1. the final boarding announcement for train number 727 with a 2:10 departure time to Seattle, Portland. 2. The same announcement in Spanish. 3. People having a

difficult time getting the change machine to work. 4. The sound of a Reese's Peanut Butter cup being opened. 5. The rustling of winter coats as people get in line to board their departing trains. 6. A football game between the Colts and the Patriots. 7. Holiday music (Winter Wonderland, again). 8. A little kid tapping on the metal lockers. 9. His father yelling at him to stop and sit down. 10. The holiday music selection has segued to 'Deck the Halls' on classical guitar. 11. I just sneezed. 12. The rumble of a train leaving the station, maybe the one to Seattle and Portland. 13. The never ending, incoherent murmur of people talking. Occasionally, a few words will rise to the top. 14. Though it's December, I swear I just heard someone walking nearby in a pair of those rubbery beach sandal 'flip-flops.' Yep! There he is. Winter coat and 'flip-flops.' 15. It's first and goal for the Patriots on the Colts five yard line. 16. I just sneezed again.

I have the advantage, if it can really be thought of in those terms, of being here and actually experiencing these events and seeing the reactions to the announcements and other events, but I'm sure you're getting mental pictures of what this place must be like, too. Wherever you are, just stop for a moment and listen to the ambient sounds around you. Which ones are natural and part of the environment normally? These effects could be looped, made to play over and over as part of the background that you notice and yet don't really notice. Which ones are rare, occasional, or one time only audio occurrences that you would need to add to the background soundscape as effects? If you are making your own ambient background loop, you could place the natural events or effects wherever you want in order to enhance your animation or create additional emotional responses. It can also be quite inspiring. Audio the visual.

Once the audio for the production has been recorded, broken down, and written on exposure sheets, you are ready to move forward to the next stage of production, Layout.

CHAPTER 5

LAYOUT

In order to animate the action described in the script and illustrated in the storyboard, the storyboard drawings need to be re-drawn onto animation paper. These drawings are called **layouts.**

These layouts will be used by the animator and background person to produce the animation artwork. You, the layout person, are setting the design of the film at this point, interpreting it, making it "animatable" while still retaining all of its graphic glory.

When working in layout mode, you are a technician in addition to being an artist. You will deal with the mechanical aspects of production like using the field guide to set up pans and zooms.

You will also translate the graphic style into character poses and background layouts. Character drawings always need to be accurate. Background layouts can be a bit looser, depending on the abilities of and your trust in, the background artist.

Layouts are done using the storyboard as a visual guide and the text on the storyboard as a timing guide. If exposure sheets are available, they can be used as the definitive timing guide. You are giving the animator close approximations of where animated events need to happen. It is the animator's job to make the 'magic' happen right on cue.

It is easier sometimes to learn by doing, so let's 'do.' Scene 5 (storyboard panels 18-24) from the cavebear storyboard in the Storyboard and Design chapter seems like a good choice of scenes to layout and animate because they are fairly simple but still offer a variety of tasks to be learned. The storyboard is almost completely **voice over,** meaning the characters don't speak or **lip sync** to the recorded track. The descriptions are done by the voice-over narrator except for the pterodactyl art critic in panel 40 who actually speaks his line and therefore requires lip sync. Get comfy at your animation station, sharpen your pencils, and grab a stack of paper and a field guide. We're about to start.

LAYOUT NOTE:

Since the layout drawings will be used by the animator, the paper used to draw them should be the same size and type as the paper to be used by the animator and assistants. The type of paper used for the layouts that are going to be given to the background artist isn't important, but it is vital that all layouts use the same registration system and be accurately registered.

This is a good spot to explain and define one of the most important tools you will use in animation: the field guide. The **field guide** is a sheet of 15 mil acetate (three times the thickness of a regular acetate cel) with a grid printed on it. This grid is actually a representation of the full film frame divided into smaller film frames or "fields," all sharing a common center. It

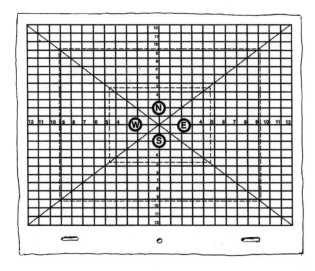

is used to draw and indicate frame sizes and camera movement in the animation environment.

There are two sizes of field guide: 12 field and 16 field. 12 field measures 10.5" x 12"; 16 field measures 12" x 16". In traditional animation, 12 field is the most common size; 16 field, being larger, is used when more detail is needed or when a larger area of art environment needs to be traveled over (zooming in or zooming out). For this exercise, we'll use the more common 12 field guide.

The largest field on the 12 field guide is 12 field (was that too obvious?). The smallest is 1 field. You navigate around the field guide using map coordinates: North (up), South (down), East (right), and West (left). The center of the field is used as the identifying coordinate point. For example, a camera move that begins fairly wide (say, 8 field) at the upper left-hand corner of the frame to a small field (how about 4 field) in the lower right-hand corner of the frame would be indicated as 8 field, 4 North/4 West to 4 field, 8 South/8 East.

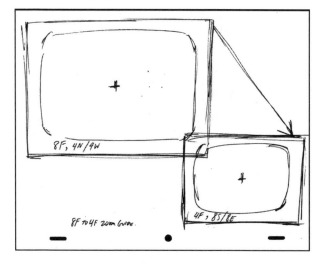

Shot sizes can also be approximately defined as they relate to the animation field guide. Wide shots are 9-12 field, medium shots are 6-9 field, and close shots are 6 field and smaller.

Using these storyboard panels as guides, let's analyze the scene that they represent. We will then break the image down into separate layout elements.

ANIMATOR'S NOTE:

If the storyboard drawings are clean and accurate enough, you can enlarge them on a copier and trace over them.

Though this exercise sounds like it is primarily written for a traditional cel on film animation production, the same basic procedure works for digital animation also. There are some advantages and shortcuts that are available in digital that aren't there in traditional, and with a bit of experience they'll just become a natural part of your layout process, but for the basic, learning purposes of this demo, it's easier and clearer to explain things in simple film-related terms. There's a digital section coming up, but it's probably better if you get the basics here before skipping ahead.

Let's suppose that we have an approved prerecorded track and a set of exposure sheets that have been analyzed or 'read.' Exposure sheets aren't always available at the layout stage of a production, but they can really help if they are. If the actual production sheets aren't available, making a rough test or scratch track and taking rough, approximate timings from it can be a big help.

Panel 18 is a zoomed in view of the cave 'room.' In panel 19, the cavebear slides into the scene, and in panel 20 we see him in his final position, standing in front of the cave wall that he is going to use as his canvas. He is standing near a 'table' with a piece of vine charcoal on it that he will pick up and use to draw with. Through a window, we see trees, mountains, and clouds in the sky. There's also the doorway through which the bear entered. In the middle area of the drawing, we have the cavebear standing partially behind his bed. In the foreground, there are stalagmites

and stalactites framing the scene, and potentially obscuring parts of the cavebear. We will use this frame (panel 20) of the storyboard as a guide for the layouts since it gives us the fullest view of the scene.

The scene can be broken down into these layers and in this order:

Clouds/sky/trees/mountains/cave = Background
Cavebear = an Animation layer
Vine charcoal = an Animation layer
Stalactites/stalagmites/bed = Overlay

If you're not xeroxing the storyboard panels up to size and tracing them off, it's a good idea to start off with a rough sketch of the scene using the storyboard panel as a guide. The rough sketch can be very rough. It needs just enough information to be able to plot your moves.

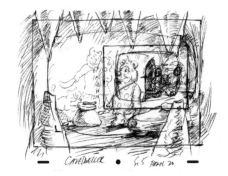

A rectangle around the area in the background in frame or panel 18 can be drawn in at this stage. This will be the area that the camera ZOOMS OUT from. To get the entire frame into view, we will need to zoom all the way out to 12 field center. If you're laying out the scene for yourself, you can work from a rough layout like this, but if you are laying out the scene for an animator, you'll need to add more detail and break it down further. The animator will use this layout guide to know where the fields are and how large to make the actions of the

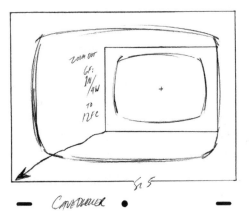

character in order to make sure that the animation is inside the visible area. For accuracy, lay the field guide down on the rough field layout drawing. Lay a piece of paper on top of the field guide and draw a rectangle around the field areas. This scene starts at a 6 field, 1 North, 4 West. This means that the camera will be zoomed in to a 6 field size and offset one field above the center of the frame and four fields to the right. With a different colored pencil, draw the TV cutoff areas in both fields.

Layout Note:

The TV Cutoff and Title Safety areas are the areas of the screen that are guaranteed to be seen by the viewer, regardless of the age or style of television being viewed. It is a graphic safety measure from the days when television screens were more rounded at the corners. The rectangular film frame's image being broadcast was cut off on the top, bottom, and sides by the rounded corners and available area of the television screen.

In order to make sure that the important parts of the broadcast image are seen, you have to make sure that it appears within the TV cutoff area, approximately one and a half fields smaller than the overall field. Title safety is the area where a title is guaranteed to be seen. It is a bit smaller than the TV cutoff. A safe bet is two fields smaller than the overall field. Composing and setting up the animation with its end viewing form in mind guarantees fewer problems, if any at all, later in the production.

Next, you will label the fields and write the instructions, describing the action that the camera is to take. Give the guide the appropriate scene number and production name and you've got your field layout for the scene. We're now ready to layout the background.

To do the background, draw or trace the cave walls, the cave entrance and exterior hills, trees and sky onto a piece of paper. Make sure to keep the important parts of the composition, the parts that must be seen by the audience, within the TV cutoff. The drawing needs to have the important items and areas that the character will be interacting with. The degree of 'tightness,' meaning accuracy or detail, depends on how the background will be rendered for its final version. If you're handing it out to a background artist or if it's being rendered in 3D or collaged, the amount of detail in the illustration should be enough. It shows the accurate location of the 'props' in the scene and gives a general idea of where the light sources are and where the shadows are falling. Since the character is entering the scene through the door near the window and needs to appear as if he is coming into the room from the other side of the doorway (essentially, being revealed as he slides in), you'll need

CAVE DWELLER ● R 5 BG-5

to settle on the final shape of the door and make a registration line for the animator and background artist. The animation and background need to match this line as exactly as possible.

LAYOUT NOTE:

In traditional cel on film production, backgrounds are top-pegged, meaning the peg holes in the paper are at the top of the page. Having the drawing pegged on top makes it easier to remove a stack of drawings from the animation board. Instead of the background coming off of the pegs with the other drawings, it remains in place because your finger doesn't go underneath it. This is helpful when animating and when shooting camera. The same applies to overlays. If top-pegged, an overlay can just be lifted in order to reach underneath and work with the cels.

This, of course, doesn't mean anything if you are only using a bottom peg animation set-up, in which case, you merely secure the background layer to the disk with a piece of tape at the upper corner. In digital production, having a background pegged on top would only be helpful while animating because

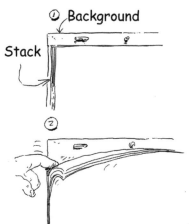

there is no cel handling when putting the animation elements together in the compositing and output stage. The background layout drawings illustrated in this book are bottom-pegged.

The Stick of Charcoal

There is also an object we need to draw. It's the stick of vine charcoal that the cavebear picks up and uses to draw on the wall. Since it is a stationary object, it needs to be drawn in its correct position on a separate piece of paper until the cavebear picks it up (it will then be drawn in his grasp). For the sake of simplicity, let's call and label the vine charcoal 'chalk.' We can now move on to the character.

CAVE DWELLER   •   CHALK

— CAVEDWELLER • 55 — BEAR 1

— CAVEDWELLER • 55 — BEAR 2

Bear 1: the character slides into the scene. He *registers* to the registration line that represents the doorway. Note how the character appears to be entering the room from the other side of the doorway.

Bear 2: The bear scampers up to the foreground.

— • — BEAR-3

— • — BEAR-4

Bear 3: The bear at his final position.

Bear 4: The bear reaches for and picks up the stick of chalk.

Bear 5: The bear holds the stick of chalk and sizes up the wall.

Bear 6: The bear reaches forward and begins to draw. He is going to be drawing the mural, so his action needs to cover the entire area of the mural so that it will appear to be drawn on. In this scene, the bear has been set up to start drawing at the top of the mural. Placing the layout of the mural drawing underneath the layout drawing you're making will help you draw the character in the correct positions.

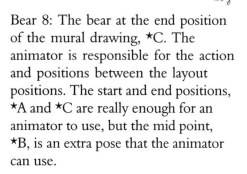

Bear 7: The bear at the final position of mural drawing. These two drawings were done with the mural layout as a guide. Bear 6 is starting at the top of the banana, ★A. Bear 7 is the bear at the saber-toothed tiger's tail ★B, the mid point of the mural drawing.

Bear 8: The bear at the end position of the mural drawing, ★C. The animator is responsible for the action and positions between the layout positions. The start and end positions, ★A and ★C are really enough for an animator to use, but the mid point, ★B, is an extra pose that the animator can use.

CAVE DWELLER • S. 5   MURAL-1   BEAR-9

The mural drawing as it appears when fully 'drawn' on the wall.

Bear 9: The bear stands back to admire his work.

There is one more thing to draw as a separate element. The overlay. This drawing includes the stalactites, stalagmites, and bed.

Like the piece of vine charcoal, the stalagmites and stalactites that are hanging about in the foreground and the bed need to be drawn onto a separate layer. They will become the top layer, held throughout the scene with action going on underneath. This kind of layer

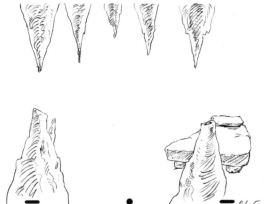

OL-5

is called an **overlay.** In order to speed up the frame-by-frame shooting of the animation camera operator, this layer needs to be drawn with the pegs at the top of the drawing. This way the camera person doesn't need to remove the layer when changing the animation cels underneath.

Director's Note:

At this point, the layout drawings could be timed (using existing exposure sheets or audio track), shot on film or video, combined with the scratch track or actual production track, and used to make a test of the animation or animatic. If you're working digitally, the drawings can be scanned and composited with the existing audio to produce the animatic, probably in the form of a Quicktime movie. Regardless of your production method, the animatic will give you a good idea of how the character and environments work together in motion. The motion is, of course, limited; the more layouts, the smoother the action.

Digital Layout

As mentioned earlier, the previous steps were aimed at the traditional animation approach—animated artwork to cel, painted, and combined with the backgrounds, shot onto film. When using digital animation, you follow the same basic steps, but you have a few advantages.

Here's a brief overview of doing layout for digital animation. We'll use the same storyboard panels as a guide.

Field Guide

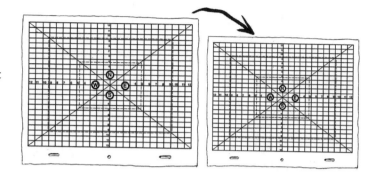

The transparent, punched, plastic 10.5" x 12" field guide that you used for the film output layouts can be used if you're laying out and animating on 10.5" x 12" paper. If you're using a different size paper, most commonly, 8.5" x 11", you can reduce a regular field guide to fit by xeroxing onto transparency, or having a Photostat on acetate made. A traditional (12 field) field guide available from Cartoon Colour Company and other suppliers measures 12.5" by 10 3/8." Reducing it by 82% will shrink it down to 10 1/4" by 8 3/8", enabling you to have a field guide that fits on an 8.5" by 11" page. This custom field guide beecomes your basic fielding system.

Carefully and accurately drawing an extension of the center line of the field guide to the edge of the page and, using this line as a guide, punching registration holes on a cel punch, will give you a field guide to use in an 8.5" x 11" format.

When working in digital format, you can zoom in all the way to a 1 field or smaller if you scan in your artwork at a high enough **DPI** (**d**ots **p**er **i**nch). In addition to composing you layouts within the traditional TV cutoff area like you do in a traditional production, in digital

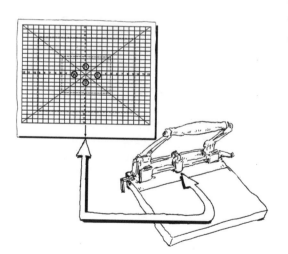

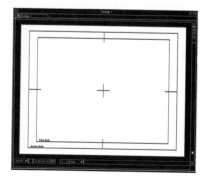

you can also use your animation or compositing program to generate an accurate field guide. Most programs have a **Title Safe** and **Action Safe** area or adjustable grid that can be displayed and printed out.

No matter which field guide you decide to use, you should be consistent and use it for the entire project.

Working with the Rough Layout

When doing layout in a digital production, you can use your rough layout and mark off the frame areas to indicate the camera moves just like doing layout for film by using your 8.5" by 11" field guide. To do so, lay your field guide on top of your cleaned-up background

drawing, lay a piece of paper on top of the field guide and, using the rough layout as a guide, mark off the frame areas of the zoom out/camera move.

Now you need the separate elements that will be used by the cavebear.

In addition to drawing the elements individually, you can use a digital shortcut. In

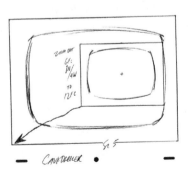

the traditional production, we talked about earlier, separate drawings were made for each individual layer. When working digitally, one cleaned up layout drawing can be used to make all of the layers needed. Let's assume that you've already drawn the background that you want to use and scanned it into your computer. (Scan the artwork in at 144 or 150 DPI, 100% size.)

It's always a good idea to make a back-up copy of the artwork you're working on. In your animation program, use the lasso tool to select the objects needed, copy them, and paste them to a separate layer. Do this for all of the needed elements. Once all of the elements have been separated from the background, you will need to fill in the area on the original background layer where the items were previously positioned.

Use the 'rubber stamp' or 'clone' tool (Photoshop or similar program) and fill the missing areas with appropriate line work from adjacent areas on the background. You can also cut and paste artwork from the background, resizing, distorting, and smoothing it until it blends in and works behind the objects.

Whatever method used, you should now have the same separate elements as before. They will need to be displayed in your animation or compositing program in the same relative order as before. Stalactites on the very top, followed by the vine charcoal layer, the animation of the cavebear, and the cave background interior. The exterior environment seen through the window should be on the very bottom.

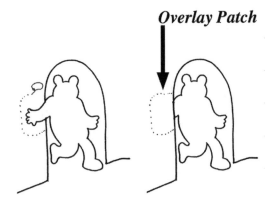

Overlay Patch

Registration Line

The point of the registration line is to make the character appear to enter the scene from behind the front edge of the doorway. When working on a digital production you don't really need to tightly conform your drawings to the registration line. Since you generally have an unlimited number of layers to work with, you can use one to add an element for another digital shortcut.

Open the background layout in your animation program. Use the lasso tool to select the area around the front of the opening to the room. Make sure it's big enough to cover the first positions of the bear; the drawings where he is still in the other room. Copy the area and paste it into a layer above the background. Make sure it matches and registers to the area it was copied from on the background. You now have an overlay 'patch' that the character will work behind. When he enters the scene, it will appear as though he is entering through the opening without having to register each drawing to the registration line.

Conclusion

OK. The scene has been laid out. Duplicates of the 'environment' elements—background, overlays, and the like—can be given to the background artist who will scamper away and make the pretty pretty, yes? The character related elements—the layouts and props (chalk)—will be given to the animator to be animated. Now we can move on to the production's entrée...Animation.

CHAPTER 6

ANIMATION

We've become familiar with and, hopefully, learned a lot so far: storyboarding, audio, and layout for starters. Now it's time to bring things to life by animating. So what is animation, anyway? The technical, dictionary definition for animation is: vivacity, ardor; the state of being alive; the technique of filming successive drawings or positions of puppets to create an illusion of movement when the film is shown as a sequence.

A more specific, animation-publication type definition is: the illusion of movement caused by the rapid display of a series of still images. When the images differ slightly and are viewed at over 10 per second, the eye perceives (smooth) motion. For our purposes and in general, that's what animation is. Actually, even one drawing per second will give a sense of motion. It just won't be very smooth or flowing motion. It would be very staccato, suitable for syncing to music beats or accenting with sound effects, but probably not full and detailed enough to convey a message or tell a story in an entertaining fashion.

But there's more to it than that. There are varying qualities of animation, based usually upon the needs of the project, the abilities of the animator, and the budget. Fewer drawings means choppier action. The action can be smoothed out a bit by 'favoring' extremes, instead of drawing straighter, more typical, mechanically placed breakdowns and inbetweens where drawings are placed exactly (as close as possible) in the middle of two others.

Straight Inbetween at mid point between Extreme #1 and extreme #2

Another indicator of smoothness and quality is the number of frames each drawing is held when being shot or recorded for playback. This is called **timing.** Animation is timed using 35mm film footage as the basis of measurement. There are 24 frames per second. Therefore, in order to make the smoothest possible animation, you would need to make 24 drawings for every second of animation. This is called animating on 1s. The same effect and smoothness can be achieved by holding each drawing for 2 frames (2s). 2s are the default animation rate in traditional animation. 3s tend to be a bit jerky if not spaced properly. 4s are even jerkier, but begin to be useful if you're working with a strong music or sound effect beat.

Different animators will give different definitions of what good, high quality animation is. A person that does beautifully drawn but motion limited, Japanese styled animation (Anime), will tell you that 4s are just fine and that 3s are marvelous. Old Saturday morning animation guys will say that only 2s will do. An old Disney guy will tell you 1s are the greatest and only way to go (they are, if you've got a huge budget and an army of assistants to do the actual drawings). The more drawings you have, the smoother the action. The fewer drawings you have, the choppier the action.

Here's your first exercise in animation.

Basic Motion

Get some flipbook pads (from your nearby office supply store) and try this exercise.

Exercise 1: Animate Your Name (it doesn't get simpler than this)

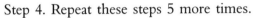

Step 1. Write your name on the bottom page of a note pad.

Step 2. Lay the next page down on top of the bottom page. Write your name again, this time slightly higher, say, a distance of 1/4 the height of the letters.

Step 3. Do it again. Lay the next page down (page 3) on top of the second page. Again, write your name at the same increment, 1/4 the height of the letters.

Step 4. Repeat these steps 5 more times.

Step 5. You are now on page 8. Keep writing your name slightly higher and higher on successive pages, but to diminish the monotony, start writing your name a bit smaller and smaller.

Step 6. Repeat these steps 8 more times.

Step 7. You are now on page 16. Continue to write your name, but move it toward the right-hand side of the page while continuing to make it smaller as it exits from the scene.

Step 8. Repeat these steps 8 more times until your name is a tiny dot in the distance on the right hand side of the 24th page.

Step 9. Rejoice. You're an animator.

You just created the basic throbbing globule of animation. You have rendered, by hand, the same image 24 times, moving it across a 2D plane in somewhat steady increments, altering its direction, and diminishing its size. You are powerful. You are an animator. And if you aren't completely turned off by the whole procedure, you are ready for more.

Squash and Stretch

Exercise 2: The Bouncing Ball

The bouncing ball flipbook exercise is always a good one to do early in the process of learning because it can show not only the basic principle of animation, a series of drawings viewed in rapid sequence, but other 'acting' elements like 'anticipation,' 'squash and stretch,' and 'slowing-in' and 'slowing-out.'

Step 1. Draw a circle on the bottom page of a note pad. This is the ball that we will be animating. Add a small shadow and a horizon line to give us an idea of the environment. Keep it very simple because in this exercise we will be doing 24 drawings again. Later in the book, we will be using these 24 drawings to give an example of timing (remember: 24 frames per second). You should always start your flipbook drawings on the bottom page. Since animation is a sequence of drawings, you need to be able to see the drawing underneath in order to have an accurate idea of how far to move or how much to distort the following drawing. It is also much easier to thumb through (flip) the pages that way.

Step 2. Lower the 2nd page and draw another ball. The bottom of this one should be right on top of the previous circle ('registered' to it), but should be a wee bit shorter and wider. In other words, squashed, as in 'squash and stretch.' Widen the shadow a bit because the fatter ball would cast a fatter shadow. Trace over the horizon line and keep it in its position throughout this exercise. This is known as 'tracing back.'

Step 3. On the 3rd page, draw another ball, squashed about the same increment as the ball on page 2.

Step 4. On the 4th page, draw the next ball. Make this one really squashed. These first four drawings are the 'anticipation' part of the action; a small recoil, a move in the opposite direction, setting up the motion in the opposite direction. A good example of this is someone getting up out of a chair. In order to stand up from a seated position, most people don't just spring up like a jack-in-the-box. They sort of gather themselves by bending forward to some degree in order to gather some momentum, then rise from the chair. The bending forward and momentum gathering is the 'anticipation.' Of course, if you're in terrific physical shape you might not need to gather quite as much momentum, but there is always some anticipation no matter how slight.

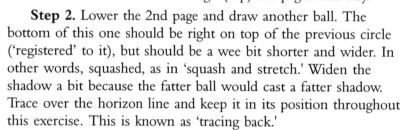

Step 5. Draw the next ball. This one is beginning to rise and return to its normal round shape. Draw the top of the ball at about twice the height of the previous, squashed ball and less squashed. The bottom remains on the ground.

Step 6. Draw ball number 6. The bottom is still on the ground, but the top is about twice the height of ball number 5. This ball is about the normal width of the ball in its regular position at rest.

Step 7. The ball that you draw on page 7 should still be in contact with the ground, but should be quite stretched. This is the 'stretch' part of the 'squash and stretch' phrase. The top of the ball is nearing the height of the bounce action.

Step 8. Draw ball 8. The bottom of ball 8 should be drawn with its bottom off the ground. The shape of the ball is still stretched out, but not as much as the previous drawing. The little shadow on the ground gives us a marker of the ball's previous position, and in this particular exercise, the position that it will return to. The shadow should be contracting inward a bit as the ball is drawn rising into the air. 'Speed lines' can be drawn in the area underneath the ball, giving an added sense of motion.

Step 9. The top of ball 9 should be drawn just a fraction above the top of ball 8, getting nearer to the top of the bounce action. The shape of the ball is returning to its rounder form.

Step 10. Draw the top of ball 10 directly over the top of ball 9. The ball has reached the top height of the bounce. The shape is round and normal. The shadow is at its smallest. Drawings 8, 9, and 10 are moving closer to the top position of the bounce action in smaller and smaller increments. The speed of the ball is decreasing in order to come to a halt. This is known as 'slow-ing-in.'

Step 11. Having come to a halt at the top of the bounce action, the ball is starting to fall back to the ground. It should be drawn ever so slightly stretched downward, having fallen a distance of about 1/8 the diameter of ball 10. The ball is drawn at such a small increment because it is slowly picking up speed as it leaves the 'rest' position. This is known as 'slowing-out.' The shadow is widening because the ball is getting closer to the ground.

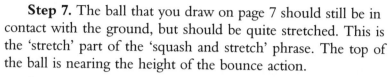

Step 12. Draw ball 12. It can be a duplicate of ball 11 but drawn as though it has fallen a distance of about half the diameter of ball 11.

Step 13. Draw the bottom of ball 13 touching the ground. The shape and size of the ball can be round and normal, like ball 1. The shadow would be the same, too.

Step 14. Draw ball 14 very similar to ball 3. Since it has fallen from a bit of a height, it would squash quicker than it would at the anticipation stage. The shadow is also drawn wider.

Step 15. Draw ball 15 squashed at least as much as ball 4. Wider shadow.

Step 16. Draw the ball as it animates up out of the squashed pose. Its shape is rounder.

Step 17. Draw ball 17, stretched upward a bit, with its bottom off the ground, having risen a distance of about 1/3 to 1/2 the diameter of the ball. The shadow will behave as it did in the previous bounce (its proportions drawn in relation to the ball; getting smaller as the ball rises into the air, widening as the ball squashes).

Step 18. Draw the top of ball 18 directly over the top of ball 17 (it has reached the top of its second bounce). The shape of the ball should be normal and round, but, you could give it a wee bit of a squash (with the top still directly over the top of ball 17).

Step 19. Draw the ball with its normal round shape with its bottom just touching the ground.

Step 20. With its bottom still touching the ground, draw ball 20 squashed just a bit, similar to drawing 3.

Step 21. Draw ball 21 slightly stretched upward and slightly off the ground.

Step 22. Ball 22 is drawn very similar to drawing 1.

Step 23. Ball 23 is drawn slightly squashed, about half as much as drawing 2.

Step 24. The last ball, number 24 is the same as number 1.

Thumb through the flipbook several times. Note the anticipation, the squash and stretch, the slowing-in and slowing-out. Though this is only a bouncing ball, these principles of animation can be applied to anything you animate. They also apply to animation done in other ways and other mediums. A bouncing ball done digitally would have the same characteristics and have the same behavior, even though each frame of the animation is computer-generated instead of hand-drawn. A character rising from a chair whether is it drawn, computer-generated, or made of clay will benefit from the use of anticipation, squash and squeeze, and slowing-in and slowing-out.

Overlapping Action

Overlapping action is another animation principle that plays an important part. Take a look at the drawing here:

Overlapping action occurs when the action of one part of an object or character causes other actions or reactions in other parts of the object. If the bouncing ball had arms or wings and reacted when the ball squashed, their reaction would be the overlapping action. When

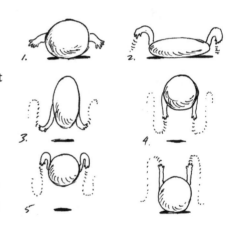

the winged/ armed ball reached the top of its jump, the arms would still be trailing behind it and would arrive after the ball started its descent (overlapping action). Basically, like your luggage, all the parts of an object or character don't arrive at the same place at the same time. By the way, those little dotted lines coming from the fingertips of the ball's arms are not just there for decoration. They are indications of other principles of animation: 'follow through'

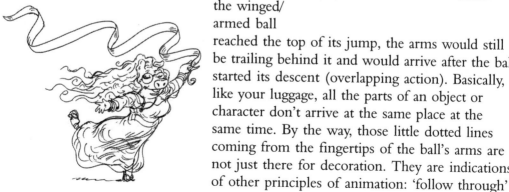

---

and 'paths of action.' An object in motion follows a curving path of action based on its previous position. If you wave a rope, a ribbon, a flag, or any long pliable thing through the air, you can see the path that it makes. This is the **path of action** and it is based on the positions of your hand as it moves. The object itself (rope, ribbon, flag) is **following through.**

There is an exercise to help you learn overlapping action in the Appendix.

Animator's Note:

Sometimes the terms 'slow-in' and 'slow-out' are interchanged, depending upon the motion described, the person you're talking to, or the computer program you're working in. Basically, you can 'slow-in' or 'slow-out' of an action or position. When you 'slow-out' of a position, you are actually 'slowing-in' to an action. This

can be rather confusing. Just know that 'slowing-in' and 'slowing-out' deal with the speed at which an object overcomes inertia. Let's use the example of a car sitting at a stop sign. It's just sitting there until it is set in motion by the driver's foot on the gas pedal, at which time it will accelerate until it reaches its cruising speed. The acceleration or gradual build up of speed is the 'slowing-in' part of the action. It 'slows-in' to the constant speed of the action. It is also 'slowing-out' of its inert, at rest position. To depict and control this action, you use a method called 'charting'. A chart is an indication of the number of drawings to be placed between two extremes. These drawings

are breakdowns and inbetweens.

The more drawings used within a specific area of action, the slower the action. The fewer drawings, the faster the action. Charting example #2 is a slower,

---

GARDNER'S guide to Creating 2D Animation in a Small Studio

'Flipping' and 'Rolling' Your Animation Drawings

Flipbook animation is a straight-ahead activity. You start on page 1 with a graphic and end up wherever your desire, goal, or available paper takes you. This technique of animation is not restricted to the flipbook. You can do the same thing on a disk; start at drawing 1 and end... when you end.

This is known as 'straight ahead' animation. When you want to see the animation, you just flip it. It's all there in order.

'Flipping' is a back and forth action between two drawings. 'Rolling' refers to viewing a sequence of drawings in order or in

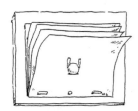

a way that puts the drawing in order. Here's how to roll a sequence of animation drawings. (These are right-handed instructions; if you are left-handed, reverse the directions or stand in front of a mirror.)

Step 1. Start with a stack of at least 5 drawings on your disk, low number on the bottom. Use the layout poses of the overlapping action ball that were made in the previous exercise.

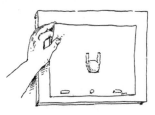

Step 2. Grasp the top drawing and hold it gently at the upper left corner.

Step 3. Pull straight forward, towards you, revealing the drawing underneath. Now lower the page back down revealing the top drawing again. You have just flipped back and forth between two drawings.

You will need to be able to flip or roll the drawings on different angles, depending upon the location of the drawings on the page underneath.

Step 4. Keep the top page in your grasp, just the way it is, and pick up the remaining pages so there's a page between each finger and one page on the disk. It should look like this...

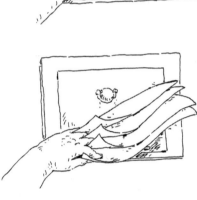

Step 5. Pull or 'roll' the drawings forward again, this time with all 4 pages in your grasp. Use an arching motion like the side view illustration. You are now 'rolling'. By the way; the drawing that is resting on the disk, not in your grasp, is viewable also.

A quick note of caution: don't grip the paper too tight. The straighter, unbent and uncrunched the paper, the smoother and easier the whole process will go. Bends in the paper tend to 'catch' and 'grab' and can really be aggravating after a while. You'll need to practice.

Flipping and Rolling while Animating

When inbetweening, you need to see the starting position of the action you're animating and the ending position of the action you're animating in order to draw the inbetween or breakdown... in between the two. The technique is the same, whether you're working over a bottom light or not:

Step 1. First, place the starting position drawing, LO-01, on the pegs of your disk. It will be referred to as the drawing on the bottom.

Step 2. Next, place the ending position drawing, LO-02, on the pegs.

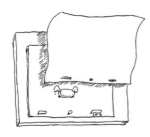

Step 3. Place a blank sheet of paper on the very top.

Step 4. Grasp the blank top sheet and the middle, ending position drawing (LO-02).

Step 5. Using the rolling technique, flip back and forth

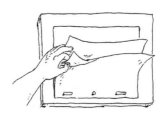

between the start and end position drawings to get acquainted with the way the motion is working.

Step 6. Lower the top, blank page, and begin to draw the inbetween, while occasionally flipping back and forth to check the motion. You are actually 'building' the inbetween.

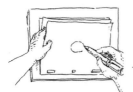  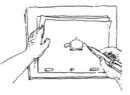 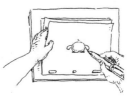

Step 7. To see the drawings in sequence, you don't have to dismantle your drawing set up and place the drawings in numerical order. You can roll them in the correct order by viewing the bottom drawing, lowering the top drawing in your grasp, then lifting it to reveal the middle drawing. This can be a bit tricky the first few times you try to do it, but with practice it gets easier.

Putting It All Together

Now that you know a few animation techniques and how to view the action as you're doing it, it's time to execute a short bit of animation. This cavebear exercise will cover traditional animation techniques as well as digital animation. Think of this as a
low budget bit of animation that nevertheless needs to look good. It is intended for digital output as well as film. I'm going to explain what I'm doing as I do it, pretending that you, the reader, are following along on your own animation set-up at home.

Set up your animation station with enough paper and drawing tools to animate 11 seconds of material: 12 drawings per second times 11 seconds equals 132 sheets of paper. It's a good idea to have at least a 10-15% allotment for mistakes and imperfection, so add another 20 sheets or so.

Along with the materials needed to actually draw the animation are the items that represent the subject matter of this particular piece of animation: the storyboard, the exposure sheets, the layouts, and the audio track.

The Storyboard: The storyboard tells you where the character should be at a given point in time. Get familiar with the board. Play the audio track as you look at the board, imagining and 'seeing' the action as you do.

The Exposure Sheets: The exposure sheets were numbered with indications for seconds (minutes and seconds if it's a longer piece) and frame numbers (every tenth frame). The audio track, once recorded onto the hard drive, was read as voice over, meaning the beginning of each word was accurately written on the exposure sheets instead of the phonetic breakdown. Before animating, you can place the layout elements in their respective, correctly stacked layers and make notes on the sheets as reminders. Also note the frame rate that is being used and if you're animating on 1s, 2s, or whatever. It determines how you indicate the animation drawing's exposures on the sheets.

The Layouts: Like the storyboard, the layouts tell you the character's location and actions, but take it a step further by providing actual drawings to manipulate. Layouts can actually be used as animation extremes if they were accurately drawn in the style of the spot with the right animatable poses. The layouts in this demo are named and numbered "Bear-01" through "Bear-09."

The Audio Track: Playing the audio track as you look at the storyboard and flip through the layouts to determine their relationship to the exposure sheets can be very useful. The obvious use is for a character's lip sync, but it can also help define the tone and attitude of the character(s) in the scene. Not only will you see the action as defined by the storyboard and layouts, but additional potential bits of motion as well.

Getting Started

Place the layouts on the pegs in animating order (low number on the bottom).

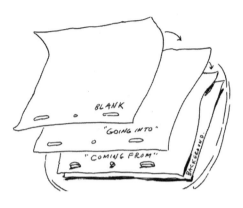

Roll through the layouts as though you were checking animation extremes while you refer to the storyboard and listen to the track. Imagine or "see" the action, rolling a drawing into view as its place in the scene is reached on the audio track. Do this a few times. You'll see additional bits of action that can occur in addition to the intended, 'laid out' action.

Once you're familiar with the scene, 'sketch in' the action on the exposure sheets by placing the layout drawing number on the frame that looks like it will work best on. You can also draw a tiny sketch of the layout pose in the 'action' column to help you visualize the action.

The choices of timing for this exercise are all completely personal, as yours should and will be when you do your own animation. If you are following along, you can choose different timings and frames to have animation events happen. Not all action is exactly according to the sheets and charts.

The Cavebear Enters the Room

The scene is revealed quickly in storyboard panel 18. Based on the exposure sheet timing, the cavebear has about 3 and 1/3 seconds to enter the room and reach his final position near the foreground. As I rolled through the layouts, I saw an opportunity to add a bit of pause and scamper to the action, then have him run up to CAMERA quickly to reach the indicated final position. The cavebear does the rest of the acting in the scene from this foreground position.

I'm placing the Bear-01 layout at frame 19, about 2/3 of a second into the

scene. This is about the point where I think the bear would end his slide and start heading toward the foreground.

I'm placing the Bear-02 layout at frame 57, about 2 1/3 seconds into the scene. This is the cavebear running up toward the final foreground position. Stored in the back of my mind is the thought that there is a 1 1/2 second piece of time to do SOMETHING with between the Bear-01 and Bear-02 poses.

I'm placing the Bear-03 layout at frame 81, 3 1/3 seconds into the scene. This is the cavebear at the final foreground position.

I'm placing the Bear-04 layout at frame 91, about 3 3/4 seconds into the scene. The cavebear has reached down and now has the piece of chalk in his hand. I make a mental note that at this frame of the exposure sheets, the chalk would no longer be exposed as a held drawing in its own layer, but would be drawn along with the bear. This means that an 'X' would be placed at this frame on the chalk's layer to indicate that it is no longer there.

I'm placing the Bear-05 layout at frame 149, about 6 1/3 seconds into the scene. The cavebear poses, pauses, and sizes up his canvas, preparing to burst into action.

I'm placing the Bear-06 layout at frame 207, about 8 2/3 seconds into the scene. The cavebear leans/stretches toward the wall, placing the tip of the chalk on the wall to begin his drawing. I've decided that the cavebear will rapidly draw downward then sweep back upward to complete the mural. Regardless of the actual production method used (revealed by a mask, scratch-on, drawn-on frame-by-frame), this is where the mural will begin to appear on the wall.

I'm placing the Bear-07 layout at frame 223, about 9 1/3 seconds into the scene. This is the end pose of the cavebear's first drawing sweep, the downward action. At this point, the mural is going to appear on the wall half completed.

I'm placing the Bear-08 layout at frame 240, 10 seconds into the scene. This is the last frame of the cavebear drawing on the wall. The entire mural is visible on the wall.

I'm placing the Bear-09 layout at frame 251, 10 1/2 seconds into the scene. The cavebear proudly looks at his creation.

That's the basic 'rough sketch' of the action. You could stop and make a pose test or animatic of the animation as it exists in the exposure sheets and get a rough approximation of the scene. The exposure sheets look like this after placing the layouts in these locations.

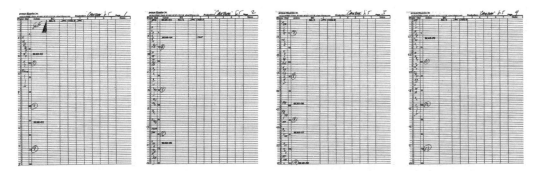

The next step is to go from layout indications to actual animation extremes. There are times when the layout drawings can and should be used as actual animation extremes. If the design of the spot has to conform to a very rigid standard, then the animation designer can make the actual layout drawings or poses to be used by the animator. This is one of those times. The layout drawings can now be given their appropriate numbers. At this stage of the exercise, we really don't know the exact locations of the animation extremes so they will retain their layout names and numbers until their position in the exposure sheets is defined.

Back to the beginning of the scene. This time through, I want to define and add the areas where additional action will take place. I don't want to fill in all of the drawings, just the basic extremes. Before beginning the animation stuff:

Place the background layout on the animation disk and tape it at the upper left-hand corner (if you roll the drawings with your left hand, otherwise the upper right-hand corner). This layout will serve as a guide as you animate the cavebear in the 'environment' (the room). You could also use the doorway registration line layout, at this point, if having the entire background seems distracting or confusing. Later, we will need to know the location of the chalk and the wall, so I've chosen to use the entire background layout drawing. Use whichever one you're most comfortable with.

I'm choosing frame 3 as the first frame of the cavebear sliding into the room. On layer 3 of the sheets at frame number 3, I've written BE-1, the name and number of the drawing to be done.

Since the cavebear is going to be drawn and animated to the next pose (the layout, now extreme, Bear-01), I should rename and number the 'Bear-01' drawing as BE-09. I can also *expose* the rest of the drawings in that entire section (exposing = writing their numbers at the appropriate frame of the exposure sheets), numbering them BE-02 through BE-08.

At this point, I'm also going to flip back and forth between the two extreme drawings and mentally describe and define the action. I think that the cavebear will need to slide into the scene abruptly and slow-in to the pose at BE-09 (sort of like that Tom Cruise action in 'Risky Business'). I can make a chart of this action on the BE-01 extreme.

I could also stop and do an additional drawing, the breakdown, but that might be a bit premature at this early, 'sketching-in-the-action' phase. (It might seem more logical to choose the first frame instead of the third frame, but I want to have a set-up of the room without the character in case there is a decision to extend the previous scene or add sound effects of the character approaching the room. The scene can always be edited at a later time to show the character already partly in the room. If extended time is needed, you have a couple of frames to freeze frame or loop.)

Place the BE-09 drawing on the pegs, followed by a blank sheet of paper. Label the blank BE-01. Draw the cavebear's hand where it would make its first appearance in the scene, registered to the doorway opening on the background, on BE-01.

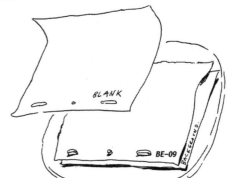

If you're working on a light table or over some sort of bottom light, note the position of BE-09 as it appears through the blank sheet of paper on top and draw the hand as it would appear entering the room. If you are working without a light, flip back and forth between BE-09 and the blank page to get a mental 'picture' of the cavebear's position and draw the hand. Regardless of the technique used, since the bear is sliding into the room in a straight line, the hand should be drawn directly across from the bear's hand in BE-09.

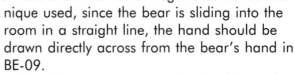

Since I've got your attention, here's another little note. You may notice that I refer to single digit numbers as having a zero as a place marker for the "tens" place (e.g., BE-01 as opposed to BE-1). This is because the drawings, when scanned for digital output, require a place marker in order to show up in their list order in the production's computer directory.

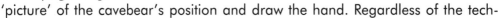

The midpoint between BE-01 and BE-09 is right about here.

Place BE-01 on the bottom of the stack with BE-09 on top and 'flip' back and forth to view the action. Once you're satisfied with the action (minimal at this point), make some sort of mark near the name/number of the drawing to distinguish it as an 'extreme' pose. This can be a helpful tool when flipping through a completed stack of animated drawings looking for key poses to fix or alter.

Place the Bear-02 layout drawing on top of the stack and roll through the drawings, analyzing and imagining the action as you do: The cavebear needs to come to a stop, then run up toward CAMERA in the foreground, reaching the Bear-02 pose at frame 57. There are 38 frames, slightly over 1 1/2 seconds to accomplish this action. The cavebear could just slide to a pause, then start running up to this pose, or he could do something less straightforward. I'm going to bring the cavebear to a faster halt, then have him quickly turn toward the foreground pose and scramble a bit, running in place. It might be a bit funnier than the straighter motion, it gives an opportunity to place an additional sound effect, but it also gives me an opportunity to show a simple cycle. Also, looking at the Bear-02 pose again, the bear could be in the middle of a *leap* instead of in an airborne running pose. That's the little scenario for this section of the scene.

The cycle of the bear is the pivot point between the BE-09 pose and the Bear-02 pose.

Place a blank piece of paper on top of BE-01 and BE-09. The beginning pose of the scrambling cycle has been drawn at frame 26, 8 frames (1/3 of a second)

---

from BE-09, and numbered BE-13. The cavebear's left leg is forward and his right leg is back, having just 'pushed off.' Fill in the numbers on the exposure sheet between BE-09 and BE-13. Make your 'extreme mark' on BE-13.

This is one of those spots where you can stop and work out a problem or an action: the cycle. I want it to be fast and simple. The cycle will be four drawings. Place a blank sheet of paper on top of BE-13 and draw the legs in their opposite pose; right leg forward, left leg back. Label this drawing BE-15. The cycle is halfway completed. The drawings with the cavebear's feet touching the ground remain to be done. Write the chart for the cycle on BE-13. Note that the final drawing of the cycle, BE-16, 'hooks up' to BE-13, the first drawing of the cycle to complete the cycle.

Place BE-15 on top of BE-13, followed by a blank piece of paper. Flip back and forth between BE-13 and BE-15 and draw the inbetween, BE-14. This drawing will have the cavebear's left foot making contact with the ground while the right leg comes forward. When completed, place the drawings in order and roll them to view the action. The next and last drawing in the cycle is BE-16. Place BE-13 on top of BE-15, followed by a blank sheet of paper. Flip back and forth between BE-15 and BE-13 and draw the inbetween BE-16. This drawing is similar, but with the right foot on the ground and the left leg coming forward. When completed, place the drawings in order and roll through them to view the action. Write the complete cycle on the exposure sheets. I'd like the action to last about a second, so the cycle is written in the sheets three times, taking us to frame 51.

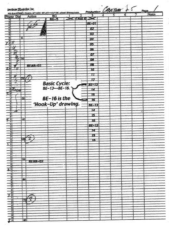

Place the Bear-02 layout on top of the stack, followed by the Bear-03 pose. Flip through the drawings. This portion of the sequence, from the scrambling to the cavebear's pose in the Bear-03 pose needs to be continuous, so the drawings for this sequence of the animation can be written onto the exposure sheets. Bear-02 at frame 57 gets renamed and renumbered as BE-20 and the Bear-03 pose at frame 81 becomes BE-32.

Flip back and forth between BE-20 and BE-32. As I look at this action it really does look more like a leap than a stride. Animating from the leap to the standing pose is another one of those spots I think needs to be resolved. Place a blank sheet of paper on top of BE-32, flip the drawings and imagine the action. The cavebear is approaching the BE-32 pose with the speed and weight of a cavebear. The way I'm 'seeing' it, when the bear 'hits the mark' with his feet, his upper body will continue to animate forward past the pose, then while attempting to gain his balance, overshoots the pose again bending backwards, then finally settles into it. There are 24 frames, one second, to use for the animation. I'm going to break the action down into one-third of a second chunks. Flip back and forth between BE-20 and BE-32 to draw the extreme BE-24 at frame 65. The cavebear's right foot has landed in the final position and will stay in that position throughout the action. The cavebear's upper body is leaning forward, off balance. When the drawing is completed, place it in order and check the action.

Place a blank piece of paper on top of BE-32, flip back and forth between BE-24 and BE-32 and make the next extreme, BE-28 at frame number 75. The bear is leaning backward, but not as far as he was leaning forward because he's regaining his balance.

Place the artwork in order and roll through it to view the action. There are 10 drawings on the pegs at the moment, so it might be getting a bit difficult to roll through the drawings. When there are a lot of drawings on the pegs, the top drawings tend to slip off of the pegs when you flip the drawings. You can remove all of the drawings except BE-32. Place the Bear-04 layout on top of BE-32 followed by the Bear-05 layout. Roll the drawings to view the upcoming action. From the pose in BE-32, the cavebear reaches over and grabs the chalk from the stone taboret (Bear-04) then 'sizes up' the wall he is about to draw on. Take a look at the exposure sheets and notice that there is a bit of animation that needs to be added between the Bear-04 and Bear-05 poses to fill the 58 frames (approximately 2 1/3 seconds) of time on the sheets. The director and layout artist have set the goal of the animation and told their 'version' of the story so to speak. As the animator, here's where you tell your version of the story and make an entertaining path to the goal. Should the cavebear stay in the BE-32 pose and do some eyeblinks before reaching over and picking up the chalk? Should he excitedly fumble around with the chalk while picking it up and sizing up the wall? I've decided to add a pose of the cavebear pausing to check out the piece of chalk after picking it up *("Let's see now,... I've got this piece of chalk in my hand...),* then animating into a pose of him looking up at the wall *(...and I can draw a picture on that big surface...),* then animating into the Bear-05 pose *(...and I can draw it in that general area of the wall).* I like that scenario, so a couple of additional extremes will be added.

Remove the Bear-05 layout from the stack of drawings on the disk. Flip back and forth between BE-32 and the Bear-04 layout. Number the exposure sheets down to frame 91, the location of the Bear-04 layout. Rename and number the Bear-04 layout BE-37. Flip and view the action.

I want the bear to 'slow-out' of the BE-32 pose and snap in to the BE-37 pose, so that action gets charted on BE-32. Also note that the bear has picked up the piece of chalk, so it will no longer appear on the taboret. From this point forward, the chalk no longer needs to appear in its own layer on the exposure sheets, so place an "X" in the chalk's layer of the exposure sheets at frame 91 to indicate that it is no longer there.

Place a blank sheet of paper on top of BE-37 to draw the next extreme drawing. This pose has the cavebear standing with his legs a bit wider apart and his hand on his hip as he looks at the piece of chalk. As for timing and exposing the drawing on the sheets, I'd like the cavebear to reach this upright pose in the same amount of time he took to reach over to the BE-37 pose (10 frames) and in the same manner, 'slowing-out' of the previous extreme and 'slowing-in' to the next extreme. So this drawing is named and numbered BE-42. Let's not break down this action right now, but we do need to chart the action on BE-37. Flipping back and forth between BE-37 and BE-42, I think this action needs to slow-out from BE-37 and snap into BE-42, so the chart will reflect that.

The cavebear just standing there is a bit boring, so the pose will be punctuated with a couple of eyeblinks. Place a blank piece of paper on top of BE-42 and label it BE-44. Draw only the cavebear's eyes closed. Make a note on the drawing next to the area where the cavebear's head would be that will remind you or the assistant animator/inbetweener and the person doing the ink & paint that this drawing is a 'trace-back' drawing.

ASSISTANT ANIMATOR'S NOTE:

A trace-back drawing is a drawing that has only a portion of it animated but needs to be a complete drawing of the character or object. Trace-back drawings can be done for a couple of reasons. The first and primary reason is speed, meaning that the animator doesn't have to actually draw the complete character. The second reason is that trace-backs save you from needing to have an extra layer to keep track of on your sheets and in the production. A third reason is accuracy. This works best in digital. If you had a character that had to be held absolutely still while a part of its body animated and didn't feel that it could be accurately done by human hands, a trace-back could be done by combining the animating portion of the drawing with a static version of the drawing.

Place a blank piece of paper on top of BE-44 and label it BE-43. Flip back and forth between BE-42 and BE-44 and draw the inbetween position of the cavebear's eyelids half-closed or half-open, depending on your world view. Since these drawings were so simple it seemed like a good idea to just get them out of the way.

The eyeblink we just did is a kind of cycle. This sort of cycle goes 'up and back' or 'up and down.' It starts at one extreme, animates to the next extreme, then back or down, hooking up to the first extreme as opposed to being a full action that

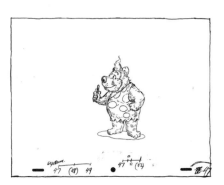

is hooked back up to the point of origin with a drawing. This cycle is written on the sheets in this order: BE-42 (point of origin), BE-43 (inbetween), BE-44 (destination pose/extreme), BE-43 (same inbetween), and BE-42 (point of origin). Indicate the cycle twice.

We also need to make a couple of charts on BE-42; one to show the drawings just completed, BE-43 and BE-44, and one to show and remind you that BE-42 will be used as the extreme for next action, not the partial drawing BE-44. Remove the two partial eyeblink drawings from the stack. They are really not useful right now because we need full drawings of the character to continue animating. Place a blank sheet of paper on top of BE-44 and draw the next pose where the cavebear looks up at the wall. The pose that I've drawn is pretty similar to BE-44. I'd like this to be a rather quick action since the poses are so close, so I'm labeling this drawing BE-47. Make an indication that it is an animation extreme drawing.

Expose the drawing on frame 119 in the exposure sheets and fill in the numbers of the inbetween drawings.

Note that this extreme hooks up to the closed eye trace-back drawing BE-44. When you do the breakdown and inbetweens of this section you can place the closed eye drawing on top of the fully drawn BE-42 extreme drawing or you can do the simple thing and just use BE-42, imagining the cavebear's eyes closed as you do the breakdown and inbetweens. Roll through the drawings to view the action. Note the amount of time used and the amount of time remaining before we

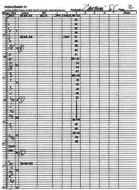

reach the next layout pose. I'd like to break up the pace a bit by having the bear stare at the wall briefly, then blink before animating into the Bear-05 pose at frame 149. Place a blank piece of paper on top of BE-47, label it BE-49, and draw the cavebear's closed eyes. Make a note that the drawing is a trace-back. Place a blank sheet of paper on top of BE-49, flip back and forth, and draw the

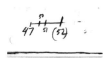

inbetween drawing, BE-48. Indicate the cycle on the sheets twice like the previous eyeblink cycle. These trace-back partial drawings can also be removed from the stack.

Place the Bear-05 layout on the top of the stack and number it BE-54 to correspond with its position in the exposure sheets. Fill in the upcoming inbetween drawings in the sheets. Roll through the drawings to view the action.

The cavebear will slow-out of the BE-47 pose and snap into the BE-54 pose. The cavebear's action from BE-47 to BE-54 needs to be charted on BE-47. The chart will be made on the BE-47 drawing because the full drawing is needed in order to draw the breakdown and inbetweens.

Once again, just imagine the cavebear's eyes closed when you make the inbetween drawings from the BE-49 closed eyes pose to the opened eyes on the breakdown, BE-52. Place a blank piece of paper on top of BE-54, flip back and forth between BE-47 and BE-54, and make the inbetween drawing. Label it BE-52. Place the drawings in order, roll through them, and view the action.

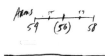

At this spot, the cavebear is going to size up the wall before springing into action and drawing the mural. I'm going to have him focus on the wall by moving the stick of chalk back and forth. To save time and drawings, instead of having the bear slowly focus with the chalk, I'm going to set this

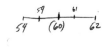

action up as another cycle. The bear will hold the chalk in the initial, closer to his face pose for about half a second, then swiftly move the chalk to its distant pose and hold it for about a half second, then reverse the drawings and bring the chalk back to the initial pose. This cycle will also be repeated a couple of times. It's the same principle as the eyeblinks, just longer. The chart for this action can be written out on BE-54 before actually doing the extreme.

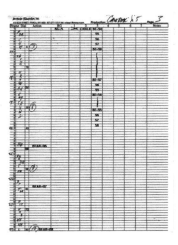

Place a blank sheet of paper on top of BE-54 and label it BE-58, an extreme. I think an 8 frame, 1/3 second action will work well here. Draw only the cavebear's arm, extended out from his body. Make a note for the assistant and ink & painter that this is a trace-back drawing. Place the drawings in order when done and roll through them to check the action. There are actually a pair of charts that could be written on BE-54. The first chart to be written is used to guide the creation of the separate arm inbetweens, BE-55, BE-56, and BE-57, shown above. The second chart to be written is to guide the creation of the inbetweens that will come after the separate arm cycles. This is a bit more complex and will be explained in a moment.

Place a blank sheet of paper on top of BE-58 and label it BE-56. Flip back and forth between BE-54 and BE-58 and draw the inbetween position of the cavebear's arm. Label it as a trace-back, place it in order, and roll through the drawings to check the action. Here are the updated sheets.

Like we did in an earlier section of the exercise, these partial drawings can be removed from the stack unless you choose to inbetween them now and get that little bit of work out of the way. As you animate more and more, you'll find and work out your own methods, approaches, habits, tricks, and work flow. Number the exposure sheets forward to the next pose, the Bear-06 layout drawing at frame number 207. If you are following along, this is what the exposure sheets should look like:

Place the Bear-06 layout on top of BE-54. Rename and renumber the Bear-06 drawing BE-62. Flip back and forth and check out the action. The cavebear stretches forward and places the chalk on the wall, the very beginning position of the entire drawing action. Similar to the previous trace-back cycles, you are using the last full drawing as an extreme, but instead of just imagining closed eyes on the character, you have an extremity in a different position. Simply imagining the arm extended on the bear would probably result in an inaccurate set of inbetweens. There are some simple solutions:

If you're using a light table, remove the stack of drawings from the disk and set them atop the previously removed stack. Place BE-54 on the bottom of the stack, followed by BE-58 (the arm/partial drawing), then the next extreme BE-62 followed by a blank piece of paper. When you flip back and forth to draw the inbetween, focus on the arm, BE-58, when you reach that area of the inbetween drawing. A variation of this method is to set up your drawings the way you normally would, BE-54 on the bottom, followed by BE-62 and a blank sheet of paper, and draw the inbetween except for the 'focusing' arm. At that point, remove BE-54, replace it with BE-58, then finish the inbetween. If you're not using a light table, trace the bear's arm onto BE-54 using a non-photo blue pencil. Set up the artwork as you normally would and focus on the blue penciled arm when you reach that part of the drawing.

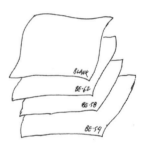

Using whichever method suits your set-up, create the breakdown drawing, BE-60. I'm using the third method, the blue pencil drawing of the arm drawn onto BE-54. Place BE-54 (with its blue penciled arm indication) on the bottom of the stack, followed by BE-62 and a blank piece of paper. Flip back and forth between BE-62 and BE-54 and draw the breakdown, BE-60. Focus on the blue penciled BE-58 arm when you reach that part of the drawing. Since the artwork is all set up to draw the BE-58 arm, it might be a good idea to just go ahead and draw the inbetween that requires it, BE-59. Because of the complexity of setting up the BE-54/58 extreme, later on, you'll be glad you got

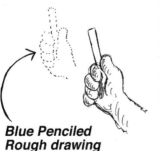

Blue Penciled Rough drawing

this out of the way. Place BE-54 (with its blue pencil drawn arm indication) on the bottom of the stack, followed by BE-60 and a blank piece of paper. Flip back and forth between BE-60 and BE-54 and draw the inbetween, BE-59. Focus on the blue penciled BE-58 arm when you reach that part of the drawing.

Make a chart on BE-60 to remind you that there is an inbetween to be done. The inbetween, BE-61, can be left until we do the bulk of the breakdowns and inbetweens later, since it doesn't require any special set up. This is a good time to look at and analyze the remainder of the animation to be done in the scene. Remove all of the drawings from the disk except for BE-62. Place the remaining layout drawings, Bear-07, Bear-08, and Bear-09 on

top of BE-62, and roll through the drawings to view the action. The cavebear has reached over to the wall and placed the chalk on it, preparing to draw. Next, the cavebear draws the first half of the mural at the teetering, leaning over, Bear-07 pose, then completes the mural drawing at the Bear-08 pose, and finally comes to rest at the final pose, Bear-09.

This is really one continuous sequence of action, free of cycles or other interruptions of the animation flow from frame BE-62 at frame number 207 all the way through to the final pose, Bear-09 at frame number 251. The exposure sheets can pre-numbered in this section because of the continuous action. The remaining layout drawings can also be pre-numbered and even pre-charted. It is always a wise idea to do your charts in pencil, though. Being able to pre-number exposure sheets can also help an animator think in terms of time as it relates to an animation drawing's number.

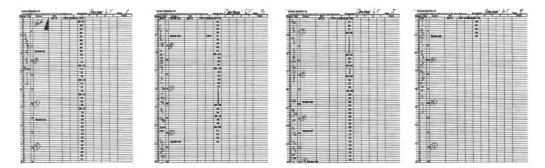

Since these layout drawings are being used as extremes, I'm going to rename and renumber them before continuing the animation. Bear-07 layout becomes BE-70, the Bear-08 layout becomes BE-78, and the Bear-09 layout becomes BE-84. The exposure sheets will also be filled in.

To complete the animation, I need to know what portion of the wall the cavebear needs to appear to draw on. For this, the layout of the mural art can be placed on the bottom of the stack, replacing, if desired, the background layout. With the mural art layout taped to the disk in the same manner as the background layout was, place BE-62 on the pegs, followed by BE-70.

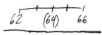

Flip back and forth between BE-62 and BE-70 to view the action and pinpoint the location and timing of the breakdown. I've decided to place the breakdown in the center of the action, making BE-66 the number of the breakdown. In addition to this, the rest of the action is charted out. The action of the cavebear's body is going to be very evenly paced because the arm will be pretty wild in order to give the illusion that the area of the wall is being drawn on. A chart is written on BE-62 to reflect this timing.

Place a blank piece of paper on top of BE-70, flip back and forth between BE-62 and BE-70, and draw the breakdown, BE-66. As I flip and make the inbetween drawing, I decide to have the cavebear *favor*, or be drawn closer to, the pose in BE-62. This is another way of slowing-in and slowing-out of poses, drawing the timing instead of relying on the drawing's placement in the chart. This technique allows you to be a bit looser when you draw, allowing

you to focus on making a nice, fluid, fun drawing instead of
stressing on making every element of the inbetween drawing
fit exactly in between the elements of the extremes.

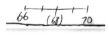

Place the drawings in order and roll through them to view the action. The action
between BE-66 and BE-70 can also be evenly paced like the
previous action. The chart for this action is written on BE-66.

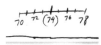

Place BE-78, the pose of the cavebear at the end of the
drawing action, on top of BE-70, and flip back and forth between
the extremes to pinpoint the timing and location of the breakdown drawing. The cavebear's drawing action should follow the
preceding action's timing, evenly paced. As I flip
through, it occurs to me that it might be nice to
have the cavebear slow-in to the final pose. The
arm still needs to move around wildly to
complete the mural. I decide to chart the action
straight and simple again, with the breakdown
drawing placed in the middle of the action (BE-
74), and do the slowing-in and slowing-out on
the actual drawing again. The chart for this
action is written on BE-70.

Place a blank piece of paper on top of BE-
78. Flip back and forth between BE-70 and BE-
78 and draw the inbetween drawing, BE-74. To give the appearance of the cavebear
slowing-in to the end pose, the cavebear's foot is placed in contact with the floor
and the upper body is drawn to favor the end pose. Looking at the finished
inbetween pose, I think the foot being back in contact with
the floor might look a bit abrupt, but I'm going to go with it
anyway. When the inbetween is drawn, place the drawings in
order and roll through them to view the action.

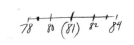

Place the last pose, BE-84, on top of BE-78 and flip back
and forth to...oh, by now you know this. This action can
continue the even pace we've established in the previous drawing action. The
cavebear needs to slow-out of the pose in BE-78 and slow-in to the end pose in BE-
84. This time, the timing will be achieved by the placement of the breakdown and
inbetweens based on the chart instead of the drawn pose of the drawing. The
breakdown will be BE-81. The chart for this action is written on BE-78.

Place a blank piece of paper on top of BE-84, flip back and forth between BE-78 and BE-84, and draw the breakdown, BE-81. As I flip and draw, I draw the majority of the character in the middle of the two extremes with two exceptions; the hand with the chalk is drawn in an upward facing pose so it will appear a bit snappier and emphatic when it hits the end pose. Also, the cavebear's face favors the end position. When the drawing is complete, remove the drawings from the disk, gather the drawings together in flipping order (low number on the bottom), and flip the animation to see the action. Once you've flipped until your heart's content, put the drawings in regular order (low number on the top), take a little break, then prepare for more work. The next step is the breakdowns and inbetweens.

ANIMATOR'S NOTE:

If we were to stop and shoot a test of the animation at this point in the production, it would be choppy and incomplete. It would work as a pose test or animatic, something to give a general idea about the action, but that's about it. To make the action smooth, we have to draw the breakdowns and inbetweens. Simply put, breakdowns and inbetweens are the drawings that

appear between the defining poses or extremes.

Breakdowns are generally the mid-point or pivot point between a pair of extreme poses. More often than not, they are the drawing that determines the point where a slow-in or slow-out occurs and is divided. Breakdowns are represented by the long vertical line in the middle of a chart.

Though slowing-in and slowing-out is generally defined by the animator's chart, a breakdown can define the action, too. By drawing an object closer to or leaning toward a pose, you can enhance a slow-in or slow-out. This is tricky sometimes, though, and some animators don't or won't trust their assistants to make this sort of timing decision, feeling it's better for the animator to draw more extremes and have the assistant and inbetweener

Partial Drawing of Animation Element That 'Favors' an Extreme.

produce drawings that just represent the mid-points of actions as accurately as possible. A way to get the best of both is for the animator to make a partial guide drawing for the breakdown. For example: An animator has an action of a ball character waving its arms from side to side that absolutely needs to be 5 drawings (10 frames) in length (Ball-01 through Ball-05).

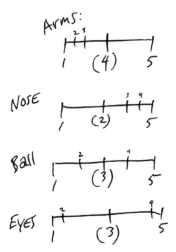

The animator also wants the overall action to be evenly spaced but the arms on the breakdown favor the starting pose. The animator could make a partial drawing and include it in the animation sent to the

assistant. The animator doesn't have to make a perfect, in-style drawing, just enough to illustrate the idea. Just the part of the character that is favoring an extreme. A non-photo blue pencil drawing works great.

Another method is to make multiple charts. The animator can make a chart for different parts of a character. As many as desired or necessary. If over-used, though, this technique can be confusing.

Inbetweens, again simply put, are the drawings placed between the extremes and the breakdowns. They tend to be the necessary filler material needed to make a smooth, delicious, nutritious, fiber filled animation movement. But like breakdowns, inbetweens can also be used to define timing and action beyond their charted function.

Doing the Breakdowns (and a few inbetweens) of the Cavebear Exercise

At this stage, we're going to go through the animation again, this time drawing the breakdowns. Like the previous run through, if there is a particular spot that we need to stop and solve a problem at, we will stop and solve the problem. The cavebear exercise explained and gave the opportunity to get familiar with the physical procedure of making a drawing between two other drawings (an inbetween drawing or a breakdown drawing). If you've been following along, you've probably got it down by now, so I'm going to stop describing every step of drawing an

inbetween drawing. The "flip back and forth between..." part of the description will be simplified because there are a lot of drawings to be done. A description of what kind of pose the drawings require, where parts of the drawings need to be placed, and why is more important.

Start by setting up your drawings with the low number on top. Place the background layout on the disk and secure it with a piece of tape. Like before, you can use the

The midpoint between BE-01 and BE-09 is right about here.

doorway registration line at the beginning of the scene and the layout of the piece of chalk later in the scene if you find the background layout too confusing. Place BE-01 on the pegs, followed by BE-09 and a blank piece of paper. Flip the two extremes and locate the mid-point of the action. A breakdown located in the exact middle of the action would be numbered BE-05. I'd like to see the cavebear in the scene a bit

earlier than that, so I'm going to make the breakdown BE-04. We can keep flipping and draw BE-04, the breakdown, OR we can use a little trick.

Once you've found the mid-point of the action, rough in the area that the breakdown drawing will occupy on the breakdown drawing, making sure to accurately draw a line on the ground plane where the

character's feet will be. Knowing where the top of the cavebear's head will be is important, too.

Remove the end pose, BE-09, from the pegs and trace it onto the breakdown drawing. If the pose of the character is rigid, you can draw the pose exactly as it is on the BE-09 extreme. If there is a bit of action, like the fingers of the cavebear opening up a bit or the torn hem of his garment flapping in the breeze, you can just trace parts of the character or do a non-photo blue pencil drawing of the character, place the drawings back in 'inbetweening order,' and use the blue penciled rough drawing as a guide to making the final breakdown drawing. Place the drawings in order, flip, and check the action. Next, place BE-04 on top of BE-01 to make the inbetween drawing BE-03. Flip BE-01 and BE-04, and repeat the previous action of finding the mid-point and drawing or tracing the pose. When complete, add a chart to BE-01 as a reminder.

Place BE-03 on top of BE-01 and repeat one of the previous techniques to make the inbetween, BE-02. Proceed through the remainder of the inbetweens between BE-04 and BE-09 and use either of the techniques just shown to produce the inbetween drawings. When completed, remove drawings BE-01 through BE-08 from the disk. They're done. Start a 'Done' pile with them and feel triumphant. Next, place BE-09 and BE-13 on the pegs and flip to find the location of the next breakdown. As I flip, it looks like the breakdown drawing needs to be placed in the exact middle of the action at BE-11. The cavebear's front foot is lifted toward the BE-13 pose and the back foot continues sliding and slips off of the ground toward the BE-13 pose. There doesn't seem to be any need to favor either extreme, so the chart for this action is written on BE-09.

Flip and draw the breakdown drawing, BE-11. When completed, place the drawings in order on the pegs and roll through them to check and view the action. Looking ahead a bit, there is a small chunk of breaking down and inbetweening that has already been done, the scrambling/running in place cycle of the cave bear, BE-13 through BE-16. This is an opportunity to do yourself a little favor. Sometimes during a production if you take a moment and get a few simple inbetweens drawn and out of the way, it will serve as a nice little treat later in the production when you're toiling away at 2:00 in the morning. A little batch of pre-drawn inbetweens can be really sweet. So while we're here, let's do the simple inbetweens, BE-10 and BE-12.

By now, you probably know how to set it up and do it, but I'll lay it out again anyway. Place BE-11 on top of BE-09 followed by a blank piece of paper. Flip, draw the inbetween, and when completed, place in order to check the action. Next, place BE-13 on top of BE-11 followed by a blank piece of paper. Again, flip, draw the inbetween, and when completed, place in order and roll through to check the action. Place BE-14 through BE-16 in order on top of the stack and roll through the drawings in sections to check the action of the cavebear sliding into the room and hooking up to the scrambling/running in place cycle. If rolling through the drawings as they sit on the pegs is difficult, remove all of the drawings from the pegs and flip the stack of drawings.

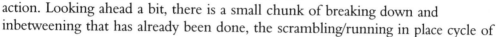

Place BE-16 on the pegs followed by BE-20 (set the artwork you just flipped through aside) and flip to find the location of the next breakdown. After flipping from BE-16 to BE-20, I noticed that the bear in BE-20 isn't a direct pose from BE-16; it's not a straight leap into the pose. I could go back and change the 'slide-in' poses, especially altering the end of the action by having the bear gather himself and actually leap into the BE-20 pose or I can make this work. I'm going to make this work. Flipping again, I see that the cavebear needs to take an intermediate step. It should make him look really anxious to reach the end poses at BE-32 and BE-37 and start drawing on the wall. Flipping again, I think the cavebear's foot should touch the ground at BE-18. Write the chart for this action on BE-16.

Place a blank piece of paper on top of BE-20, flip, and draw the breakdown, BE-18. I'm making this a straight breakdown drawing. No artificial flavoring of any kind. The arms swing into position at this mid-point between the extremes. The head and body are also coming forward at this mid-point. The left foot is in contact with the ground while the right foot is in the air behind him. When finished with the drawing, place the drawings in order and roll through them to check the action. Place BE-24 on top of BE-20 and flip to locate the next breakdown's position. This is a pretty broad action in a short range of frames. The cavebear is going into an unbalanced pose and it might be nice to get him closer to it, so favoring BE-24 will probably end up being the

answer. Let me think about this as I flip. It would look nice if the bear appeared to float gracefully near this BE-20 pose, but there isn't enough time (frames) to make that work and, anyway, he's supposed to be anxious and scrambling, so that idea isn't really a good one. Flip some more. The bear's right (forward) foot needs to

touch the ground in order for him to have a pivot upon which to teeter and slow-in to the BE-24 pose.

If I place the breakdown at BE-21, I can draw a breakdown that has his foot in contact with the

ground. The inbetweens will slow the bear into the BE-24 pose. Here's what the chart for this action looks like, as written on BE-20.

Place a blank piece of paper on top of BE-24, flip, and draw the breakdown, BE-21, as described in the last paragraph. When done, place in order, roll, and check. Since this is a slightly troubling bit of action here, I want to resolve it before moving forward.

With BE-24 on top of BE-21, put a blank sheet of paper on top of the stack and flip to locate and draw the next inbetween, BE-22. I'm making the bear's right arm a wee bit rubbery, slightly favoring BE-21 around the fingers. This will cause it to 'drag' a bit as it comes out of BE-21 and snap a bit when it reaches BE-24.

Place the drawings in order and roll them to check the action. Place a blank piece of paper on top of BE-24, flip back and forth between BE-22 and BE-24, and draw the inbetween, BE-23. As I flip to determine where the parts of the drawing go, I've decided to have the cavebear's head favor the BE-24 pose. The rest of the body is pretty much a straight inbetween drawing. The fingers on the cavebear's right hand, the one that was 'rubberized' on BE-22, have been open/flared out a little to fill the space and form an arc.

Place in order when completed, roll through, and check the action. Not bad. Place BE-28 on top of BE-24 along with a blank sheet of paper and flip to see where the next breakdown goes. I'm placing the breakdown as close to the middle of this action as possible, thus BE-26 is its name-o. As I flip, it looks like it might be nice to have the inbetween favor the extremes a bit more than they would if the normal 'simply break it down in the middle' chart was written. Here's what that chart looks like on BE-24.

Flip the extremes and draw the breakdown. When done, place the artwork in order, and roll through to check the action. The inbetweens don't look like they will pose any special problems, so I will leave them for the final inbetweening phase. Place BE-32 on top of BE-28 along with a blank piece of paper. Flip and look for the next breakdown's location. The foot coming down can be a simple mid-point breakdown, BE-30.

The body settling into position can be a simple mid-point breakdown, too. This looks like a pretty straightforward breakdown situation with a couple of exceptions: the arms might look nice if they favored BE-28 (it might give a little snap to the whole thing). And why not overlap the head a bit? Have it come forward past the pose slightly then hit the final BE-32 pose? Flip and draw the breakdown, BE-30. When finished, place the artwork in order and roll through the drawings to view the action. The inbetweens, BE-29 and BE-31, shouldn't pose any problems, so we'll leave them for the final inbetweening phase.

Right now, BE-32 should be the most recent extreme in use. Place BE-37 on top of BE-32, followed by a blank piece of paper. BE-32 was charted during the animation phase.

The chart shows that we're slowing-out of BE-32 into BE-37, with the breakdown, BE-35. Flip the extremes again to verify that it's still a good idea. Yep. A bit of exaggeration on the hand that reaches over to pick up the chalk might be nice. It becomes a mini-extreme. It looks like it should slow-out like the rest of the drawing, so no additional chart is needed. Flip and draw the breakdown, BE-35. When done, place the drawings in order, roll through them, and check the action.

The inbetween, BE-34, could be drawn with the hand favoring BE-32. Instead of stopping and drawing the entire thing, I'm going to make a quick non-photo, blue pencil rough indication/ partial inbetween that I'll finish on the final inbetweening run through. When done, place the partial drawing in order in the stack, then...

Place BE-42 on top of the stack, followed by a blank piece of paper. BE-37 also has a chart with a predetermined breakdown. Flipping back and forth between BE-37 and BE-42 to find the location of the breakdown, BE-40, reveals another rather uneventful, straightforward action. The cavebear's hand being placed on the hip could use some emphasis as it reaches the BE-42 pose. This 'favoring' move can be done on the drawing by elevating the arm on the breakdown and having it snap into the BE-42 pose. Flip the drawings and draw the breakdown, BE-40. When completed, place the drawings in order and roll through them to check the action.

Place BE-47 on top of BE-42 followed by a blank sheet of paper. Note the charts on BE-42. One chart is for the eyeblinks that occur here and have already been done. The other chart is for the present action. Flip to find the location of the breakdown, BE-46.

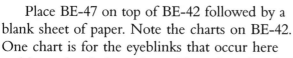

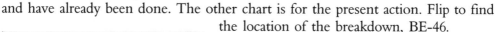

This is very simple. The head tilts up, the hand with the chalk lowers, and the hand on the hip loosens a bit. Sweet. Flip the drawings and draw the breakdown, BE-46. When finished, place the drawings in order, roll through them, and check the action.

Note the two charts on BE-47. One is the chart for the eyeblinks that have already been done, BE-48 and BE-49. The other chart is for the breakdown we're about to do, BE-51. Place BE-52 on top of BE-47, followed by a blank piece of paper and flip back and forth to draw BE-51. When completed, place the drawings in order and roll through them to check the action. This is another straightforward breakdown drawing, slowing-out from BE-47 into BE-52.

Place BE-54 on top of BE-52 and flip back and forth between them. It doesn't look like it presents any special problems so let's leave this inbetween, BE-53, for later. Note the two charts on BE-54, one for previously done artwork to be addressed in a moment, and the other, a guide for the next breakdowns and inbetweens to be done. We have reached the point where we made trace-back drawings of the cavebear's arm and hand, holding the piece of chalk and moving it back and forth to 'focus' and 'size up' the wall. Place the previously done drawings, BE-55 through BE-60 on the top of the stack and roll through them, just to check and maintain a good mental picture of the animation's 'flow.' The stack of drawings is also getting thick on the pegs, so this is a good spot to remove them, place them on the 'done' stack, and place BE-54 on the pegs in preparation for the next work. Flip through them to see how it's going. Feeling a sense of satisfaction? Good! Realizing that animation is a lot of work, but with a really nice payoff? Good! Place BE-62 on the pegs on top of the mural layout. If you were using the doorway registration line, remove it and replace it with the mural layout. Place BE-66 on top of BE-62 followed by a blank sheet of paper. Note the chart on BE-62, then flip back and forth between the extremes to draw the breakdown, BE-64.

BE-64 is quite straightforward. Nothing special. The cavebear's tuft of hair on top of his head might offer some fun. When finished, place the drawings in order on the pegs, roll through them, and check the action. Place BE-70 on top of BE-66 along with a blank piece of paper and flip back and forth to locate the next breakdown's location (BE-68). BE-68 is

heading toward an unbalanced pose. Parts of him should get there 'early' to accentuate that off-balance look. If I make his head and drawing arm favor BE-70, it should help to accent and give a bit of weight to the BE-70 pose. Flip and draw the breakdown, BE-68. When finished, place the drawings in order and roll through them to check the action. With the extreme BE-70 on top of the stack, place BE-74, followed by a blank sheet of paper on top of BE-70 and flip to find the location of the next breakdown, BE-72.

When we animated this section earlier, it was decided that the cavebear would need to draw wildly with his arm while the animation of the rest of him stayed fairly evenly paced. Just for the heck of it, let's have the cavebear do an unexpected move on a breakdown. Instead of going in a nice, evenly paced arc from BE-70 to BE-74, let's make him dip down with his drawing action. That nice arcing line can be established on the couple of inbetweens that will be drawn in this area of the animation later. It could be interesting. When done, place the drawings in order, roll through them, and check the action.

Place BE-78 on top of BE-74, followed by a blank sheet of paper. Flip to locate and draw the breakdown, BE-76.

Let's repeat the previous action, having the cavebear make another unexpected move on a breakdown. Doing it once might be abrupt, but like a musician hitting a bad note during a solo, if you repeat it, it wasn't a bad note, it was an adventurous addition to the music. The same can apply to art. Everything else on the breakdown is evenly spaced. As I flip, it looks like the inbetween BE-77 could favor BE-78. Flip back and forth between the extremes and draw the breakdown, BE-76. When done, place the drawings in order and roll through them to check the action. Place BE-81 on top of BE-78. Note the chart on BE-78. We are going to be slowing-out from BE-78 into BE-81. Place a blank sheet of paper on top of the stack, flip back and forth between the extremes, and draw the inbetween, BE-80.

This drawing should be drawn directly at the mid-point. A simple breakdown. When completed, place the drawings in order, roll through them, and check the action. Place BE-84 on top of the stack (it's gotten thick again, but we're so near the end...) and note the chart on BE-81. We slow-in to BE-84, so BE-82 is the inbetween drawing we're doing.

Flip back and forth between the extremes to

draw the inbetween. When completed, place the artwork in order and roll through the drawings to view the latest action. Remove the drawings from the pegs, place them with the rest of the completed drawings, and flip through the pile of animation. Nice, huh? The exercise is almost done. The last part is the inbetweening phase. Put the artwork back in order with the low number on top. Take another break.

The Last Bit: The Inbetweens

The final drawings to be added to the sequence of animation are the inbetweens. If the scene was shot as a pencil test at this point, it would be a combination of 2s and 4s except for the parts that need more than one inbetween.

A lot of inbetweens have already been done in this exercise. Fewer than half of the total drawings remain to be completed. There were situations where doing all of the inbetweens at a particular point in the action took advantage of a tricky or difficult set-up that would have been time consuming, tiresome, or frustrating to set up again at a later stage. Tracing the sliding cavebear on BE-01 through BE-09, animating the partial arms, and using two drawings as an extreme at BE-54/BE-58 are the most notable examples. It's often best to get simple things like eyeblinks out of the way. Instead of describing the order of set-up for each and every extreme, I'm going to simplify things for this end section. You already know that:

- The extreme you're 'coming out of' goes on the bottom of the stack.
- You check the chart on the extreme that you're 'coming out of.'
- The extreme that you're 'going in to' goes on top of the extreme that you're 'coming out of.'

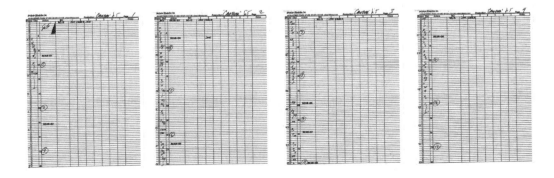

GARDNER'S guide to Creating 2D Animation in a Small Studio

- You place a blank sheet of paper on top of the stack.

- You flip back and forth between the extremes, finding the location of the elements of the breakdown or inbetween drawing being done, and...

- When completed, you flip the drawings or place them in order on the pegs and roll through them to check the action.

So, I will simply note the inbetween to be done, flip the extremes, and give a description of the drawing or make a comment on it. If you're following along, you can just go ahead and make the inbetween on your own.

The first inbetween to be done is BE-17, between BE-16 and BE-18. It looks simple and straightforward. You might want to try having the foot that's coming forward favor the BE-18 pose. The next inbetween is BE-25. It's a very straightforward inbetween, but the back foot could drag and favor BE-24 or elongate a bit. Next, is BE-27. It's straight, but could favor BE-28 on the foot animating down. Next is BE-29. It's straight with no favor. BE-31 is straight with no favor.

BE-33 and BE-34. We have a partially drawn inbetween to complete with BE-34.

The cavebear's hand was drawn favoring the BE-32 pose. The rest of the pose on BE-34 can be a straightforward inbetween drawing. Note the chart on BE-32 and draw the BE-34 inbetween. The BE-33 inbetween should be a straightforward piece of cake inbetween.

Next up, BE-36. Pretty straight. You could favor the BE-37 pose when you draw the hand that is animating up. Be aware of that the bear is about to pick up an object, the chalk. If you draw the hand close to the chalk on your inbetween, make sure you register it to the chalk, giving the appearance that the fingers are going behind it in order to wrap around it.

BE-38 and BE-39. Both inbetweens are basically straightforward. We added a little extra 'something' to his arm that is about to land on his hip with emphasis. In hindsight, a second chart specifically for that arm could have been done indicating a 'slow-in' to the BE-40 pose. Again, that is hindsight, but you might consider favoring it on the BE-39 inbetween drawing. BE-38 can just be a totally straight inbetween drawing.

BE-41. The chalk can slightly favor the BE-42 pose. The arm coming down can have something added to emphasize the action; speed lines or the arm hair trailing a bit.

Animator's Note:

Speedlines are lines that are drawn behind an object in motion to accent the illusion of motion. They are used primarily in still, single image forms of art like comic books or illustrations, but can be put to good use in animation.

Speedlines can be used to 'fill in' an area

behind an object in motion. This can be very helpful when you have an object that needs to cover a larger distance in a short period of

time (fewer frames) and you want the action to appear smoother, not abrupt. If you use speedlines on more than one inbetween drawing in succession, you can draw fewer lines, closer together, on the inbetween that is closer to the next extreme's pose. This gives the appearance that the lines are 'catching up' and can be very effective.

BE-45. You're using BE-42 as the 'coming out of' extreme, imagining the eyes closed. It's a straightforward inbetween drawing beyond that little consideration.

BE-50. You're coming out of BE-47, imagining the eyes closed as you draw the inbetween, BE-50. It's straightforward.

BE-53. Straight, but maybe favor the BE-54 pose with the chalk.

A reminder: we've reached the part of the animation where the bear draws wildly on the wall. The arms are drawn in various positions to give the impression that he is drawing loosely, while the rest of the bear is pretty much inbetweened in a straightforward manner. I'm going to simply describe the inbetween drawings that I made, with comments or reasons for drawing them in the positions chosen, if necessary.

BE-61. The drawing arm is drawn in a lower position between the two higher positions. It gives a rapid, scribbling-sketching feel that I used a lot in this area of the animation.

BE-63. Another lower position in relation to the higher positions on the extremes.

BE-65. Same approach.

BE-67. A break from the scribble-sketching action. More of a straight inbetween, favoring the BE-68 pose. It should give the appearance of a sweeping drawn stroke.

BE-69. Back to the scribble-ish action. The bear is heading toward that off-balance pose, so his head favors BE-70 a bit.

BE-71. This is a fairly straight forward inbetween. The drawing sweeps downward to sketch in that lower left-hand corner of the mural.

BE-73. This is a straightforward inbetween, including the drawing action.

BE-75. The drawing hand bends backwards to draw the cave girl's shoulder. Everything else is straight ahead.

BE-77. Straight except for the drawing hand straightening out to draw a bit of the cave girl's skirt.

BE-79. A straightforward inbetween.

BE-83. This inbetween favors the end position, BE-84 a little bit, though it really didn't need to.

Now that all of the animation artwork has been completed, there is an additional piece of artwork to make. It is a mural drawing guide. The appearance of the mural on the wall will be done using artwork made in the digital ink &

paint department. It will also be used in the Camera, Compositing, and Output chapter. These methods will be easier and faster than doing a lot of traceback drawings to animate the mural onto the wall. The Mural Drawing Guide needs to be made from the animation drawings that draw on the wall, BE-62 through BE-78. Each drawing is placed on the pegs and the hand and arm holding the chalk are traced. Each hand/arm segment needs to be labeled so you will know which frame it corresponds to. By the time you get to BE-78, you should have something that looks like this drawing.

Label the drawing MDG-01 (Mural Drawing Guide) or something like that and scan it with the rest of the artwork when you get to ink & paint.

That's it! The drawings are all done. Remove whatever you've got on the pegs, put it all in order and flip it to view the completed animation.

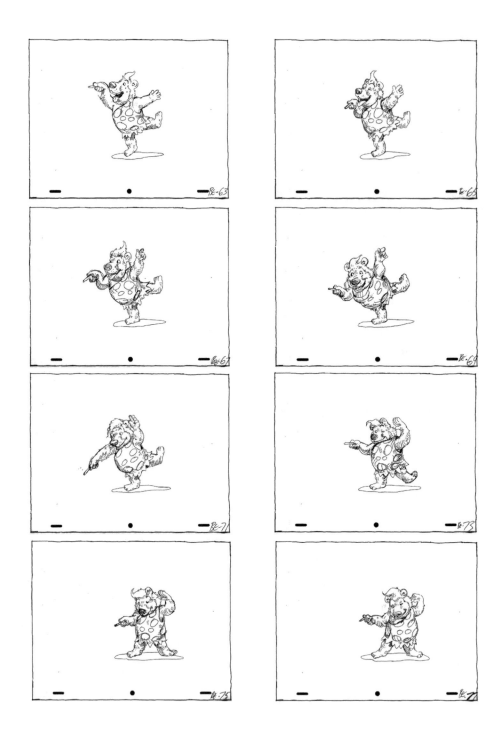

GARDNER'S guide to Creating 2D Animation in a Small Studio

Viewing the Animation: The Pencil Test

The animation has been completed. The breakdowns and inbetweens are all in place. You can flip the stack of drawings and get a general idea of the flow of the motion you've animated, but in order to truly see the animation, it needs to be recorded on to film, video, or digital media and played back at the correct frame rate and speed. It's time to shoot a **Pencil Test,** also known as the PT.

In addition to checking the quality of the animated motion, pencil tests can be used to check more mundane, but vital, aspects like composition; how the animated elements look in relation to the background elements. Making sure that everything is in registration is also checked again here at the pencil test phase. There are a few methods of making a pencil test, most of which can be used regardless of the mode of production.

Video Animation Systems

The fastest and easiest method for producing an animation pencil test is to use a Video Animation System. Video animation systems have been in use for a number of years. You get fast and immediate results from a video animation system because you're shooting directly on to videotape which, as

soon as the frames are recorded single frame, can be rewound and played back to view the animated motion. The system can be set up right at the animator or assistant's workspace. People who have been in the animation industry for a while remember or maybe even still have one of the old Lyon & Lamb Video Animation Systems.

These systems aren't easily available anymore, though you might find one on Ebay or from an animation company that is getting rid of one. The new video animation system that is available and widely used is the L-MO'S (Lightfoot Mobile Studio) or ALL IN ONE Animation Workstation, both made by Lightfoot Ltd.

Video animation systems enable you to test your animation at any time. They are configured and used in a way similar to a regular animation camera. The main components are a surface with pegs that match your peg system and a video camera attached overhead. You place your animation on the pegs a drawing at a time and shoot the number of frames per drawing that you have indicated on your exposure sheets. The output from your shoot can be viewed on videotape or input into a computer.

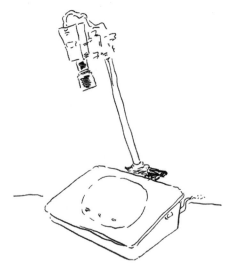

Shooting on Film

In traditional cel on film production, the PT is shot, naturally, on film with an animation camera stand. If the camera stand is outfitted with a video camera, then the animation can be viewed on video. In days past, pencil tests were usually shot on black and white film stock because it was cheaper and had same day developing. PTs generally don't need to be of very high quality since they're used primarily to check the quality of the animation, so black and white was just fine. Labs that reliably do black and white are pretty scarce these days.

Shooting a PT on color stock is an excellent opportunity to also view the color models and backgrounds that may have been completed to this point. It is important to view your color work at this stage of production, in the medium that the final product will be delivered in—film, video, etc. Artwork doesn't always look the same when it's viewed on film or video. If the PT was shot on film and needs to be viewed on video, the processed film can be submitted to a videotape facility and transferred to video. A videotape facility can also digitize the film for digital viewing or manipulation. The process of doing a traditional cel camera shoot is explained in the Camera, Compositing, and Output chapter.

Digital Pencil Testing

If producing animation in the digital domain, the artwork can be scanned into the computer system, composited, and combined with the background elements and rendered in a digital format like a Quicktime, MPG, or AVI for viewing, critiquing, or even outputting to film or video, if necessary. The process of making a digital pencil test is explained in the Camera, Compositing, and Output chapter.

The Importance of Exposure Sheets

Regardless of the method used, a vital part of any pencil test are the exposure sheets. They are used as a guideline for the actual recording or shooting of the artwork onto film or video. They tell you how many cel 'levels' you have, what element is there, and where they are in relation to each other. In other words, which level or layer is laying on top of what other level or layer.

Your audio information—analyzed voice over, music beats, and other audio events—is indicated on the sheets, so they are also very useful to the music and sound person. Whoever's doing the editing—cutting the film together, coordinating the elements, and putting them together into your final product—needs the exposure sheets because they have exact timings of all the audio and visual elements and events. This is needed for traditional or digital. Having the sheets can save time and time is money.

ANIMATOR'S NOTE:

Sometimes the artwork isn't complete at the pencil test phase. Perhaps it's a very rushed deadline or the assistant's dog ate some of the inbetweens or something else caused a gap in the drawings. Fear not. A pencil test can still be done. You will have to make the artwork that DOES exist work. This can be done by either experimenting with frame rates or selectively shooting drawings for longer than their originally intended exposure. Most animation is set up to be animated on 2s, or as explained earlier, two exposures per drawing. A

combination of 2s and 4s can work very well or exposing the entire incomplete section of animation on 3s can also work well, depending upon the drawings that are missing. If the spaces are wide, try 3s instead of 2s and 4s. You'd be surprised how forgiving the eye is.

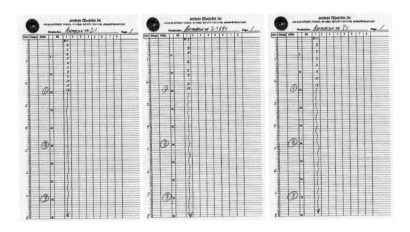

The Pencil Test and Audio

Sound tracks, if recorded, can be lined up and played with the pencil test animation in order to check the accuracy of any lip sync or other audio elements that need to be in sync with the visual elements. Adjustments are then made to the animation and are re-shot until the animation is correct. Audio can also be adjusted to bring everything into sync, showing the value of keeping the audio tracks as separate elements. If the animation is being done to a voice track, then the voice elements are certainly already in existence and available for adjusting. The pencil test phase is also a good time for the animator to try out or experiment with sound effects and music, getting a feel for what might work with the animation, before sending it off to the music/sfx person.

If the pencil test looks good and you are pleased with it, you're ready to go to the next stage of production—adding color in Ink & Paint.

Chapter 7

Ink & Paint

The animation has been completed. It looks absolutely wonderful. You're happy with it. And even the client is pleased with the results.

But there's something missing. The element that brings the character forward, making it stand out from the background. The element that helps to focus the viewer's attention on the desired parts of the scene's composition, the part that sets the mood and time.

It's color.

The basic process of applying color to your animation is pretty straightforward whether you're working in traditional cel animation mode or digital mode. Both methods require you to get the animated artwork into a form that enables the addition of color. In traditional cel, it's inking or Xeroxing. In digital, it's scanning or digitizing. Both methods share the same approach to basic animation coloring: getting flat color into the drawn areas of a character or object in order to support the line art. In traditional, it's flipping the cel over and painting on the back. In digital, areas are filled with the click of a mouse. Adding detail like texture or shading to the artwork can be done in both modes. In traditional, detail is added to the drawn side or **surface** of the cel. In digital, the colored artwork can be filled with gradients or textures or even pictures instead of flat color or further manipulated in a variety of paint programs. And finally, both methods require a similar amount of dedication, patience, accuracy, and focus. Not a very glamorous description for a phase of production that brings about such rich and colorful results, but an accurate one.

The process of traditional cel painting will be explained first to give a bit of background for the entire technique, followed by the digital ink & painting process.

The Steps in Traditional Ink & Paint

Step 1. The drawings need to be transferred to acetate sheets called cel.

Step 2. The cels need to have color applied to them, usually on the back side so that the line can show through.

Step 3. The cels are then allowed to dry (or induced if you're in a rush).

GARDNER'S guide to Creating 2D Animation in a Small Studio

Step 4. If desired, permanent marker, china marker, air-brushed colors, or any art material that will adhere to acetate can be applied to the surface of the cel to add dimension and additional color to the designs.

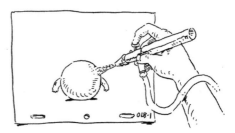

Step 5. The cels are cleaned and checked on top of the scene's background to make sure that everything registers.

Step 6. The artwork is sent to camera to be shot on film or recorded onto video.

This a basic

description of the steps in traditional cel ink & paint. Let's look at each step a bit closer.

Getting the Artwork Onto Acetate

There are two primary ways of getting the animation artwork onto acetate: inking and Xeroxing.

Inking is the original method of getting artwork onto a transparent surface. When hand inking, registration of the paper to cel is extremely important. Place each drawing on the inking board in sequence, place a cel, with the tissue between it and the drawing, over the light and begin to ink, tracing the animation art onto the cel.

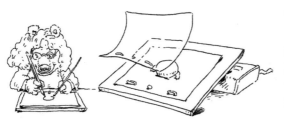

The early technique of using a fine sable brush to trace thick and thin lines that were used by Disney and others has been replaced for decades by the flexible pen.

Steel pens (sometimes called 'dip' pens because you dip them in ink) give a varying width line depending on the flexibility of the pen and your own touch.

Technical pens give a consistent line depending on the point you are using. Smaller numbers being finer lines, larger numbers being heavier ones.

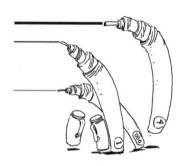

Fine line sharpies or other permanent markers are easy to work with and give excellent results, but have a drawback; the chemicals used in the markers produce fumes, so they need to be used in a well-ventilated space. The same applies to paint markers; use them only in a well-ventilated space.

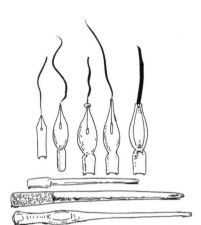

Stabilo pencils and china markers (also known as grease pencils) can also be used to trace the lines but they are more fragile than ink and can be easily wiped off when handling the cels.

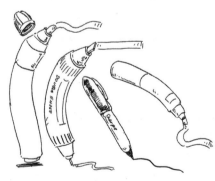

In order to keep the surface of the cel clean and to ensure that the ink will stick to the surface of the cel, a glove should be worn to keep the oils from your hands from getting on the cel. White cotton gloves originally worn by film editors and lab technicians who handle delicate film have been adopted and adapted by inkers and painters.

Xeroxing is a mechanical means of getting your artwork onto acetate. It eliminates the need

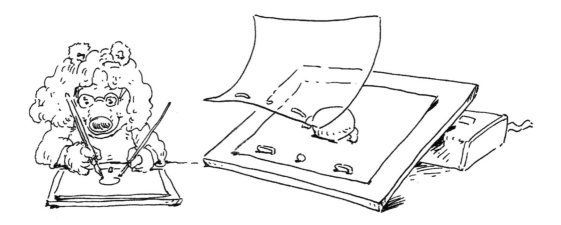

for an inker and eliminates the possibility of inaccurate drawing on the cel since it exactly duplicates the animator's drawings. Of course, this means more work for the animation team because the drawings have to be clean and in the style of the production. Animation that has been done in this 'clean' way is **Xerox ready.**

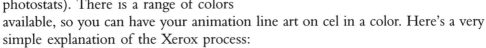

Most professional Xeroxing is done on copy cameras (cameras and stands that have been designed to make photostats). There is a range of colors available, so you can have your animation line art on cel in a color. Here's a very simple explanation of the Xerox process:

1. The image is projected onto an electronically charged metal plate with registration pegs attached to it.

2. The areas of the plate where the lines appear are electrostatically charged.

3. The plate is placed in a box with toner and shaken. The toner sticks to the charged lines on the plate. A cel is placed on the registration pegs of the metal plate.

4. The plate is placed in another box containing the fumes of a chemical that causes the toner to melt and adhere or 'fuse' to the acetate.

5. After a few minutes, the cel is removed and you've got a professionally Xeroxed animation cel.

Xeroxes on acetate are very sturdy and durable if done correctly. You can apply a lot of surface shading techniques to these cels and not damage them. Also, the cels are in exact registration. One caution, though: the chemical used to fuse the toner is very similar to the chemical in permanent markers. Therefore, permanent markers can remove the toner, so be careful.

Xeroxing Using a Regular Copier

If you do a whole lot of animation and would like to economize over a period of time, you can do your Xeroxing in-house. Xeroxing can be done on regular copying machines capable of handling 11" x 17" paper, but only after certain adjustments have been made by a copier technician. Regular copy machines fuse the toner to paper or special acetate used for overhead transparencies with heat. This heat doesn't adversely affect paper or overhead transparency acetate, but it causes regular acetate cels to buckle, ripple, and even burn, making them useless (unless that's the concept of the film you're making). Adjustments can be made to the heat sensors and rollers, though, giving you a very high-quality image on acetate. Some copiers have toner that comes in a range of colors, so, like the original process, you are not restricted to only a black line. If you do a lot of animation, an in-house set-up will pay for itself pretty quickly.

The in-house process, simply explained:

1. Place the drawn artwork on the copier's glass.

2. Place a punched animation cel at the hand feed input of the copier.

3. Push the 'copy' button. Your animation cel should safely travel through your correctly adjusted copier and emerge from the other end.(A bit of prior experimenting will need to be done in order to find out which direction and position the artwork needs to be placed in and which direction the cel's holes need to face.)

Xeroxing the artwork onto cel on a regular copier requires re-registering the Xeroxed cel to the drawn artwork after the artwork has been copied onto the punched cel. This is done by:

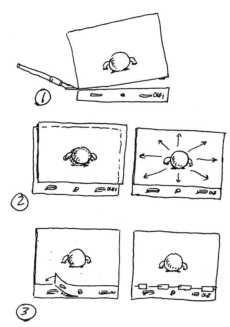

1. Cutting off the pegs of the cel about one inch from the bottom of the cel.

2. Repositioning the copied cel to match the drawn artwork, being careful and certain to match the elements from the center of the cel outward. Copiers are designed to reduce or enlarge the drawing a hairline to prevent forgery and counterfeiting, so maintain a consistent focal point as you reregister.

3. Retaping the pegs back onto the cel.

PRODUCER'S NOTE:

Even if you're not Xeroxing animation to cel, it's good to have a copier in-house. Sometimes, in the earlier phases of production, a character or object can be resized and redrawn. And there's always a need for multiple copies in the business office.

The Painting Process—Setting Up

Before the inking & painting steps are expanded and explained, let's talk about workspace and equipment. If you are a one person studio or are short on space, your animation set-up can be used for your ink & paint area. You'll need to adjust the table and disk so that the top is flat and will enable you to paint without having the paint run off of the cel.

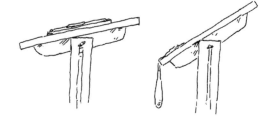

If you've got the space and budget, a second animation set-up can work as well as an ink & paint station. Since you're using the set-up primarily for painting instead of animation or layout, you can use a less expensive disk with non-moving or stationary pegs instead of panning pegs. Just turn on the light and paint. Painting over a bottom light helps you to see the thickness and 'even-ness' of the paint applied on the back of the cel.

A regular art table can also be used. Again, be careful about the angle of the table. A perfectly flat surface isn't necessary because the correct thickness/viscosity of the paint will prevent it from running quickly. Too steep an angle, though, and the paint will run, creating areas on the cel that are too thin (the area that the paint flowed *away* from) and too thick (the areas the paint flowed *to*).

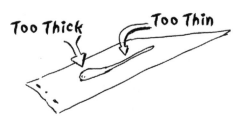

If you're using a regular art table without some sort of built-in lighting fixture, a couple of very useful, if not necessary, items are a translucent plexiglas inking board (available from Cartoon Colour Company and others) with top and bottom pegs for registration, and bottom light, a photographer's slide viewing lightbox. These two items, when placed on your desktop, replace the

disk and light unit that are part of the standard animation set-up.

For a lot less money, you can also use a fluorescent light stick.

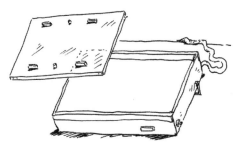

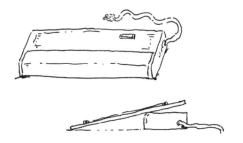

Fluorescent light sticks are designed for use under kitchen cabinets, but when used under an inking board it gives a very comfortable amount of light and places the inking board on a comfortable angle. Incandescent or regular light bulbs can also be used in lighting units, but they give off more heat than fluorescents and can make the work area uncomfortable. Actually, that's an understatement. Incandescent bulbs get hot! They don't last as long as fluorescents, either.

If you are handy with tools or are otherwise carpentry enabled (or know someone who is), you can build your own table-top animation or ink & paint set-up. There are instructions for making a simple homemade light box in the Appendix★.

In addition to a place to sit and paint the cels, you will also need someplace to store the painted cels while they are drying between colors. Shelves on a wall would work, of course, but are not the most practical approach to the problem. They are certainly not portable, which could be a problem if you needed to move your work area around in your space or were adding additional work areas. Your best and most efficient use of resources and space is to build or acquire a **drying rack.**

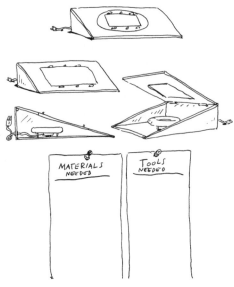

MATERIALS NEEDED

TOOLS NEEDED

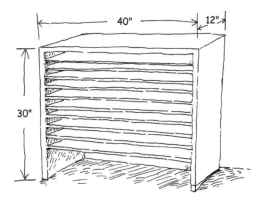

A rack that is 36-40" wide by 30" tall with about 10 shelves will give you a comfortable space that will hold approximately 30 cels, possibly more, depending on the amount of area painted on the cel. Usually, by the time you paint one color on your series of cels and start from the beginning to paint another color, the first color is dry enough to paint safely without smearing one color into another.

In addition to having a place to work, you will need items to work with.

Paint

Cel Vinyl, from Cartoon Colour Company (http://www.cartooncolour.com/), has the most comprehensive selection of pre-mixed colors, broken down into hue and value levels. The paints are available in 2, 4, 8, 16, and 32 ounce containers. You choose your colors by using their color chart.

Just about any acrylic paint with the correct consistency can be used. You can even use latex house paint, though it is harder to mix to the correct consistency and the colors are not as varied and as light fast as Cartoon Colour. If permanent markers were used to color the back of the cels, be aware that house paint pulls the pigment out of the markers. In a couple of months, the markered areas of your cels will be significantly faded, seriously affecting any possible reshoots.

Brushes

There are a lot of brushes available. Since you're painting with an acrylic water-based paint, watercolor brushes will be the best kind of brush for you to use. Though sable and other costly natural bristle brushes are wonderful and responsive when working on a watercolor painting, they are an expensive bit of overkill when painting animation. There are several varieties of synthetic

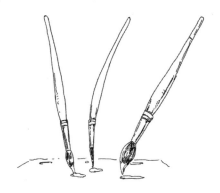

bristle brushes that are soft, absorbent, and responsive like natural bristle brushes. For animation painting, you'll need the pointed watercolor styles because you'll not only be painting large, wide-open areas of cel, but also small tight areas like eyes or freckles or that bizarre mole on Uncle Harvey's neck. Sizes 0, 2, 4, and 6 are a good starting set, and will not only work for inking, but painting also.

Other Neccesities

Polycons are small 1-2 ounce containers with attached lids used for holding paint while working. These containers are great for mixing paint to the proper consistency. Film canisters, preferably clear, that your local film processing place is holding for recycling can be used as containers for holding paint. These are a great solution and they are FREE.

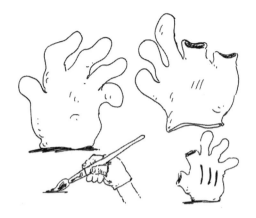

Inexpensive, white cotton gloves are used to keep ink & paint from your hands and to keep fingerprints and oil from your hands off the cels you're working on (why clean more than necessary). Many inkers and painters prefer to have the thumb and first finger trimmed back to the first knuckle to allow for better gripping of the pens and brushes. Drawing lines on the backs of the gloves to imitate old style animation characters is optional.

A water bottle with a squirt spout filled with clean water is a necessity for thinning the ink or paint to the right consistency. Your local grocery store or department store will probably have a kitchen or picnic supplies section with empty mustard ketchup squirt bottles, but if you happen to use those condiments, just hang on to the squirt bottles when they are empty, clean them out, and use them.

Slice tip on an angle to improve flow from bottle

Any old empty jar can be rescued from the trash or recycling bin and used for washing brushes and pens. Cheap fish bowls are also nice to use. Coffee cans and other metal containers tend to rust, so they are restricted to brush or pencil holder duties. It is important to keep brushes clean to prevent them from getting paint build-up. The more paint build-up you have in your brushes, the more often you have to take the time to clean them and the sooner they wear out. Clean brushes will also prevent you from contaminating new colors when changing color. Change the water often to keep things clean.

A sharpened wooden chopstick or shish kabob skewer (just stick them in a pencil sharpener to give them a point) can be used for gently removing dried drips

of paint. Be careful not to
scrape too hard and avoid
using the very tip of the
sharpened stick; you don't
want to accidentally poke
holes in the cels. The sticks
can also be used to hold the
cel flat while painting.

Painting

Animation painting is done
on the back side of the cel. The reason for painting on the back of the cel is to allow
the line drawing of the character or object on the surface to be visible. Traditionally,
the color is as flat and smooth as possible. This flat painting technique is supportive
of the drawing, allowing the line to define the object or character and motions. Can
you imagine trying to paint around all those lines on the surface?

Ink & Paint Note:

Speaking of painting on the surface, there is a last
ditch repair technique called surfacing that comes
into play if an incorrect color has been painted on the
back of a cel. The correct color is simply painted on
the front surface of the cel. This is called surfacing.

The animation drawing and the inked or Xeroxed cel
are flipped over. The animation drawing should end up
drawing side down with the cel on top and the inked or Xeroxed side facing down.
This method protects the inked or Xeroxed surface of the cel and leaves the cel
ready to be painted on the back.

It is best if you take the time to turn each cel and paper over in the manner
described above before you begin to paint. It saves time overall and will keep you
from 'breaking your rhythm' as you paint. It is also a good time to get an idea of
how many cels will fit on your paint rack. If you have a rack that is in the neighbor-

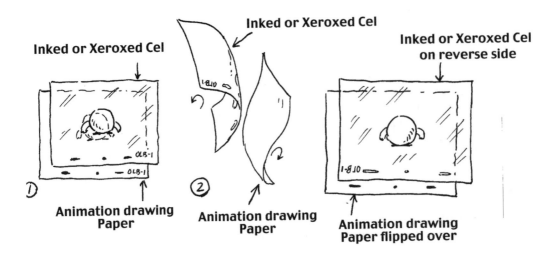

Inked or Xeroxed Cel

Inked or Xeroxed Cel

Inked or Xeroxed Cel on reverse side

Animation drawing Paper

Animation drawing Paper

Animation drawing Paper flipped over

hood of 40" wide, you can fit three cels on each shelf if they're placed horizontally, or four, if they're placed vertically, allowing for a very slight amount of overlapping in very safe parts of the cel, like the peg hole area.

A very important thing to remember is to make sure that the wet painted areas of the cel, whether they're placed side-by-side on the rack or overlapped, are FLAT.

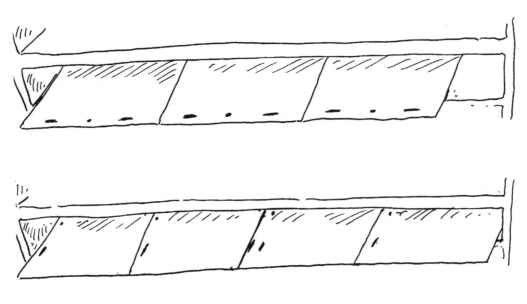

If any part of the wet area is in the curved part of the cel, the paint will run downward and make a thick area, leaving a thin and less than opaque area.

With all of your cels flipped and sitting on the drying rack's shelves, and the rest of your painting area is set up, you are ready to paint.

When doing basic animation painting, you do not need to place the inked or Xeroxed cel on the pegs of your inking board or disk because the image is already in register on the cel. It is easier to paint if you can easily turn the cel to avoid damp areas; the registration pegs can get in the way. To avoid bumping into the pegs, turn the board over and paint on the flat side over the light box. If you are using an

animation lightbox unit or one of the units that was described earlier in the chapter, remove the pegs or pegbar from the set-up.

Registration is sometimes important, though, like when you are using a technique called **self-line**. Self-lining means that you will be inking or painting an object or area in the same color you'll be using to paint and fill the area with. Cheeks, lips, highlights, or shadow work on characters are usually where you'll use this technique. These lines should be drawn or painted in register first, using the registration pegs, before flipping the board over to do the painting.

Because you will be painting on a slight slant, your paint needs to be the right consistency. If the paint is too thick in consistency, it will cause streaks. Too thin will cause runs. To get the right consistency of paint, add water to the paint in the container you're using (polycon, film can, etc.) and stir gently with your brush handle until you get the right consistency.

There are times when you may actually need to have your paint thick in consistency. In order to paint in a technique called **dry brush** (a technique for painting streaky textures like speed lines), you'll need thicker paint; straight out of the bottle works best. To paint transparent clouds or

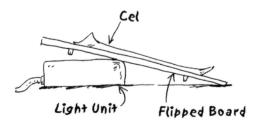

shadows you need thinner than usual paint or paint that has been thinned with water and an acrylic medium or paint 'extender.'

Applying Paint

When painting, the brush full of paint needs to be 'puddled' in the middle of the area to be filled and pushed to the midway point of the line dividing the color areas.

The paint on the cel needs to be opaque and even. Painting over the light box enables you to see thin areas and whether or not you have painted as close to the line as possible.

No matter how carefully you stir the paint in the container, bubbles can occasionally form and end up on the cel. If there are bubbles in the painted area, they can be removed by gently lifting and thumping the cel under the painted area.

When painting animation, you will be working with a group of about 20-30 cels at a time, depending upon the number of cels you can fit on your drying rack(s). The most efficient way to work is to paint one color at a time on all the cels, then return to the first cel and begin painting the next

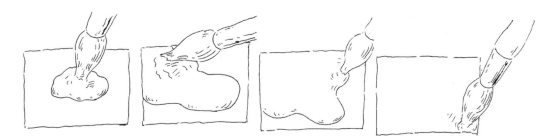

color. By the time you've painted one color on all of the cels and return to the beginning, the first cel has enough dry edges to safely paint the next color. If the next color is not adjacent to the first color, you don't have that worry; just paint another color on the group of cels. You are safe to paint the next color as long as the edges of the previous colors are dry. Continue in this manner until all of the cels are painted. It really is an assembly line type of activity.

Ink & Paint Note:

Paint small areas like eyes, teeth, freckles, and polka dots first, and then when these are dry you can safely paint over them to fill the rest of the area. For example. If this character with the dreadlocks and the freckles were a character you were working on, you would paint him in this order.

• Teeth, whites of eyes and highlights in eyes, throat, freckles, nose.

• Eyebrows, hair, tongue, if the throat area has dry edges, and shirt.

• When the small areas are dry, paint the large areas on top of the smaller areas; face, inside mouth.

Drying

Allow cels to dry thoroughly before cleaning. If you're in a hurry, you can always speed the drying process along by using a hair dryer on a low heat setting. Don't overdo it, though. The paint will dry with cracks that resemble parched desert or the cracquelure effect in Photoshop. Kinda neat looking, if that's what you wanted, but if smooth and flat was your aim, you'll have to paint over the area again to smooth and flatten it (the cracks themselves are thinner areas and are translucent not opaque).

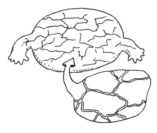

Enhancing the Design on the Surface of the Cel

Some designs require more than line and color. You can uses permanent markers, airbrush, Stabilo, grease pencil ink, paint, or any art material you desire that will adhere to acetate to draw, paint, or otherwise add an additional bit of depth on the surface of the inked & painted cels. Any art material that adheres to acetate can be used to enhance the design on the surface of the cel. Grease pencil (China Markers) and Stabilos give a nice gritty look, but also may cause problems when being shot under camera if used too thick. Bits of the waxy line can flake off and adhere to the camera's platen glass (used to hold the artwork in place) during the shot. It takes the camera operator a longer time to shoot and keep everything clean. It is safest to use materials that are durable and permanent. If you use an ink or another wet medium, make sure it will dry to a non-sticky state to avoid unwanted transfer of color.

Final Cleaning

No matter how careful you are when you ink or paint cels, wearing gloves and the like, cels tend to accumulate dust, fingerprints, paint splatters, and other things that need to be removed before the artwork is sent to the animation camera. Dirty artwork can flicker and distract from the final production. A few moments spent at the end of the ink & paint phase can make a difference.

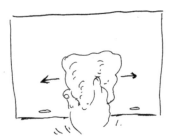

- Final cleaning, polishing, and fingerprint removal can be done with an anti-static cloth.

- Simple dust removal can be done with a black velvet cloth.
- Wipe the cels from side-to-side (East-West) because the lights at the camera service are set up in a side-to-side configuration, and are less likely to reflect off of horizontal scratches.

Once dry and clean, the cels can be flipped back to right side up. You may want to replace the animation drawings with plain paper to prevent any damage from humidity to the original art or just to keep your original drawings in the safety of your studio. Be absolutely certain that the cels are dry because sometimes paint isn't really as dry as it feels. When it has been stacked, additional moisture can come from the painted side of the cel.

Checking

Once the cels are clean, they are ready to be **checked.** This is done by placing each cel on top of the completed backgrounds and checking to make sure that all of the elements in color on acetate have maintained their registration. The exposure sheets are used when the artwork is checked, so it is also an opportunity to make sure that none of the animation drawings have been missed or forgotten in the process. When checking is completed, the artwork is ready to be shot onto film.

The Steps in Digital Ink & Paint

This is where the computer really comes into play. All interaction with the artwork is virtual and digital, not physical. It's clean and dry; humidity doesn't hamper your production. No waiting for cels to dry. No scratches or dust visible over dark backgrounds. The brilliance of color, if you're into brilliant color, is thrilling. There are a wide variety of techniques that can be used, taking you to a world beyond that of regular cel painting. There are a variety of cross platform programs like Painter or Photoshop that can be used to add color or special effects to the scanned animation. Animation programs or any program designed for the production of 2D animation have their own built-in ink & paint modules.

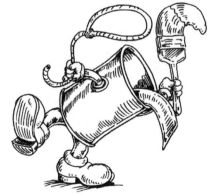

The first step in digital ink & paint is to get the artwork into a form that enables you to color it digitally.

Scanning

The process of getting your 2D or other artwork into the computer is called **digitizing**; in other words, turning your artwork into digital data. Though it can be done using a variety of means, the most common way is scanning it in. This is the method used instead of Xeroxing or inking the animation artwork onto acetate in order to add color and opacity to it.

Activity not recommended; can void your warranty.

There are a number of ways to digitally input or digitize artwork. Some techniques using digital and video cameras are shown in the Experimental Animation chapter later in the book. For the purposes of traditional animation, the drawn 2D artwork needs to be input with as little distortion as possible while retaining registration. The best way to achieve that is to use a flatbed scanner. Once it's been placed on your hard drive in this manner, a wonderful world of digital techniques opens up to you.

Scanner Software

Your computer controls the functions of your scanner through the device's software. Scanner software, though different in interface design, is generally all the same in principle and contain the same elements and features; size adjustment of the image, output type, output resolution, color, and picture adjustment (contrast-dark & light).

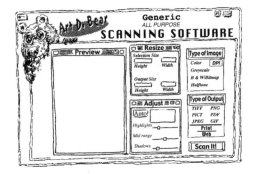

But your specific hardware and software have their own specific techniques and approaches. The parameters that you set when you scan your artwork determines what you are able to do with your artwork and the quality of it later in your production. An explanation of the features found in most scanner software will help you make the correct choices. When you scan, you follow these basic steps.

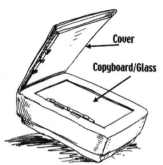

Step 1.

PREVIEW. The preview area shows you the artwork in a window of the interface with default or automatic image settings. A selection marquee appears around the area of preview image that is to be scanned.

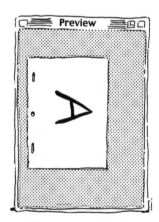

- You can adjust the scan area selection by grabbing a side of the selection marquee and resizing it or simply click outside of the selection marquee area to de-select the image and then redraw the desired selection area. If you're scanning from pegs or your artwork has been placed along the long side of the scanner glass, it will have to be rotated so it is correctly oriented.

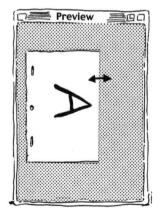

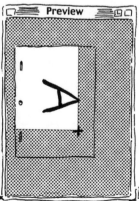

Step 2.

Choose the TYPE OF IMAGE. When you 'Preview' an image, the software automatically chooses the image type based on the information it scans from the artwork. If the artwork is primarily black and white, the software will assume that you want a black and white **bitmap** setting. If the artwork is primarily black and white but with gray elements, the software will choose **grayscale.** If the artwork is primarily black and white but the paper it was drawn on has any sort of color tint to it at all, the software will preview it as **color.** You have to be careful. You need to manually select the type of image you are scanning; color, black and white drawing (bitmap), continuous tone grayscale, halftone, etc. You may also have the option of adjusting the resolution (or DPI).

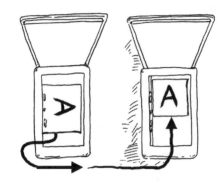

Most traditional animation tends to consist of a black or other dark colored line drawing. Your objective is to get a

nice smooth, non-jagged (anti-aliased—a word that will be explained shortly) line quality. If you are scanning a dark line drawing, your scanner software will probably default to 'black and white drawing' or bitmap mode. This type of scan will give you a jagged, bitmapped, aliased line quality unless you scan at a high resolution (200–300 dpi).

Higher resolution means larger file, especially after color is applied.

Ink & Paint Note:

A way to get a nice smooth line at a lower resolution (72-150 dpi) is to scan your artwork as grayscale types and adjust the brightness and contrast using the 'Adjust the Image' feature to give yourself the smooth, dark line you're looking for.

Step 3.

ADJUST THE IMAGE. This is where you adjust the brightness, contrast, and color or accept the software's interpretation.

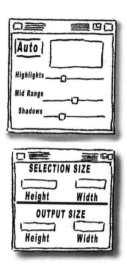

Step 4.

RESIZE. If necessary, you can resize the image for optimum use and output. Resizing is usually shown as Height, Width, and Scale with a choice of measurement units available. For example, if you're scanning a scene of 'locked off' (static; no camera moves) animation that will be output to television (648 x 486 pixels), you would scan your artwork to fit within that output size. It is best to scan your artwork at or near its final output size because that eliminates the possibility of distortion or other problems later.

If your animation will be used in a scene with zooms or other resizing, you should scan it at its largest size so the 'blown up' resized image will not appear distorted by large bitmapped, jagged lines. Boosting the resolution can also accomplish the same thing, but again, higher resolution means larger file size.

Step 5.

DO IT. When all of the elements are correct and adjustments have been made, hit the button that will "make it so." This will bring up the final "Save" dialog box where you can....

Step 6.

Name the file and choose the TYPE OF OUTPUT (also called OUTPUT PATH or PRINT PATH). This is where the type of image is set, GIF, JPEG, TIFF, PNG, etc. Hit the button that makes it all happen and you're scanning. TIFF is a

---

high resolution format, but file sizes tend to be huge. JPEG, the more common format, is considered 'lossy' (meaning lower resolution), but is a format much easier to handle via email, web, etc. GIF is usually very low (72 dpi, or that of your computer screen), making it undesirable for printing purposes.

Resolution

Resolution is the measure of how many dots per inch (dpi) are scanned into the system or printed from it. The higher the number of dots per inch, the higher the amount of detail there will be in the image, and the smoother and clearer the image will be. This is important because the

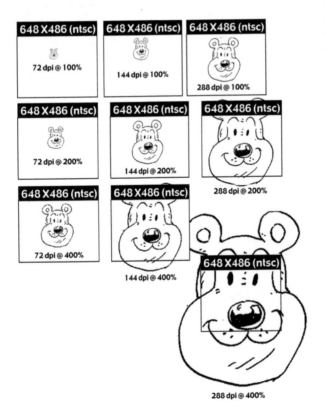

artwork that you scan into the system is **bitmap** art, artwork that is based on and displayed by the grid of teeny tiny blocks (dots) called **pixels.** The grid of pixels is measured in inches and the higher the number of dots per inch (dpi), the sharper, clearer, smoother, nicer, better the quality of the image scanned. Illustrated here is a drawing scanned at 72 dpi, 144 dpi, and 288 dpi.

Compare the smoothness and clarity of the lines at 100% and magnified by 200% and 400%. Also note the size of the artwork at 100%. The 72 dpi comes in at its exact scanned measurement in relation to the screen. The scans at a higher dpi come in proportionately larger. In animation, resolution

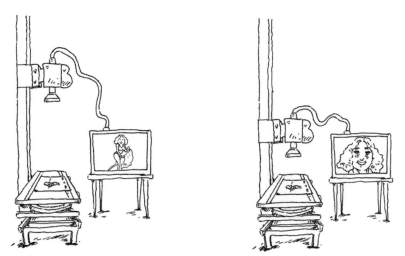

comes into play most during a zoom in. In a regular, animation camera/film zoom, the camera *zooms in* or out on a piece of artwork. The artwork may pan from side-to-side, but it is in a fixed location, the camera compound.

In a computer/digital zoom, the 'camera' is actually the screen and is stationary. In order to simulate the action of a camera zooming in to a closer shot, the artwork is magnified or reduced. The closer the 'camera' gets to the zooming image, the larger the artwork has to be in order to maintain or reveal the desired clarity and detail.

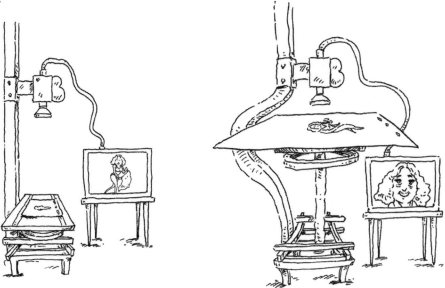

You've probably seen animated artwork on television or the web that has a blocky or chunky appearance, especially on the edges. This is due to low or insufficient resolution. This is also called **aliasing.**

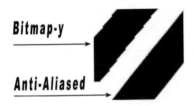

Eliminating this unwanted phenomenon is called **anti-aliasing.**

There are programs that will anti-alias existing artwork, essentially breaking the larger, chunky pixels down into smaller smoother ones, but the best way to avoid aliasing is to scan your artwork with an adequate DPI at the very beginning.

Vector Art

Vector art, artwork that has been generated in a program such as Adobe Illustrator, Macromedia's Freehand or Flash, or Toon Boom, or converted from bitmap in a program like Adobe Streamline, is artwork that will retain its original look, sharpness, and clarity when reduced or magnified.

Vector artwork is based on and displayed by lines and curves that pass through an infinite number of non-gridded points (unlike the finite grid/points of bitmap), forming areas called *vectors.* Color information is contained inside the enclosed areas and in the lines that form the edges and outlines of the vectors. You are actually manipulating mathematical data, the stuff that computers love.

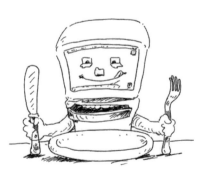

Vector files, being data, are smaller files which is why they are perfect for use on the internet; smaller file sizes mean faster downloads. Bitmap art can be *vectorized*—converted to vector art. This process is done by 'tracing' the lines and converting the data. This can

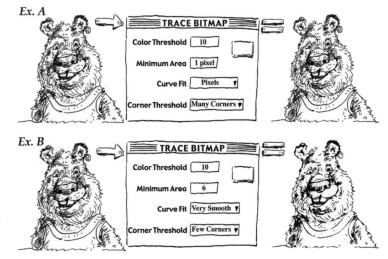

Ex. A

TRACE BITMAP
Color Threshold | 10
Minimum Area | 1 pixel
Curve Fit | Pixels
Corner Threshold | Many Corners

Ex. B

TRACE BITMAP
Color Threshold | 10
Minimum Area | 6
Curve Fit | Very Smooth
Corner Threshold | Few Corners

be a blessing or a curse because complex bitmap art that has been vectorized can end up being a larger file than the original. The more accurately the lines are 'traced' and vectorized, the larger the resulting file. Tracing a complex bitmap drawing at a lower, less sensitive, and accurate setting can generate an interestingly different style of drawing. Simpler, more graphic. Something else to experiment with.

Ink & Paint Note:

A very important piece of artwork to make and have is a scan guide.

A scan guide is similar to a field guide. The field that you animated the scene at can be traced onto

paper or acetate then placed onto the scanner's plate and scanned as a guide. This guide will enable you to scan additional or revised artwork

from your scene and have it at the same size and proportion as the original scans. You can include the scene number, job number, and field that the scene was animated at or you can even note the scan settings for future reference. It's good to have a mark at the center of the scan area as an additional registration or orientation point. If you're scanning multiples, which you will more than likely be doing, and you would like to have a representative drawing from your scene as the scan guide, you should make your scan guide on acetate

and lay it down first, followed by the piece of artwork. This will show you the artwork's position in the scene.

Scanning an Actual Production

Before you begin your scanning session, it is important to set up the directories that will be holding your scanned data. For the purposes of the examples in this chapter, let's continue to work with the animation from the cavebear project.

- On the hard drive or hard drive partition you're planning to use, make a directory/folder of the overall project. This directory/folder will serve as the overall container of all the sub-directory/folders and files related to the project and can be named "Cavebear Demo."

- If the cavebear production had more than one scene, you would create additional directory/folders inside this main directory of the project for the additional scenes. In addition to folders for the scenes, it helps the organization of a project to have separate folders for Storyboards, Layouts, Audio, and Animation files (original scans and rotated files ready to be worked with) and any other elements used in the production. Backgrounds that will be used in the production can be stored in the individual scenes that they will be used in if not stored in their own separate folder. If you are working in a style that requires some initial set-up work to be done in an image editing or drawing program and you want to retain the ability to easily make changes to the background artwork, you can store these set-up files in a background directory/folder. Separating and storing files in this way can help the animation program that you use access the needed files faster since the files will be in closer proximity to each other and not spread out all over the hard drive.

A word of caution: Once you place an item in a particular directory/folder and begin to work with it in your animation or compositing program, leave it there. Some programs may not be able to find the files once they've been moved from the place where the program originally accessed and made use of the file. If a file is moved, you will get a dialog box telling you that the file is missing or otherwise unavailable, or the program may make a 'place marker' for the file. In any case, the file will be missing and you will have to re-enter it into your digital exposure sheet or timeline.

INK & PAINT NOTE:

If this were an actual production, you more than likely would have scanned some design drawings into Photoshop or some other image editing program and added color in order to make color models to view and approve. You may have experimented at that point and, hopefully, saved the settings. Use 'em if you've got 'em. This gives you a bit of a head start, not only for scanning, but for ink & paint, too.

If, however, you're new to scanning and don't have any pre-made, favorite familiar useful settings, you'll need to do a bit of experimenting. Open Photoshop or whatever image editing software you're using and scan a sample piece of artwork from the scene you're

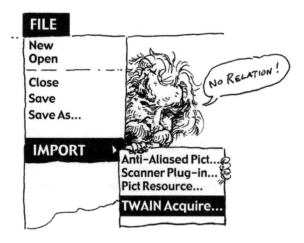

working on to determine settings for brightness and contrast, size, and resolution. Scanning into Photoshop or an image editing program will allow you to make test scans, view them, and make adjustments to them until you get the results you want. You can also experiment with color or effects, seeing how certain brightness and contrast settings work with the colors or effects you've chosen. When you find the settings you want, save them as a preset in your scanning software or at least make note of them. *The ideal setting is the one that gives you lines that are crisp and black and nicely resolved so they don't appear 'bitmappy'.* Once you've determined the settings that you want to use, go into your scanning program. In Photoshop or an image editing program you have to reset the scan image area each time you acquire a scan.

When you're scanning a large number of drawings you cannot afford the possible inaccuracy of resetting the scan area each time. If you fail to scan all of the drawings with the same dimensions, the animation won't register accurately and will shift positions erratically. The shifts may be tiny, but they can be an unwanted detraction from your intended animation. Also, having to reset the scan area for each drawing scanned is time consuming.

When you scan a large number of drawings in your scanning program, you can set scanning parameters for the entire session by scanning one piece of art. You can set the size of the scan, the resolution, and the brightness and contrast settings, then scan your scene(s) of animation or, better and safer, **save** that group of parameters as a preset to use in future scanning sessions, if your scanning program has that option available. This is where the scanning guide comes in:

- Place the scan guide face down on the pegs attached to the copyboard glass and 'preview' it in order to set the scanning area. This scan will appear in the scan area of the software interface throughout your scanning session. You can choose your image settings after selecting the scan area using your scan guide. Once you've scanned the guide for reference, remove it before scanning your actual artwork.

- Place your animation artwork to be scanned face down on the pegs, close the lid, and scan away.

Numbering Scanned Files

As mentioned in the animation chapter, the files that you scan into the scene directories/folders need to be named and numbered to match the identifying numbers on your exposure sheet. In order to have the artwork available in numerical order, use zeroes as placeholders. A system for numbering files so they fall into correct order in your directories/folders was explained in the animation chapter. Here it is again, in a different context. Instead of A-1, A-2, A-3, etc., use a single zero as a placeholder (A-01, A-02, A-03) if there are 99 drawings or less. Use two zeroes (A-001, A-002, A-003) if there are 999 drawings or less. Keep adding zeros as place holders as you keep advancing into those higher thousands. And get a pillow because scanning can be time consuming.

Using the information presented so far, and if you're set up for it, go ahead and scan the cavebear drawings that you animated in the Animation chapter.

And remember, always back up. Files can get corrupted in mysterious ways, so what may seem like excessive backing up can actually come in handy.

At this point, the animation drawings have been scanned and exist as digital data on your hard drive. There are

partially drawn images, shortcuts called 'tracebacks,' that were drawn when the scene was animated. These files need to be opened in the ink & paint module of your animation program or an image editing program, completed and checked, then saved as complete images. Once completed, the files can be inserted into a digital

exposure sheet or timeline in your animation program, timed to match the exposures in the original paper sheets, and used to output a digital pencil test.

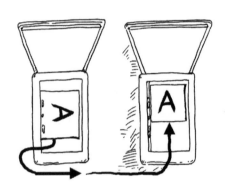

Once a pencil test is approved, the next step in production is to add color to them. Before leaping into that activity, it is a good idea to get familiar with what animation programs can do.

Animation Program Features

There are tools and functions that are common to most, if not all, animation programs such as Macromedia's Flash and Adobe's After Effects or Photoshop.

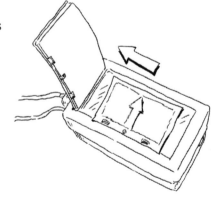

Basic toolbox items:

All programs have a toolbox or tool menu where you can access the tools and functions of the program. The icons may be different in each program, but they function in a similar way. These toolboxes are divided into areas containing tools that access functions in a particular mode.

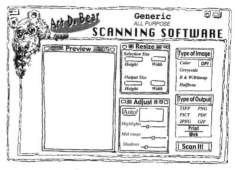

- There are **Paint and Draw** tools that enable you to create new artwork in the program or enable the scanned artwork to have color or effects applied in a variety of styles and modes and turned into the style of artwork made at the design phase.

- There are **Selection Tools** that enable you to choose or *select* an entire drawing or an area of a drawing to alter, work specifically on, or add effects to.

- There are **Image Altering Tools** that enable you to affect an entire drawing, a selected portion of a drawing, or the area of a drawing that is being drawn on with the tool.

- There are **General Purpose Tools** that enable you to do basic things like move the image around in the file's window, magnify the image, rotate the image, etc. The **Text Tool,** which enables you to add text to a file, is included in this category.

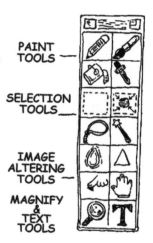

PAINT TOOLS —

SELECTION TOOLS —

IMAGE ALTERING TOOLS —

MAGNIFY & TEXT TOOLS

Paint and draw tools:

The **Pencil** Tool gives you a hard edged, bitmappy line. There is also a **Paint Brush** Tool that has adjustable edges, from hard to soft. The Pencil and Brush tools have adjustable sizes, measured in pixels. Their transparency is also adjustable. There is a **Pen** Tool usually used to draw bezier curves and lines. The **Airbrush** Tool gives a size adjustable soft-edged line. The softness and transparency is also adjustable. The Airbrush Tool continues to build up color as long as the mouse button is pressed, unlike a regular Brush tool that makes a line of fixed size and color and of the specified opacity. The **Eye Dropper** Tool is used to select a color from the artwork and make it the foreground, usable color.

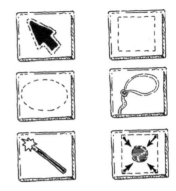

Selection tools include the standard **Arrow** Tool that allows you to select the entire file or objects that exist as separate entities, like a file that has been previously selected and saved as an area. There is also a **Marquee** Tool. This Marquee Tool is rectangular by default, but can be changed to an oval/round shape. The **Lasso** Tool is used for freehand selection of objects; you draw the selection area 'by hand.' The **Magic Wand** Tool is used to select enclosed areas. Click the Magic Wand inside an enclosed area and, depending upon the sensitivity the tool was set to, will select the color or range of similar colors in the area. Some programs have **Shrink to** or **Magnetize to** Tools. These selection tools enable you to draw a selection marquee or freehand shape around an enclosed area, group of lines, or color and have the selection snap, enclose, and select the area. This is a useful tool for selecting an entire painted character and setting it up for an alpha channel.

Selection tools can be adjusted for sensitivity; the higher the sensitivity, the more specific the selection. An example. You need to select a curved, anti-aliased line to be copied, cut, and pasted. With lower sensitivity, you will select the line, the grayed pixels along the edges of the line, and some of the background pixels. With higher sensitivity, you will pick up the dominant color only and leave behind the lighter anti-aliased pixel surrounding the selection area, so when you copy and cut the line, you will have a cleaner cut. Selected areas can also be expanded (encompassing a larger area around the selected object) or contracted (shrunken to select an area smaller than the selected object).

Image altering tools:

A **Blur** Tool blurs, softens, and de-focuses the part of the image it is used on. The settings are adjustable by size and intensity like a Paint tool. A **Sharpen** tool does the opposite, making the image sharper, crisper, and more intense. The **Smudge** Tool alters the pixels when you click on an area and drag the cursor. When you click and drag, you are stretching and blurring the pixels to produce a smeared and smudged effect, like rubbing your finger across an actual chalk or pencil drawing to blend it. **Darken** and **Lighten** Tools do exactly what their names imply. The Darken tool (in photographic terminology, *burning*) darkens the area that it is used on. The Lighten tool (in photographic terminology, *dodging*) lightens the area that it is used on.

General purpose tools:

The General Purpose Tools are tools that are not particularly artistic in nature, but are used for general maneuvering work. The **Hand** Tool is used to move the document around in the window. If you are working in a window and need to navigate to a different area of the document, you can use the Hand Tool to move the document to the area you want. The **Magnifying Glass** is the enlargement and reduction tool. The mode of the tool is shown by the + or - symbols in the middle of the glass. The default is magnification. The **Rotate** Tool is used to rotate a layer. Selected objects are usually rotated and moved by first selecting them, then calling up the specific command or manipulation you want to execute. Some programs give you a set of handles that appear on selected objects that allow you to manipulate them. The **Text** Tool simply allows you to add text to a document.

Preferences:

There are a lot of preferences that can be set in a program, but they don't always reside in one location. For the sake of simplicity, the ones that we will need in order to put together the demos in this chapter are shown here:

- **Cel Size:** Sets the size of the window you will compose the project in.

- **Undo Levels:** Sets the number of times you can 'undo' and 'redo' an action.

- **Tool Options:** Sets the sensitivity, parameters, and functions of tools. Usually accessed by double-clicking on a tool icon.

- **Frame Rate:** Sets the frame rate (frames per second) of the project.

- **Input Options:** Defines how the program imports, handles, or displays footage and files.

- **Output Options:** Defines what is output from the project. Audio, video, still image, with or without alpha channel, mask, etc.

- **Resolution:** Sets the dpi of the project.

- **Alpha Channel:** Defines the type of alpha channel that will be used for display purposes the project or for output.

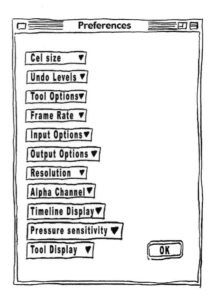

- **Timeline Display:** Defines the units of measurement used in the timeline (frames, timecode, etc.), the colors for highlighting.

- **Pressure Sensitivity:** Sets the parameters of a pressure sensitive tablet connected and used in the program (line width, opacity and color, etc.).

- **Tool Display:** Sets the display of the tools cursors (icons, brush sizes, cross hair). These Preferences become more important later on in the Compositing phase.

In addition to the tools used to manipulate the artwork, animation paint programs have a variety of modes to work in and features to work with. The following are some of the most useful. Their names may not match the exact names in the particular program that you are using, but the functions are basically the same.

- **Opaque mode:** When using this mode, the areas that you draw or paint will be filled or covered over by the current active color.

- **Paint Behind mode:** Paints behind the drawn lines, simulating the traditional cel technique of turning a cel over and painting on the back of it in order to let the drawn line define the character or shape. If you use one program to color your animation but will be working with it in a different programs, you will need to 'export' the artwork files in a file format that is usable in the other programs.

- **Gradient:** In some programs, you can draw with or fill an area with a 'gradient.' The gradients are adjustable, allowing you to choose the overall color or colors of the gradient, where the colors start and end, and the direction of the gradient among others. There are two main styles that are used and seen more often than others: a Linear, ramping gradient (one that is a solid color at one end and white, clear, or another color at the other end) or one that is Radial (radiating out from a central point). Some programs allow you to choose the location of the central point. This can be useful for painting something like a reflection on a ball. A Linear ramp is useful for painting something like a sky. Gradients can be used in alpha channels when you want one part of a character or object to be more opaque or transparent than another part of it.

Paint programs have **palettes.** This is where you choose the colors that you will use. These palettes can be represented in different styles; swatches, blended gradient areas, etc.

- Some programs allow you to 'Legalize' a palette. Broadcast television requires or at least, prefers, 'Legal' color. Because of the way the video signals are processed by television as opposed to computer monitors and higher end video, some colors do not broadcast well because they are too strong, bright, and saturated. Ever see a commercial or TV show where the red taillights on a car become way too bright and begin to appear as though the color is bleeding and breaking apart and glowing way too much, usually when the brakes are applied? Those taillights went from a 'legal' red to an 'illegal' red. 'Legality' is just the term used for this. You can't be arrested for peddling animation with 'illegal' colors, though some clients, particularly clients whose work will appear on public television, won't accept work that has colors that are 'too hot' and don't fall within a specific, correct range on their color monitoring vectorscopes.

- In addition to the tools, another important feature of animation software is a working mode that imitates an animation light table. It's usually called *onionskinning* (named after the translucent paper used by artists for tracing), but also known as Light table or Light box mode. This mode enables you to view one piece of artwork on top of one or more other pieces of artwork. This comes in handy for doing in-between work, just like you'd do on an animation light table.

Painting

Digital ink & paint serves the same purpose as regular traditional cel painting. You're adding color to your animated creation, adding that final artistic touch that turns it into a full blown masterpiece. It can also be just as tedious, time-consuming, and delivery date stress-filled as regular cel painting.

The steps in the basic process are:

Step 1.

Open the file to be painted.

Step 2.

Select colors; use a hard-edged drawing tool to close off any areas that are not completely enclosed. Use a hard-edged tool to ensure that the color will fill all the way to the darkest part of the line, past any anti-aliasing.

Step 3.

Select the Paint Bucket tool, click and fill the areas to be colored. If necessary, adjust the sensitivity of the paint bucket to enable it to fill in color all the way to the darkest area of the line.

Step 4.

When completed, choose the 'Save As...' option from the File menu, saving the color cel to the hard drive. If you want to automatically update the files in the digital exposure sheets that were made for the pencil test, you can save the files in the same directory with the same name and replace the black and white, unpainted files with the newly painted files.

Shadows

The cavebear character was drawn and animated with shadows. In traditional ink & paint, the shadows would have been inked onto a separate cel if hand inking was the method being used to get the artwork onto acetate. If Xeroxing was being used, the shadow could have just been filled in with a solid transparent black or dark grey color. Airbrushing is a technique that can be used for soft shadows, but it requires a good deal of skill and control. In digital production, shadows are easier to make and you have more opacity (transparency) and softness (blur) options with them when you composite them with the rest of the artwork.

The procedure for making shadows in digital ink & paint is:

Step 1. Before beginning to paint, duplicate the folder/directory of digital files to be painted.

Step 2. Rename the duplicate set of files. In this case, BES, where the 'S' stands for 'shadow,' would work, or whatever you think will work best to identify the files as the duplicate shadow files.

Step 3. In your animation or paint program, open the first file that the shadow appears on in the duplicate set of files and remove the character by Erasing, Selecting, and Deleting, or Painting over with white.

Step 4. Connect the lines and fill in the shadow area with black or another dark solid color.

Step 5. 'Save' the file. Proceed with this technique for the entire set of files.

When you open the character files, simply Erase, Select and Delete, or Paint over the shadow line white, then paint and save the character. The character element will be layered over the shadow element when composited.

Ink & Paint Note:

It can be a lot of fun to just play around in the paint program, experimenting and goofing around until you find the perfect color scheme for your character. However, this isn't always an available option. Your client may have specific colors in mind and they may even supply these colors. For real efficiency, work from a color model. Make a sketch or a Xerox copy of a representative layout drawing of the character and any elements that will be painted digitally. Simple color pencils can give you the basic idea of what colors you want to use. In your paint program or image editing program, reproduce the color model in the digital realm, then combine the colored in character with the background and any other environmental elements in the scene, and use this as your color model/guide.

Painting a Digital Cel

Learn by doing, right? Making this sample cel from the cavebear animation can be a good way to get to know the paint program. For the sake of illustrating the information in this demonstration, choose light or medium range colors; colors that will allow you to still see the lines in front of the color. We will assume that you've already made the duplicate set of shadow files and that the character being opened will only need to have the shadow line removed before 'Saving' the cel.

Step 1. Open a drawing file. BE-32 is a pretty good file to use. Choose a light brown color to use for the bear's face.

Step 2. Working in a 'Paint behind' mode to avoid covering over any of the drawn lines, choose the Paint Bucket and click to paint inside the face area of the character. Notice how the color 'escapes' or flows out of the gap in his eyebrow and hairline and fills the background area. Uh oh.. you've really messed up now. Naw...just kidding. Notice also that the character's left arm, legs, and suit aren't filled with color. They aren't filled in because they are completely enclosed. There are no gaps to allow the color to leak out into the surrounding area. In the main body of the character, there **are** gaps in the outside line of the drawing, allowing the color to leak out and fill the surrounding open areas.

Step 3. Perform an 'Undo' and return to the previous, un-painted state.

Step 4. Still working in a 'Paint Behind' mode, select a hard-edged drawing tool with a small brush size and close the gaps on the main body section of the ball and any other gaps you see. Use a hard-edged brush because soft-edged brushes will leave a soft, anti-aliased, un-filled area when filled with the paint bucket unless the paint bucket is adjusted to a high sensitivity. A higher sensitivity setting will enable the brush to fill in the wider range of color present in an anti-aliased line. Sometimes even a higher sensitivity won't get the color to fully fill the soft, anti-aliased edge area. Better to use the hard-edged brush.

Step 5. Select the Paint Bucket tool again and fill in all the areas of the ball character. With some experience you'll learn to spot gaps and areas on a drawing that are going to be problematic.

Step 6. Remove the shadow line.

Step 7. 'Save' the cel. The 'saved' color cel can be sent to a previously set up directory for painted cels, or, as described above, can be saved into the pencil test artwork's directory with the same name where it will replace the black and white, uncolored cel on your hard drive and update the pencil test's digital exposure sheets.

Very easy, right? And no possibility of spilling paint all over the desk or having to deal with humid weather. Ahh, digital ink & paint. Continuing on, the partial drawings called 'tracebacks' need to be completed at this point.

Digital Traceback: Eyeblinks

This is where the computer can really save a lot of time. Instead of having to physically draw the traceback drawings in an eyeblink, you can use one held pose of the character, draw only the blinking eyes and paste the appropriate eyeblink art on, then 'Save as' the appropriately numbered drawing. Though the entire eyeblink cycle is indicated on the exposure sheets (page 2, frame 101, 4 seconds and 5 frames into the piece), only drawing number BE-42 actually fully exists, so the other two drawings in the cycle, BE-43 and BE-44 have to be made. In order to do that:

Step 1. Open drawing number BE-42, the open position of the eyes.

Step 2. Erase or paint over the area where the replacement artwork will be pasted.

Step 3. Open drawing number BE-43, the half-closed, middle of the blink position of the cycle, and select the eyes. A selection tool that will 'Shrink to' or 'Magnetize to' the drawn eyes will work best, but careful selection with the Lasso, rectangular or oval tool will also work. Whatever works best for you, as long as you don't get too much background area. An excessive amount of background area will cover up things like the eyebrows or part of the character's nose, and you'll have to draw them back in.

Step 4. Copy the selection and close drawing BE-43.

Step 5. Paste the selection on BE-42. The eyes should appear in the correct position. Adjust them, if they're not.

Step 6. De-select and 'Save as' BE-43. Choose 'replace existing' when that option box appears. You have just made a new BE-43 with correct eyes and held body position. You now have the open eye position and the middle eye position. To make the closed eye position, you can leave the newly created BE-43 open, and repeat the procedure or close BE-43 and open BE-42 again and follow the same procedure used to make BE-43. Uh, let's just leave BE-43 open.

Step 7. Erase or paint over the eyes on BE-43.

Step 8. Open BE-44, the closed eyes position of the eyeblink cycle. Select the eyes, copy the selection, and close the file.

Step 9. Paste the eyes onto BE-43. Again, they should be in the correct position, but you can adjust them if they're not.

Step 10. 'Save As' BE-44 and choose the 'replace existing' option when it appears. You have just made a new BE-44 with the correct eyes and body position.

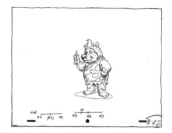

Digital Traceback: Extremities and the Like

More time saving. On page 2 at 6 seconds and 9 frames (frame 149) on the exposure sheets, the cavebear has picked up the stick of vine charcoal and is moving his arm to' and fro' (drawings BE-54 through BE-58), sizing up the cave wall before drawing on it. Drawing BE-54 is the complete drawing of the bear with his arm slightly bent, the charcoal closest to him. In drawings BE-55 through BE-58, the cavebear's arm only extends away from him. Each of the arms connects at the same spot on the cavebear's body. The same procedure that was used to make the eyeblinks can be used to make a full, combined drawing of the cavebear and his arm. But with a slight difference. Instead of adding a small element (eyes) on top of a larger

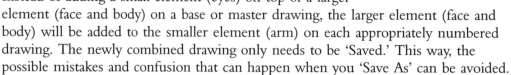

element (face and body) on a base or master drawing, the larger element (face and body) will be added to the smaller element (arm) on each appropriately numbered drawing. The newly combined drawing only needs to be 'Saved.' This way, the possible mistakes and confusion that can happen when you 'Save As' can be avoided.

Step 1. Open drawing number BE-54.

Step 2. Use the Lasso tool to carefully select the cavebear's body, without the arm that is holding the charcoal. You'll need to be very careful when selecting the area where the arm joins the body, again, not wanting to get a lot of background area.

Step 3. 'Copy' the selected area. You can leave the file open for reference.

Step 4. Open drawing number BE-55, (the cavebear's arm only, animating away from him).

Step 5. 'Paste' the selection (the cavebear's body) onto BE-55. You should now have a drawing very similar to BE-54.

Step 6. Simply 'Save' drawing number BE-55 and you've successfully combined the cavebear's body and arm.

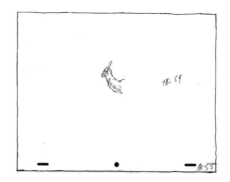

Step 7. Open drawing number BE-56 and repeat steps 5 and 6. Do the same for drawing number BE-58.

  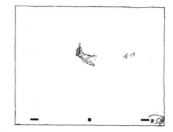

Having just completed a couple of little digital traceback exercises, you can see how handy this technique can be. You may also notice that the cycle on page 1, drawings BE-13 through BE-16, is another instance where this technique could have been (but wasn't) used. A single copy of the cavebear's upper body could have been selected and dropped on top of the sequence of animating legs. The drawings are rather small and not as detailed as the larger ones (and I didn't feel quite the need to rush things at that point since the deadline was a bit further away) so the drawings were done completely. It also serves as an example/sample.

Digital Traceback: Write-on

The way that the mural appears on screen can be done differently and easier than on cel. In traditional animation, the mural art that the bear is 'drawing' on the wall would probably be done with a lot of tracing back until the full drawing was created. Or a 'scratch off' technique (a 'produced on film' technique), where the area of time covered by the drawing of the mural would be shot backwards on film, and small areas of the artwork would be erased or scratched off. Starting at the last frame of the sequence and shooting the entire piece of artwork, the camera operator removes areas of the artwork and shoots a frame until reaching the first frame of the sequence and a completely blank, totally scratched off cel. When developed and played back, the mural would appear animated on. This technique is easier and faster in digital.

An example:

The cavebear draws the mural on the wall from BE-62 through BE-78, a 34 frame (17 drawing sequence). For aesthetic accuracy, you can make a drawing of the cavebear's arms and drawing motion, label each arm with the number of the drawing that it came from, and use it as a guide to show you what areas of the mural to select and at what number.

Step 1. Number the fully drawn mural art as MURAL-17. If you've made a guide drawing of the cavebear's drawing motion, here's where it comes into play.

Step 2. Open the guide drawing and view it in Onionskin/Trace mode in combination with the mural drawing. Select an area that corresponds with the cavebear's first 'mark' on the wall. Copy the selection.

Step 3. Create a new cel, at the same dimensions as the mural art.

Step 4. Paste the selection; 'Save' the cel as MURAL-01.

Step 5. Return to the mural in Onionskin/Trace mode. Select an area that corresponds to the cavebear's next 'mark' on the wall and the area between this 'mark' and the first one.

Step 6. Repeat steps 3 and 4, this time 'Saving' the cel as MURAL-02 Continue this procedure, selecting areas that follow the path of the cavebear's drawing motion until you reach the full drawing, MURAL-17. These cels would then be entered into your digital exposure sheet starting at frame number 207, corresponding to the cavebear beginning to draw, and continuing in order to frame number 239, corresponding to the cavebear's last frame of drawing.

These 17 digital cels will be used to make the mural appear on the wall later in the Camera, Compositing, and Output chapter. There is one more file to make here in the ink & paint section—an overlay.

Registering

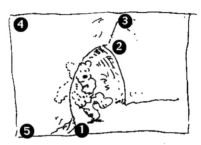

Instead of registering the character to the background in scene 5, drawings (BE-01-BE-08), the background can be broken down into an additional foreground layer (overlay) and the character can just slide into the scene behind it (the BE-08 position would be a good choice).

Step 1. Open the background art in your animation or image editing program.

Step 2. Using the 'lasso' selection tool, select the area of the artwork that will act as the overlay; the area that will cover the bear as he slides into the scene. In this case, (1) starting at the lower front edge of the cave opening, then up along the opening toward the ceiling (2), up to the ceiling (3), back to the left (4), down to the bottom of the wall (5), and then to the right along the bottom of the wall until you reconnect to the starting point (1). The line from (1) to (2) needs to be very accurate because you need to create the illusion that the bear is emerging from this area. The other lines can follow the intended direction and curvature of the area defined by the drawing. In simpler terms, it's a cave, so bumpy, jagged, irregular lines are fine. In fact, if there are any drawn lines on the artwork that can be followed that might hide the selected area, use them.

Step 3. Copy the selection.

Step 4. Create the overlay. Open a new document that's the same size as the background artwork the selection was made from. Paste the selection. It should have pasted in the exact position as the selection in the original document. When you enter your files into the exposure sheets or timeline for compositing, you can double check all of your registration. This overlay layer must be layered above the bear's animation. Name it "UL-05" (Underlay, scene 5).

Now that all of the drawings are present and accounted for, we can finish painting the rest of the cavebear files.

Opacity and Alpha Channels

When you 'Save' and replace the black and white, uncolored cels in your pencil test exposure sheets or timeline, you can immediately output a color version of your project. There is one catch, however: opacity. In

order to see the cel layers beneath it, your colored artwork will need to have some form of **Alpha Channel.** As mentioned earlier, the alpha channel is the part of a file that allows transparency. The selected part of the file will be opaque. There are a few methods you can use in order to make the selection area of the character opaque, leaving the background unselected and transparent.

Step 1. Instruct the program to ignore the background color or use the background color as the alpha channel. The default colors for this type of action are black or white, but you can usually also choose the background color (an eyedropper tool is provided) yourself. An important problem that can arise with this method is if you have an area of the object that needs to be opaque but was painted with the background color. This occurs with white eyes and teeth on a character on a white background.

A solution is to substitute the lightest gray color available to you for the color white. If a perfect white is needed in the project, you can make adjustments in a compositing program like Adobe After Effects.

Eyes will also be transparent if white is used as alpha

Enclosed areas will be opaque if a 'magnetize' or 'shrink to' Selection tool is used unless the background color is ignored.

Step 2. Use a selection tool that 'magnetizes' or 'shrinks down' to fit around the character. The character is selected and will appear opaque over the background. This method works well if there is an option for the tool that allows you to select enclosed areas like the area between the character's legs in the example art.

Step 3. Use a 'Magic Wand' type selection tool and manually select the areas that need to be transparent. Once this selection is made you can select the inverse of the selected background area, thus selecting all of the character, including enclosed areas, or manually select the areas that need to be transparent and save them as the selection.

When you open the artwork to use it in your animation program, instruct the program to invert the alpha, thus giving you the selected, opaque character with a transparent background.

Step 4. Add a 'key color' to the background area of the artwork to make the alpha channel/transparent background. A color that isn't used anywhere on the character is used. Traditionally and by default, programs use blue or green as key colors, but in reality, any color can be used. Whichever method is chosen, your animation program will have to be instructed to recognize that method when you open the exposure sheet containing the color files.

Some Additional Thoughts on Digital Ink & Paint

As you choose the final colors that will be used for the production and make your color model, it's a good idea to paint a patch of color on the cel near the area of its use. This will make it easier to paint an entire scene's worth of cels without having to seek out the correct color each time or possibly selecting a color that is close to, but not exactly the same hue. You simply use the Eyedropper/ color selecting tool to choose and activate the appropriate color and paint. Depending on the size of the project you're working on, you may end up with a lot of cels to paint. In order to complete your project on time, on or under budget, and with as much of your original allotment of sanity intact, you'll want to establish a solid, efficient working procedure. You'll develop your own techniques as you work, but the following are a couple of good things to do:

- Take a quick but accurate look at the cel to be painted.

- Close off as many of the gaps as possible. You probably won't be able to get them all at the beginning, but the more you're able to see and close off at the beginning, the fewer times you'll have to change tools. The Paint Bucket is the fastest way of filling areas, and the sooner you can get to it and stay in that mode, the faster the project will go. Let's be honest. The people that work in the ink & paint departments of professional studios aren't sitting there with headphones on because they're intensely excited by the work they're doing.

- Get as comfortable as you possibly can. A really good chair...get a really good chair.

- Take an occasional break. Give your eyes and wrist and mouse-clicking finger and area that comes into contact with the chair a couple of moments off.

Output a Color Test

Open the pencil test exposure sheets and check to see that all of the black and white pencil test files have been replaced. If you do not see the background behind the color files, you will have to instruct your program to recognize the alpha channel selection in order to see the correct transparent areas. Open you program's Preferences and make the necessary adjustments. When the background is visible behind the character animation, rename your exposure sheets, identifying them as the color version, by the 'Save As' method. Output another Quicktime and enjoy.

With the animation completed and colored, it's time to move forward to the phase of production where the environment of the production is done: Backgrounds.

CHAPTER 8

BACKGROUNDS

Backgrounds are the environment of each scene. They set the style and location. Backgrounds also complete the design and set the form of the composition, enabling the animated action and placement of the characters to complete the composition. If you see a framed background on someone's wall and the composition is perfectly balanced, there probably wasn't much action going on in the scene. The term background in this chapter also refers to elements that are used as foreground elements, like overlays, underlays, and the like. Any non-animating element that requires artistic rendering is a good, loose definition that we can work with.

Background artwork can be rendered using traditional techniques and materials, then scanned into the computer, and used in a digital production. Background artwork can also be produced in a totally digital mode, then printed out and used as background or overlay elements in a traditionally produced animated film. It's art, so no restrictions, right?

Backgrounds are based on layouts; therefore, the background artist works closely with the layout artist. In order to make sure that the backgrounds don't distract from the action of the animation, the layout artist, animator, or assistant animator provides 'path of action' drawings for the background artist to follow. Path of action drawings show the character's or animated object's areas of activity.

Using this path of action guide, the background artist can put together a composition that doesn't contain elements that will distract from the animation action. It will also help to prevent the rendering of important scene elements in areas that can be obscured by the animation or are outside of the TV cutoff area. Of course, if there are some subversive little bits of graphic stuff or inside jokes to the checker or camera person that the background artist just HAS to put in there, they can be placed in a position where the character actually CAN obscure them a bit.

In traditional cel animation, backgrounds are generally flat artwork rendered on fairly heavy watercolor paper or a type of thick paper/thin board called Bristol board.

Several techniques can be used to execute the background artwork in traditional animation; even more if you're working in digital mode.

In traditional cel animation, the main limitation on the background techniques that can be used is the way in which they will be combined with the overlaying cel animation when shot on the animation camera table. For best results during the camera shoot, the artwork needs to be flat. Background artwork with high and low areas will distort the cels above it and cause unwanted shadows and lighting problems.

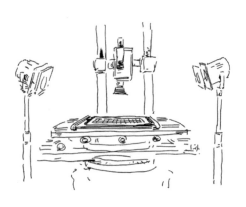

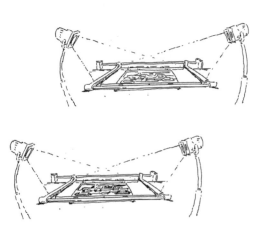

Materials

The following is a brief overview of some the materials and techniques often used in the background phase of traditional cel animation.

Watercolor, or some form of it, is the most versatile of the techniques and has been used the most in traditional cel animation. Watercolors have been used for everything from thin washy effects to full blown imitations of Old Master's oil paintings.

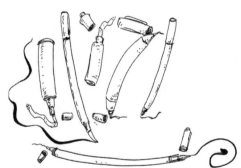

Dry media—like pencils, color pencils, pastels, oils pastels, and charcoal or conte crayon—need to be sprayed with workable fixative or some sort of coating medium in order to protect the artwork, prevent smudging, and keep the material from transferring to the animation cels that will be laid on top. Spraying workable fixative requires a well-ventilated workspace.

Water-based markers on Bristol board or heavier paper are fast, dry, and easy to use. You can blend the colors with a small amount of water and get a very nice watercolor effect. The amount of water applied should be very small. Use too much and the paper or board may buckle, causing problems later when the artwork is shot under camera.

Permanent markers on board or acetate work well, though they need to be used in a well-ventilated space because of the fumes. Markers on cel, though, can be sticky. Let the cels dry thoroughly before stacking and shipping. If using marker on Xeroxed cels, use caution; the chemicals in the marker can dissolve and remove the Xerox.

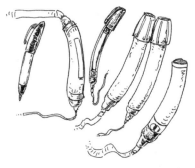

Collage and cut paper is a fun technique. Juxtaposing and resizing background elements can lead to some very creative solutions. Technically, collages can have overlapping edges that build up causing high and low areas on the background. These high and low areas cannot only cause registration problems, but under the plate on the camera stand can produce a lot of cel shadows. The problems can be worked around by photographing or color Xeroxing the artwork, creating a piece of flat art that won't pose any problems. This technique is mentioned last because it can be even more rewarding if done in digital. If you are new to computing or have limited experience with the techniques, collage is a good bridge to digital backgrounding. The same image overlapping and juxtaposing is used, but you have so many instantly available options like duplicating the artwork, resizing it, or altering the color.

Traditional Registration

Paying close attention to registration is vital in the rendering of backgrounds. The background artist isn't just making beautiful artwork for the sake of making beautiful artwork. The artwork is serving a function; the animation has to work on top of it and in some cases, be in perfect registration to the background. If a character has been animated to enter a room, like the cavebear in the earlier exercise, it has to appear that the bear is entering through the doorway, not materializing through the wall or in the space between the boundaries of the opening.

Dry media rarely cause registration problems. You just execute the artwork, spray some workable fixative on it, let it dry, and air out so it doesn't reek of fixative, secure a piece of acetate on top of the finished artwork to protect it, (marking it 'PROTECTIVE CEL; REMOVE BEFORE SHOOTING' or something like that) and send it off to camera.

Wet media like watercolors and inks can definitely cause registration problems, mainly buckling, and shrinkage of the paper. Since watercolor is a common back-

ground technique, it is important to know how to use it in a way that won't create problems. This can be done by using a technique called **stretching a watercolor.** When you stretch a watercolor you are pre-shrinking and tightening a piece of watercolor paper and setting it up so that the actual paint doesn't cause ripples, shrinking, buckling, and distortion.

Stretching a Watercolor: The Technique

This is a useful technique that many people learned early in their art education, but is sometimes overlooked and forgotten. You are going to need some materials to accomplish this task:

- Your background (BG) layout.
- Your lightbox set-up with disk or taped on pegs.
- A peg strip. This is a small length of paper or cel that has been punched in the animation system, Acme or Oxberry or whatever, that you are using.
- Some regular ol' scotch tape for taping the peg strip to the finished background to complete the registration process.
- Something to draw with, usually a pencil. If you draw with something permanent it can be difficult to adjust in order to make the registration perfect later.
- A sheet of watercolor paper, at least 1-1/2 inch or larger, all the way around your layout. Watercolor paper comes in a variety of thickness or weights. Since the BG is the bottom level, you want something fairly substantial, so a medium to heavy weight works better than a really light weight. Sturdier, too.

- Old fashioned package sealing tape (paper tape).
- A small sponge or 3-4 paper towels.
- A flat wooden board, a few inches larger than your sheet of watercolor paper.
- A clean sink or tub that's large enough to place the sheet of watercolor in and allow to soak for a while after the layout information has been drawn on it.

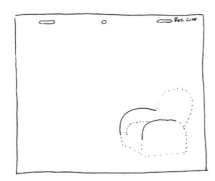

Step 1. Before beginning on the actual background, tracing the areas that need to be in register from the layout onto a cel using a fine line permanent marker can be helpful. It will give you a crisper, easier to see image to trace from, and prevents any possible spilled water or color damage to the original layout drawing. It also gives you a durable drawing to use for double checking with the animator or ink & paint persons, making sure that the animation adheres to the registration lines on this cel. In the long run, it is simpler to adjust a single piece of artwork, the background, than dozens, hundreds, or even thousands of painted cels. This cel will be used later when you're checking the registration on the finished watercolor BG. Just put it aside for now, though.

Step 2. Working over a lightbox or the light under your animation disk, trace the background layout onto a piece of watercolor paper. High-quality papers like Fabriano or Arches are best. The sheet of watercolor paper needs to be at least an 1"-1 1/2" larger in all directions than the sheet of paper that the layout is drawn on. Trace the layout drawing information onto the watercolor paper;

marks at corners of the layout drawing.

pay close attention to any areas that need to be in register to the animation. Trace the peghole positions, too, because this piece of artwork will have to be accurately registered later and the pegholes give you a guide for doing this. Make small marks to indicate the corners of the layout drawing. This tells you how far from the edge you can tape the watercolor down and where to cut to remove it from the board it is stretched on.

Step 3. Have your board, paper tape, and paper towels ready near the sink or tub. The sink or tub will need a few inches of water in it; enough to completely cover the watercolor paper, allowing it to float and soak and become thoroughly wet. There are artists that soak their paper overnight especially if it's really a heavy-weight paper. Experiment. See what works best for you. This can take anywhere from 10 minutes to a half hour. So run an errand or feed the dog.

Step 4. When the paper is thoroughly soaked, remove it from the water, letting the excess water 'drain' off of it into the sink or tub. Place the soaked piece of paper in the center of the board.

Step 5. Take a paper towel and gently 'dab' at the edges of the paper, removing more excess

water. An inch or two from the edge will do, being careful not to cross over into the area of the watercolor that will be on screen.

Step 6. The watercolor paper needs to be taped down to the board. Measure four lengths of paper tape, one for each edge of the paper. Make sure that the paper tape is long enough to overlay at the corners. Do not lay the tape down on the wet areas of the board because it may stick.

Step 7. Make sure the paper is laying flat on the board, then moisten the tape and apply it to the edges of the paper.

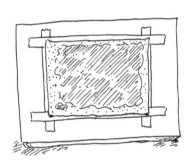

Step 8. When the tape is applied, take a couple of paper towels and lay them down flat on top of the wet watercolor paper and gently remove the excess water from the surface of the paper. Just laying them on top of it, allowing them to soak up the

excess and then peeling them off is the simplest way. You can pat the paper towels if you like, but you don't want to rub the paper towels and paper because you might smudge or damage the drawing underneath.

Step 9. If you're looking for a real 'wet into wet' kind of thing, now's the time. If you are going to use a more detailed technique, you can allow the paper to dry thoroughly before applying the watercolors. This can take at least an hour or two; maybe longer, depending on the weight of the paper. But there are a few ways to speed up this process.

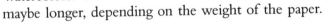

You can use a hairdryer and speed dry the paper. A higher setting is ok, but

don't get too close. Move the hair dryer back and forth to get an even amount of hot air on the artwork. Also be aware that there's going to be a tiny bit of shrinkage in the drawing, even if allowed to sit and dry slowly and naturally. Speed drying with a hairdryer can cause a bit of extra distortion.

You can use a lamp to speed up the drying process. Lamps tend to focus their heat in a smaller area than a hair dryer, so you will need to check the drying process often and move the lamp around to get an even distribution of the lamp's heat.

You can use a small portable heater to speed up the drying process. Portable heaters blow an even amount of hot air in only one area at a time, so like

the lamp technique, you need to check the heater often and move it to different positions to dry the watercolor paper evenly.

The watercolor paper is now stretched and ready to work on.

Step 10. Paint the watercolor.

Step 11. When the painting is completed and allowed to thoroughly dry, it is removed from the board to prepare it for use. You can carefully remove the paper tape from the edges or use a utility knife to carefully cut around the edges and remove the artwork from the board. If using a utility knife to remove the artwork, use a metal ruler or some sort of rigid straight edge between the knife's blade and the actual artwork area to prevent any accidental slicing of the actual artwork.

Step 12. The BG will need to be registered to the layout drawing. You can punch peg holes in the background where you drew them, but you shouldn't expect the background to line up perfectly, because, as mentioned, there is a tiny bit of shrinkage that occurs and the chances of it lining up completely accurate are pretty slim. A more accurate method is to go ahead and punch the background, then slice off the punched pegs in the area between the pegs and the layout's drawing area.

BACKGROUND NOTE:

For easier and faster shooting at camera, place the pegs at the top of the background art. If the background is meant for a digital production, regular bottom pegging will work just fine. Refer to the Layout chapter for a more in depth explanation of the reasons for top or bottom pegging.

Step 13. Place the layout drawing on the pegs over the lightbox. You can, for additional clarity, place the fine-lined registration line on a cel that was drawn earlier on top of the layout drawing or use it by itself.

Step 14. Place the peg strip you just sliced off (or a previously punched cel's peg strip) on the pegs.

Step 15. Place the finished background over the layout and pegs and line up the background to the layout and/or registration line so they are in register. The markered registration lines are easier to see than the layout on paper.

Step 16. Tape the pegs securely to the finished background, and you're good to go. Here's where that really accurate fine line markered registration cel comes in again. You can double-check the registration by laying that fine line markered registration cel on top of the background while it's

still on the pegs and seeing if everything is in register. If not, make the necessary adjustments: A bit of watercolor can be applied to make corrections, but it can't be very wet. A bit of pencil or color pencil can be used to add definition to a watercolor or tighten up areas for registration.

The finished stretched and watercolored background.

Background Note:

There is an alternative to stretching watercolor paper before painting on it. You can use a watercolor block. A watercolor block is a pad of pre-stretched watercolor paper. The pad of paper is bound on all four sides with glue except for a small area where a dull-edged blade can be inserted to separate the top sheet of paper that was painted rom the rest of the pad after the painting is finished and dry. The painting is then registered, pegged, and prepared for production just like you would for a regularly stretched watercolor. The drawback to working on a watercolor block is that registration is more difficult because you can't use a lightbox and accurately trace the background layout's drawing registration lines onto the watercolor paper. You can come reasonably close, though, by projecting the layout drawing onto the block of paper or

tracing the lines on the back of the layout drawing and rubbing them onto the watercolor block's top sheet. The trade off in time used to register the artwork as accurately as possible in relation to the time spent stretching the watercolor is something you'll have to determine for yourself. If you don't have characters or objects registering to the background, you don't have a problem. If you're scanning the background into the computer, you have a lot of digital tools that can help you touch up or alter areas of the artwork that need to be in register.

Final Check

Final checking is pretty much exactly that; checking for the final time that everything is OK before the artwork is sent to camera and recorded onto film or video. The closer you get to the final output medium, the more difficult and costly the corrections. Hence, final checking done by a knowledgeable person known as a **checker.**

A checker needs to be a very thorough person. Using the exposure sheets, the checker is the person that basically sets up the animation elements the way the camera operator will, making sure in advance that:

- everything is painted correctly;
- all the levels will work according to the exposure sheets;
- all the elements are clean and undamaged;
- all the elements are in register; and
- all the elements are there.

Any problems that the checker finds are sent back to the department that is responsible for that area of production. The corrections are made and that portion of the job is re-checked.

BACKGROUND NOTE:

Place protective cels on background art before sending it to camera. Protective cels on finished background art are very important. There are an infinite number of coffee spills, sweat droplets, and flying insects looking for areas to land on and taunt you into sending them to their next incarnation. These bits of cosmic flotsam, for some reason, find animation

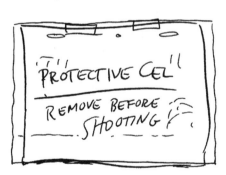

backgrounds the item of choice when interacting with this dimension. Hours and hours of work can be ruined by any of these little guests coming into contact with artwork. Fixing their damage can affect your deadline, causing your animation empire to crumble, and sending you into the world of UBJs (Uniformed Burger Jockeys). Sacrifice a simple animation cel, tape it carefully and securely to your background, and label the cel "PROTECTIVE CEL; REMOVE BEFORE SHOOTING."

Packing up for Final: The Checklist

- The finished cels, packed securely for transport.
- The finished backgrounds, packed securely for transport.
- The exposure sheets, correct and clearly written.
- Names and contact numbers for the person or persons coordinating the project that the camera operator can call in order to get clarification and answers.
- A copy of the storyboard for the camera person in case the question answerer/contact person isn't available.

The painted cels and finished backgrounds are now ready to be taken to final camera and recorded onto film or video if you're producing in a traditional cel to film mode.

Digital Backgrounds

Though you may not get the same physical joy that you receive from actually feeling the texture of the pencil or pen or brush as it moves across the surface of a nice piece of paper, or the smell of the ink or wet watercolor paper, you can still have a rewarding experience when you do backgrounds in digital mode.

If you're working digitally, you have a variety of programs that can be used to generate background art; Photoshop plug-ins and Painter Chief, are two examples. These programs can simulate watercolor and any other painting technique or effect and can generate combinations of techniques and effects that can't be done effectively in the real world. Want to mix oil paint with watercolor? You can do it digitally. Want to simulate an expensive, feature film type multi-plane camera effect on an educational film's low budget? You can do it digitally. There is no worry of wet paint or bits of china marker or paint chipping off and sticking to cels. If you prefer actually painting artwork to digital painting you can, of course, paint an actual background and scan it in to your computer system. You can further enhance it once it has been digitized. A couple of key points to remember when doing digital backgrounds:

- Just like traditional cel animation, your backgrounds are based on your scene layouts.

- Unlike traditional, the layouts can be scanned into your computer system and actually painted on, using them as the base background drawing. This virtually ensures correct registration.

Digital Approaches and Techniques

There are paint programs, like Painter from a company called Procreate, that simulate traditional media and techniques like watercolor, pastels, airbrush, and crayon among others. Copies of your layout drawings can be painted on directly or placed in a layer and used as a guide to paint over. Photoshop also works well for this sort of background.

You can achieve a great deal of depth if you use 3D for your backgrounds. 3D backgrounds can be set up from a layout drawing but it's a bit more difficult to set up the registration. When using 3D it's a good idea to set up the 3D environment, print out a rendering of the background, and use it as a guide to animate on.

In spite of the flexibility of digital production, it is still important to have things in register and maintain that registration throughout the different steps of production. In the end it saves time and money doing things correctly the first time as opposed to a 'fix it in the mix' attitude.

A Few Digital Registration Techniques

Three techniques for registering animation to a background are presented here. The first is to emulate the traditional cel method of accurately and carefully drawing your animation in register to the background. The second technique makes use of a registration line for background elements (similar to the one used for registering a watercolor background in this chapter). The

registration line from layout is used in all three techniques and is used digitally, ideally, because a single drawn line is crisper and easier to see than the actual colored background.

The first technique emulates the traditional cel method of accurately and carefully drawing your animation in register to the background:

Step 1. Scan your background drawing and registration line into your computer system along with your drawn animation. Make sure it is the exact same size, rotation, and resolution (dpi) as your animation drawings.

Step 2. In your animation program or program that you will be doing your ink & paint in, open the registration line drawing.

Step 3. Select and copy it.

Step 4. Open the drawing that needs to be registered. Paste the registration line into the animation drawing file.

Step 5. Cut away or paint the same color as the file's background over the 'excess' part of the drawing (the part that needs to be registered to the background). The registration line is now part of the animation drawing. Continue with the technique to register all of the drawings that need to be registered.

The second technique makes use of a registration line for background elements (similar to the one used for registering a watercolor background in this chapter). This alternate method works well if your animation program has a lightbox or onionskin feature (the ability to open two or more files and view them in a translucent mode, allowing for tracing and comparing). If not, altering the opacity level of the artwork will also work.

Step 1. Scan your background registration line into your computer system along with your drawn animation. Make sure it is the exact same size, rotation, and resolution (dpi) as your animation drawings.

Step 2. In your animation program or program that you will be doing your ink & paint in, open the registration line drawing.

Step 3. Open the drawing that needs to be registered.

Step 4. Turn on the onionskin or lightbox feature and cut away, or, using the file's background color, paint over the excess part of the drawing and register the drawing to the registration line.

The third technique is the simplest. The area of the background that needs to be registered to can be copied, cut, and pasted into a layer above the animation, giving the appearance of the animation registering to the background. This works best in a situation where the animation appears behind an object or section of the background. You can have several of these layered registration areas in a scene. In traditional animation, you would be adding excessive cel levels to your shoot, adding time and cost to the shoot, and dulling your background color.

Digital animation makes it easier to experiment with a wide variety of styles, techniques, and variations than traditional 2D animation. The best way to learn more about digital backgrounding and digital artwork in general is to experiment. Set aside a bit of time as often as possible to just play with the programs. The results can lead to a lot of different personal approaches and shortcuts, but more importantly, they can be incredibly inspiring and lead to some new directions in your personal art.

Having the animation completely colored and some sort of background created, it's time to put it all together in Camera, Compositing, and Output.

CHAPTER 9

CAMERA, COMPOSITING, AND OUTPUT

By this point in the production, you've done the Storyboard, Design, Layout, Animation, and added color in Ink & Paint and made a Background. The client's needs and concepts have been visualized in a distinctive graphic style with full motion and brilliant, tantalizing color. In addition to the visuals, the audio track, your highly creative and insightful collaboration with the audio person, is waiting to be combined with the final picture.

If you're producing in traditional mode, it's all there in that neat, polished stack of

acetate or other materials that were used in the graphic realization of your epic. If you're producing in digital mode, your hard drive is stuffed and throbbing with the files. A lot of time and effort has gone into the production so far.

But now what? Flip the cels or show the production on a laptop door-to-door?

That stack of artwork has to be recorded to a form that can be

viewed by the client and the masses clamoring for your artistic gift. And those digital files need to be compiled, composited with the background, and output to its final viewing medium. If you produced in traditional cel mode, it's time for **Camera.** If you produced in digital mode, it's time for **Compositing and Output.**

Camera Time

If you're a student at a well-equipped school or a person working for a company that has their own equipment, you probably have access to an animation camera stand and someone with the expertise to at least guide you through your shoot. You may even have someone to shoot it for you.

But if you don't have direct access to an animation camera set-up, like the rest of us, you will need to find an animation camera service. There are a few ways to get the information that you need:

- One of the best ways is to contact other animators or animation companies and get recommendations. Animators are generally helpful and generous with information.

- If you contact an animation company, it might be helpful to have the name of a specific person to talk to. You can often get names by looking through trade publications and finding promos, announcements, or showcases of recent work. These free showcases usually contain the names of the people and facilities involved in the production. This can also be a way of finding people and places to send samples of your work if you're seeking employment or commissions.

- Media industry related directories have comprehensive listings of services and suppliers.

- Film labs are also useful sources of information. The film that the camera service shoots has to be developed, and the labs are a vital part of the entire process. If the folks at the lab aren't actually acquainted with absolutely everyone, they have at least heard of them and probably have their phone number.

- The 'motion pictures' section of your phone book's yellow pages is where camera services are listed along with film labs and other related services.

When you make contact with the animation camera service, there is important information to get:

- **Their hourly rates.** Sometimes the guy with the lowest price isn't the best deal. One camera person may give you a quote of $100.00 per hour and another may give you a quote of $150.00 per hour, both estimating a two-hour shoot.

$200.00 versus $300.00. No-brainer, right? But if the $100.00 per hour guy doesn't take good care of his equipment and is inexperienced, inefficient, or just plain slow and doesn't shoot your job in the amount of time quoted, that bargain can turn into a financial problem in a hurry. Go with the reliable, more experienced person, with the better reputation. Though they may initially be more expensive, in the long run they will probably be the better choice. You will seldom regret it.

- **An estimate of the amount of time it will take to shoot the job.** This can be difficult to do over the telephone. Most camera persons will want to see a storyboard, exposure sheets, or a color model. The style of the animation can determine the amount of time needed to shoot the job. Two levels of animation durably

Xeroxed on cel without additional surfacing is easier, faster, and cheaper to shoot than two levels of delicately airbrushed animation that requires careful handling.

Contact as many services as possible, getting as much information as you can. Ask them how the labs have been running. Are the labs processing film on time?

Has the quality been good? Has there been any lost or damaged footage or negatives? Is it the holiday season? Are the lab folks augmenting the normally pervasive vapors with Styrofoam cups of *distilled revelry juice?* It happens.

When You Find a Camera Service...

There are things to be discussed with the camera person.

Confirm the budget. Get a re-confirmation of the amount of time (therefore money) that it will take to shoot the job. Make sure there haven't been any price hikes since you last spoke with your camera person. Jobs are almost always quoted at the bid stage, but sometimes they don't start in a timely fashion. Weeks or months can pass.

Go over the job with the camera person. It is a good idea to check over the artwork and exposure sheets with the camera person before the actual shoot.

Occasionally, there are little things that can be missed by the checker or things that have been set up incorrectly or perhaps there was a misunderstanding about how to set a particular piece of artwork or effect. If there is anything that needs to be fixed or adjusted, you can take care of it before the shoot begins. If a background was pegged at the bottom and should have been pegged at the top and the camera

person has to stop shooting your job to fix the problem, you will be charged for the time.

If possible, it's a good idea to go over a job with a camera person at the storyboard stage, early in the production, thinking of the camera person as a member of the creative team. A camera person, because of their knowledge of the equipment and the full range of what it can do, is usually able to offer some very good suggestions for effects and techniques that can add to the visual impact of your job. Going over the storyboard helps to cement this relationship and get everyone on "the same page," so to speak.

While going over the storyboard, the camera person may also see alternate approaches and can offer suggestions that can help you achieve your desired effect in a way that might be easier, and therefore, cheaper to shoot. Over time, as you gain experience, you'll instinctively know what can and can't be done from the very beginning of the production, and can wait until you're ready to shoot a pencil test before talking to the camera person. For the novice, however, earlier is better. Discuss the storyboard, discuss the effects you want, and discuss the exposure sheets. Make sure that you've numbered the sheets correctly and that you've included all of the artwork that corresponds to the exposure sheets. Also remember to ask how the lab has been running. If there have been any problems, you'll want to know about them and allow yourself a little extra time, if needed.

Inspect the artwork as you discuss the sheets. If you're having any effects shot that involve artwork or masks that you have prepared, double check them here at the animation camera facility, on the actual equipment that will be used to shoot the job, if possible, even though you already did it at the *final checking* phase of production. This may sound like a rather excessive amount of checking, but you will be glad later when there are no surprises.

Understanding the Process

Whether you're a professional with an actual budget, a student with some bucks to spend on a project, an animator who feels the need and desire to control the entire project in a 'hands-on' way and shoot the animation yourself, or simply hiring a trained professional with their own equipment, it's a good idea to know something about the animation camera stand and what it's capable of doing.

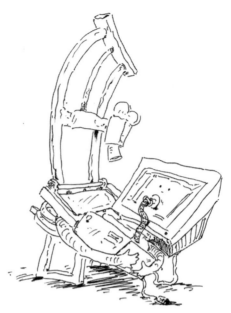

Another reason to have at least a slight familiarity with the animation camera is because a lot of functions that originated with the traditional animation camera are imitated or duplicated in animation and compositing software.

With that in mind, here's a bit of information about animation camera stands. Not enough to start a career as an Animation Camera person, but enough to soften the "quizzical-deer-in-the-headlights" expression that can occur when faced with unfamiliar machinery and practices.

The Camera Stand: A Little Anatomy Lesson

Animation camera stands come in a wide variety of configurations. The one illustrated here is based on one of the higher-end Oxberry stands.

The *camera* (1) can be an 8mm, 16mm, or 35mm film camera or video camera. Attached to the camera is a stop frame motor that allows the camera to take single frame shots or continuous running footage shots. Attached to the lens of the camera

GARDNER'S guide to Creating 2D Animation in a Small Studio

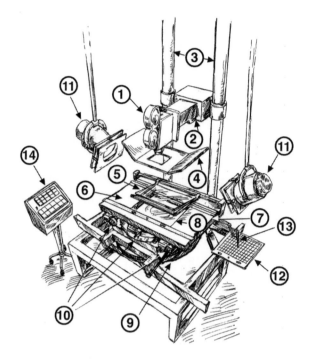

is a device called the *follow focus*. This follow focus unit maintains a clear and sharp focus while the camera is executing zooms or vertical trucks (moving up or down the vertical column, moving in and out). The camera, motor, and follow focus are mounted to a *carriage unit* (2) on a vertical column, or on a more heavy-duty professional set-up, a pair of *vertical columns* (3). Attached to the camera carriage unit is the *shadow board* (4). The shadow board is a board covered with matte black cloth that has a hole in the center for the camera lens to focus and shoot through. This shadow board prevents the camera and other items positioned overhead from reflecting off of the surface of your reflective artwork or the *platen* (5). The platen is a pivoting, floating pane of glass in a frame used to hold the artwork flat, minimizing cel shadow or other problems that arise from the various thickness' of artwork. The platen is attached to the camera table or *compound* (6). The compound is the part of the animation camera stand that holds and handles the artwork. In a pinch, a cup of coffee can be placed on it. The thick, wooden surface has *pegbars* (moveable rulers) with sets of pegs attached to them (7). These rulers can be held in a stationery

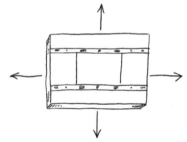

position or moved from side-to-side in order to pan the artwork. In the center of the table is a rectangular opening with a piece of glass inset in it (8). Installed under the opening is a light unit used for bottom lighting effects. Underneath the wooden tabletop is the drive mechanism and a rotating disk. The mechanism and disk enable the compound to travel in the compass directions related to the *field guide* (N, S, E, W, and points in between) and to rotate the compound 360°.

The handles and frame counters located on the front of the compound are used to control the moveable rulers and compound elements. They can be cranked by hand, but most modern, high-quality stands are motorized and connected to a control unit for ease of use and accuracy. Positioned on both sides of the compound/tabletop are the *lights* (11). These lighting units are set at angles of 45° relative to the camera. This angle keeps the light from reflecting up into the camera lens. On most animation stands there is also a device attached to the compound called a *pantograph* (12).

The pantograph is used to help shoot complex camera motions. The motion that the camera is supposed to follow is drawn on a piece of animation paper as a guide, in registration and in relation to your field guide. This drawing is placed on the pantograph where the *pointer* (13) is used to track the move and align the tabletop to the drawn guide. The actual frame where the camera shot needs to happen can be indicated by marks on the guide's indication line or can be calculated by the camera operator using the computer aided *control unit* (14). The number of frames of the move and the distance to be traveled by the compound, and camera if there's a zoom indicated also, are key bits of information needed in this calculation's equation.

All of these parts come together, as needed, in the process of shooting an animation job.

There are issues that can arise after an animation shoot. If there were problems during the shoot or mistakes made, they can, and probably will, lead to the animation having to be shot again. This is called a **re-shoot**.

Paying for Re-shoots

The dreaded re-shoot argument—who pays for what. Naturally, it depends on who screwed up. If you have checked everything well and are certain that everything is in order, and have taken the time to involve the camera person before the shoot, most camera people will respect that and cut you some slack if there is some deep hidden problem that occurs. Especially if you're a valued customer. There are no guarantees in that regard, though. If the mistake was yours, be prepared to pay for it.

If the camera person has a spasm and ruins your artwork because an alien spacecraft emerges from the air conditioning duct, bumps into the camera column during one of the zoom or pan moves, and causes a noticeable glitch...well, that re-shoot is on the camera service.

If the lab messes up your footage during development or printing, their general policy is that they are only responsible for the cost of the film stock they brutalized,

not the re-shoot of the animation that produced the film stock that was brutalized. A bad deal, yes. It's one of those things you really don't miss when you're doing your animation in the digital realm.

Hanging out at a camera service can be one of the most educational things an animator can do. Camera people are generally amongst the most helpful, most straightforward, information-sharing people you will ever work with in the field of animation. And at some point, they've met just about everyone in the local animation field, have worked on a wide variety of projects, and usually have some very interesting and enlightening stories to tell.

A key point in dealing with the animation camera part of production is if you set up your job correctly from the beginning, it will benefit you in the end. You will save time and money and probably learn something in the process. A good deal for all concerned.

That's the traditional approach. Now the digital.

Compositing and Output

Compositing and Output is the final phase of a production. The combination of visual elements, animation layers, background elements, and even audio, if completed, is done at this stage. Visual effects can be added, audio adjustments made, and color correction can be done. The final output size and format is chosen. And everything else needed to polish the production and set it up for perfect output and presentation to the world. Having the animation completely colored and some sort of background created, it's time to put it all together.

We touched upon Compositing and Output in the Animation chapter when we reached the pencil test part of the production and introduced scanning and an animation program's ink & paint functions when we painted the animation files. In the Background chapter we prepared a color background. It's time to complete the project by combining and compositing the elements and outputting a digital file for viewing.

An Overview of the Compositing and Output Process

Once you get the artwork scanned and rotated as it is now, you'll want to see the action of your animation in real time, at the speed that it was intended to be seen at. To do that, the information in your paper exposure sheet needs to be transferred to your computer program's digital equivalent of exposure sheets: Digital Exposure Sheets and Timelines.

Digital exposure sheets are similar to the paper exposure sheets that you use when you animate. They not only contain the basic information like the field size, name, and identifying number of the art files, the duration of the exposure (1s, 2s, 3s), and the position of the artwork in relation to a camera move, but additional information like the actual numerical position of the artwork in relation to a camera move, artwork size, amount of anti-aliasing, and alpha channel information (transparency). Digital exposure sheets are frame-based instead of time-based (minutes and seconds).

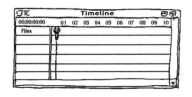

Timelines can contain the same information as exposure sheets, but are horizontally oriented and time-based instead of frame-based, though they can indicate frames if that's the preference chosen. Timelines are the default mode in programs used for video or Quicktime movie editing like Adobe Premiere Adobe After Effects. Macromedia's Flash program has a frame-based timeline interface.

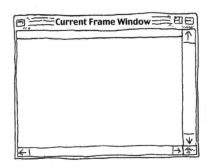

Information is entered into the exposure sheet or timeline by clicking on the frame in the layer that you want to enter information into, and opening a file in that frame. Some programs allow you to enter several files into the exposure sheets at a time. Some require you to enter one at a time. If you have a layer of animation where all the files are going to be using the same parameters, you can select individual files or an entire layer and enter the size, position, compositing, or alpha channel information or other types of information for that layer.

The Current Frame window shows the composited or combined elements in the current frame of the exposure sheets or timeline. This enables you to view and check your of animation as it's being worked on.

When the animation files have been placed in the digital exposure sheets or timeline, matching the paper sheets, you can output the animation. Some programs have internal output methods. These are forms of outputting motion that can only be viewed in the program. For a very first viewing of a piece of animation, a pencil test, these internal output methods, if available, are a good idea. They usually render fast and don't take up a lot of hard drive space if you choose to save them. Everyone can gather around the monitor for viewing.

A Quicktime movie is probably the best and most useful digital format to output the pencil test to since it is a cross platform format that can be output to video or compressed and sent to a client via the Internet.

Compositing and Outputting the Cavebear Animation

To explain and demonstrate, we will composite and output the cavebear animation that we've been working on. At this point, the files have been scanned and colored in ink & paint. Since the files are in color, we will be compositing and outputting a complete color version of the animation.

If we had put done this after the animation was completed using the files in black and white we would call this the pencil test.

This exercise is set up using two methods. The first is a frame-by-frame, exposure sheet method. The animation, background, and all elements are all composited and output from the same program.

The second method is a timeline method. The animation will be output with an Alpha Channel from the animation program and combined with the background layer in a timeline based compositing program like Adobe After Effects.

Compositor's Note:

A couple of very important pieces of equipment to have near you when you are doing digital work is a writing utensil and inscribable surface. In other words, pen and paper.

There are a lot of numerical settings involved in digital work, the sizes of cels, the positions of cels, camera moves, the colors used, the preferences

used...lots of numbers and things that can be easily forgotten if you have to reproduce the project on a different computer or

revise it in the future. Any kind of reliable pen, pencil, or crayon will do. A more permanent way of keeping track of things is to use a journal. A cheap, lined, collegiate ruled notebook or a binder loaded with three hole punched paper can prove to be a very valuable thing when a client calls back in three months and needs you to reproduce a particular job with some minor changes because there's been a shakeup at the corporate level and the new managing partner's sister-in-law doesn't like the color of the curtains in the background (believe me, it could happen).

The information that was created and used in the paper exposure sheets when the cavebear was animated needs to be transferred to the digital exposure sheets or timeline of the animation program you're using in order to view the animation. As a guide, here are the sheets.

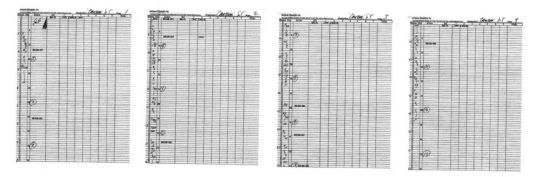

There are some basic Preferences to be set before beginning the session. Preferences differ according to the program, but there are some that are common to all.

Step 1. Create a new exposure sheet or timeline document in your animation program.

- Set the program's output settings, preferences, or whatever it uses to indicate frames per second. The cavebear animation was done on 2s @ 24 frames per second, so, the setting for your program's frames per second preference is 24 frames per second.

- Set your output frame size according to the final output product's destination—TV, internet, etc. The cavebear animation is intended for video use, so the frame size is 640 x 480. Set the onscreen viewing mode so you can see the underlying layers that have been entered into the sheets. With the Preferences set, the fun can begin.

Step 2. Take a look at your paper animation sheets and note the number of layers needed for the scene, a total of 6 (Background, MURAL, Chalk, Bear's shadow, Bear, and Overlay). Select a layer above the 6th layer.

COMPOSITOR'S NOTE:

Here's where the adjustments for size, position, and transparency take place. Animation programs display images at 72 dpi. Our artwork was scanned at 144 dpi, so it is going to appear much larger when opened and displayed. Therefore, it has to be adjusted.

Step 3. Open the field guide/scanning guide that was used when you animated the scene. Adjust the guide to make it fit correctly in the program's display window. The outer frame lines on the guide should be at the outer edges of the window. Make sure that the action will fit within the TV cutoff area by turning on your program's TV cutoff guide or indicator and double-checking.

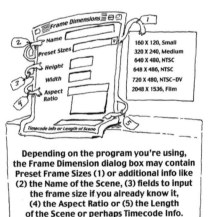

Depending on the program you're using, the Frame Dimension dialog box may contain Preset Frame Sizes (1) or additional info like (2) the Name of the Scene, (3) fields to input the frame size if you already know it, (4) the Aspect Ratio or (5) the Length of the Scene or perhaps Timecode Info.

Step 4. Enter the settings in your frame dimension dialog box because they should apply to the rest of the artwork that will be entered in these exposure sheets. *Note the settings* on a sticky note or in your journal. Remember, though, that this scene starts at a close shot of the bear sliding into the room and zooms out to its final wide shot, so these settings will represent the scene at its zoomed out, wide shot position.

Step 5. Select the bottom layer at the first frame of the exposure sheet to enter the background art. Background layers are labeled 'Background' in some programs and just plain old Layer 1 in others. Open the Background file and adjust it for the close-up part of the scene. Refer to your layout sketch to adjust the composition of the frame. Enter the settings in the frame dimensions dialog box. Again, note the settings.

Step 6. Extend the background file (thus, exposing it) to frame 50, the last frame of the background that will be used at the close-up position.

Step 7. Leave the next layer, Layer 1, blank for now. This is the layer that will hold the MURAL artwork when the cavebear draws it on the wall. It remains blank until frame number 207 (corresponding to BE-62) where the series of cels MURAL-01 through MURAL-17 will be entered.

Step 8. At the first frame of the exposure sheet on the next layer, Layer 2, open the file called "Chalk" or whatever the writing instrument was labeled. This element is 'held' (static) on its layer until the cavebear picks it up at frame number 91 (BE-37). From that point on, the layer will be blank.

Step 9. At the third frame of the exposure sheet on the next layer, Layer 3, open the file labeled BE-01. This layer is where the cavebear's animation will be 'exposed' ('exposed'... exposure sheets). This file is being opened at the third frame because the cavebear doesn't make an appearance until the third frame of the scene.

Compositor's Note:

As you open and enter the BE files, you will also need to open and enter the cavebear's shadow files and give them the same settings as the BE files.

Step 10. Adjust the cavebear's artwork to match the background position and size by entering the frame dimension settings from the background file in Step 5. Since the bear was animated in register and relation to the background and scanned in at the same dimensions and resolution, it will remain in the same register and relationship as long as the files share the same settings. The sheets are now set up to work.

Step 11. Enter the cavebear's animation files into Layer 3. Each file should be at the initial adjusted settings, and each frame of the digital sheets should match the paper sheets: BE-01 @ frame 3, exposed for two frames, BE-02 @ frame 5, exposed for two frames. Continue entering the files on Layer 3 until you get to frame 50.

We need to move from the close-up shot (Position A) to the wider shot (Position B). There are a couple of ways to do this, depending on the program you're using. They both accomplish the same thing, just in different ways. To continue this exercise, we will execute the zoom out in a frame-by-frame method. The alternate method, a timeline approach, will be used and explained in a later exercise.

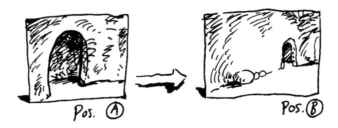

Pos. Ⓐ   Pos. Ⓑ

Compositor's Note:

All files have parameters that can be edited and executed; size, location of the file in the frame, and opacity being the main ones.

Programs that use a frame-by-frame method, the mode we're working in for this exercise, may require that you enter the file with one set of settings, then re-enter the file when you need to perform some action on that file. You are actually making keyframes by entering and re-setting the file manually. You would then instruct the program to create the inbetween frames. The program creates the individual inbetween frames of the zoom. In the case of our pencil test and zoom out:

The background and overlay are entered at frame **1** and given the close-up settings.

The background and overlay are extended to frame **50**, the last frame of the static, close-up position.

New instances (re-insertions) of the background and overlay files is entered at frame **51** with the close-up settings. This frame represents the first frame of the zoom out.

At frame **61,** a new instance of the background and overlay files are entered and adjusted for the wide shot. You could just enter the layout guide settings that you made on the top layer and entered into your journal or on sticky notes. See? Useful, huh?

Instruct your program to create the inbetween frames of the zoom out (frames **52** through **60**). This action is program specific, so you'll need to check your program's manual or help files for the specifics on how to perform this task.

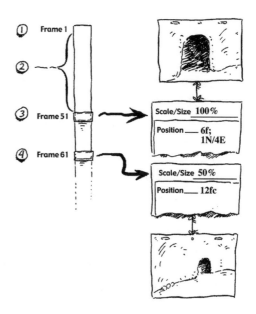

ANOTHER COMPOSITOR'S NOTE:

Hey what about the cavebear? The bear is animating forward during the zoom. He started the scene with the file parameters as the background, and since he was animated in register to the scene, he needs to have the same parameters as the background at the wide, zoomed out position. The same procedure that was used for the background can be used for the cavebear. There are, as there so often seems to be in digital production, different ways to accomplish this. This is probably the easiest one:

• At frame 51 the first frame of the zoom out, enter the bear's file, BE-17, at the close-up settings.

- At frame 61 the last frame of the zoom out, enter the bear's file, BE-22, at the wide shot settings.
- Depending on your program's features and methods, instruct the program to adjust the size and position of the artwork, creating the zoom and insert the correct inbetween drawings BE-18 through BE-21. This will bring us up to the current frame, frame 61.

Step 12. Here at frame 61, extend the background file, with its wide shot settings to the end of the pencil test, frame 295.

Step 13. Continue to enter the cavebear's files (the BEs) with the wide, zoom out settings. When you get to frame 91 (BE-37), you will notice that there are two pieces of chalk visible, one sitting on the rock in the background and one in the cavebear's hand. At this frame, make sure that the 'Chalk' artwork's level is terminated. Crossed out. No longer entered. Its timeline indicator does not extend beyond this frame, if a timeline mode is being used. Following the animation exposure sheets, enter the remainder of the cavebear's files to the end of the scene at frame number 295, noting and double-checking at certain key points:

- Frames 101-114: The bear's first eyeblink cycle.
- Frames 129-140: The bear's second eyeblink cycle.
- Held frames at frames 149, 169, and 187.

Step 14. At frame 207, enter the sequence of 17 MURAL art cels.

The files are all entered into the digital exposure sheets.

Step 15. Output the pencil test. Some programs have internal output methods. These are forms of outputting motion that can only be viewed in the program. For a very first viewing and testing of a pencil test, these methods, if available, are a good idea. They usually render fast and don't take up a lot of hard drive space if you choose to save them.

A Quicktime movie is probably the best and most useful digital format to output the pencil test in or just about any other stage of your project.

Output for Compositing in Other Programs

Animation programs are designed to enable you to create, compile, composite, and output your entire project. A convenient, 'All in One Package' solution to your animation needs.

But there are situations where you may find it necessary to output your animation for use in another program.

Perhaps someone else is preparing the background files or you're doing animation to be used over live action and the project is being composited by someone else, somewhere else.

Perhaps the effects available in a program like After Effects or Boris are needed or desired (drop shadows, color change, special titles, special effects, snow, rain, etc.) and your program doesn't do that sort of thing well, if at all.

Whatever the reason, you can output individual layers and sync them up in a compositing program like After Effects, or video editing program like Premiere or AVID, or other editing programs. To do this, you will need to output your animation with an Alpha Channel or key color.

As explained in the Ink & Paint chapter, where animation files were prepared for compositing, an Alpha Channel is the part of the file that allows transparency (the opaque area is the matte). It can be made by selecting the desired areas of a file or it can be made by selecting a particular color to be used as the transparency area.

The program you're using will have specific Alpha Channel options and instructions for their use that you can get familiar with. Here's a quick bit of information regarding color keying, though.

The terms **bluescreen** and **greenscreen** are used when referring to color keying. They are used as the background area behind the character or object that is to be composited. Blue or green are not the only colors that can be used. Any clean, flat color will work as long as it doesn't reoccur in the footage being keyed. If you're using a normal key blue and the character has a blue collar on his shirt in a similar color range, you're obviously going to have problems.

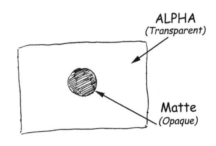

Occasionally, the key color can overlap the pixels on the edge of a keyed image and affect the appearance of the image, creating a fringe of unwanted color. This occurs when the edges of the animated image are resolved or anti-aliased, at output (resolving and anti-aliasing = graying out the line's curves to give a smoother look as opposed to a blocky, chunky bitmap appearance, as explained in the Scanning section of the Ink & Paint chapter).

When the footage is keyed out in After Effects or the compositing program you're using, you have options for the sensitivity of the color key. High sensitivity will key out a wider range of the color and 'eat into' the image's outline giving you a jagged edge and negating the output resolution. A lower sensitivity will key the pure color and a lower range of it, leaving the image's outline, including the grayed out, resolved portions of it.

Though you can extend or reduce the area of key selection (thickening or thinning the lines), or 'feather' the selection (softening or re-resolving the lines), it can be helpful to just prevent the problem up front by using this little tip.

COMPOSITOR'S NOTE:

For an animated image with a black line, a dark blue/black can be used as a key color instead of the usual and common blue or green. When the animation is resolved at output, the edge pixels are resolved with the dark blue/black color of the background, instead of the default white background that most programs employ or a color that will give you an unwanted color at the edges of your image. Fringe is nice for your 60's day parade, but not welcome at all on compositing day.

To show how all this comes together and demonstrate the ease and versatility of the medium, the cavebear animation will be output from the animation program with an Alpha Channel, and combined with a background in a compositing program. That's the basic goal of the exercise. But there's more:

- The first exercise will use the same background as the previous animation program exercise, but show an alternate ways to execute the zoom out.

- The second exercise will show how to composite the animation over a 3D background that has an animated zoom out. Some things to consider when making the 3D background are also discussed in the exercise. An alternate way of making the mural appear on the wall (using a 'masking' technique) will also be a part of the upcoming exercises.

Exercise 1:

Preparing the Animation Elements

The animation needs to be output from the animation program as a Quicktime movie to be combined with the background, shadow, chalk, and overlay elements.

Step 1. In your animation program, open the cavebear's exposure sheets.

Step 2. Make sure that all of the files are there and that everything is registered properly. The exposure sheets are ready for output, combining the background and static art layers with the animation layer. For this exercise, though, we want to output the animation with an Alpha Channel but without the background.

Step 3. Depending on your program's layer handling features and methods, turn off the non-essential, non-animating layers: the background, the chalk, the overlay. You may be able to simply click an icon to make the layer invisible and non-rendering or you may have to actually remove or delete the files from the layers. Advance forward in the exposure sheets, checking to see that only the character is displayed over the empty, default background.

Step 4. You can choose the background color for your program to generate behind your animation as it renders the output. You will also need to select the appropriate resolution options for smoothness of line, and whatever available options are provided by your program.

Step 5. Choose the appropriate output display options if offered. Some programs allow you to select the nature of the display to output. In addition to the Normal display, you may be able to output a Mask (solid black silhouette of the animation layer with a white background) or Reverse Mask (a solid white silhouette with a black background). This can come in handy if you need to output a mask or a shadow for compositing. In After Effects, for instance, you can place the solid black shadow on a layer under the animation layer, adjust the opacity to about 50%, and apply a 'fast blur'—an instant drop shadow that will mirror the animation. You can take it a step further and distort the shadow with Scale, Rotation, and Transform tools to give it perspective. If the character's shadow wasn't animated and prepared in ink & paint, this is an alternate way to create shadows.

Step 6. Output a Quicktime movie of the animation. The animation component is ready for further compositing.

Animation saved as a mask can be used as a shadow.

The mask can be placed on a layer under the animation and given a lower opacity number, making a very effective shadow.

The shadow can be manipulated with 'Transform' tools, adding perspective to the shadow.

Check and Prepare the Background and Prop Elements

Check to see that the Background, the Chalk, and the Overlay artwork is all the same size and resolution, making sure that they will all be in register when they are entered into the compositing program's timeline. This can be done in your animation program or in an image-editing program like Photoshop.

Putting It All Together

This method allows you to enter a file into the sheets or timeline and have a variety of actions executed on that one specific instance (entry into sheet or timeline) of the file. In this method, the background file is entered and a **keyframe** is set. A keyframe is a frame that holds the information for the properties of a file in a particular frame. The size of the file, the location of the file in the frame, the opacity of the file, etc. These, among other things, are its properties. When you want to change the values of the properties of a file, you enter a new keyframe at the location on the timeline that you want those changes to begin to take place, and the location on the timeline that you want those changes to have been completely executed. In the case of our exercise:

Step 1. Open a new document with timeline in your compositing program. Depending on the program you're using you will need to select the output size, the frame rate, the timeline's display method (timecode, minutes and seconds, frames), and a variety of other options and preferences for the compositing session. Because we are duplicating the output from the animation program, this session needs to have the same parameters:

640 x 480 for the output size,

frames for the display method, and

24 frames per second for the frame rate.

Step 2. Import the files needed for the session. For this exercise, we will need the Quicktime movie of the animation we just output, along with the Background, the Chalk, the Mural art, the Mural 'write on' guide, and the Overlay.

Step 3. Insert the files at the first frame of the timeline. For the purposes of this demo, we will call it frame 1, though there is usually an option enabling you to call the first frame of the timeline frame 0.

Step 4. At this first frame of the timeline, we adjust the artwork for the close-up shot and enter the information into the file's data.

Step 5. Using the exposure sheets as a guide, at frame 51 we need to indicate that it is the last frame of the background at the static, close-up shot and the first frame of the zoom out to the wider shot.

Step 6. At frame 61, we would enter the settings for the wider shot, thus indicating that the zoom has ended.

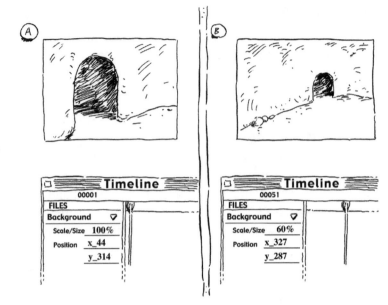

Step 6. The program creates the inbetween frames of the zoom.

Scroll through the timeline or output a little Quicktime to check the motion so far.

The last element to add is the Mural's appearance on the wall. In the straightforward, animation program exercise, the mural was 'drawn' on the wall in a series of individual digital cels. An alternate way of creating the mural's appearance on the wall is to use the masking techniques available in a compositing program like Adobe After Effects.

Step 1. Insert the mural artwork at frame 207 of the timeline and extend it to the end of the scene.

Step 2. At the same spot on a separate layer, insert **MDG**-01 (the multi-armed **M**ural **D**rawing **G**uide of the cavebear drawing the mural on the wall from the Animation chapter). Adjust the opacity so the guide is translucent enough for you to see through it.

Step 3. Depending upon your program's features and methods, bring up the window that enables you to add and manipulate a file's mask.

Step 4. Apply a mask, and edit it so the mural isn't visible in the current frame of composition window.

Step 5. Using the translucent multi-armed guide, step through the timeline on 2s and animate the shape of the mask so that it appears as though the mural is being drawn on by the cavebear.

When completed, scroll through the timeline and check the motion. If it looks good, you can render and output the project.

Exericse 2:

An Animated 3D Background

The second exercise uses the cavebear animation, but with a different background approach. We will assume that the background layer was created in a 3D program and that the zoom out was part of the 3D rendered Quicktime. This situation requires a few different steps at the beginning of the project.

In the traditional method used to produce the animation used in the preceding exercises, the animation was registered to the layout drawing. In this case, using a 3D background layer with a pre-built zoom, the 3D would be created using the layout as a guide. The 3D background elements would be modeled and arranged and the rendering camera would be lined up to match as closely as possible or desired, to the layout. The animation exposure sheets would tell you where to create the zoom out or other camera events.

There are two basic approaches to the 3D. The first approach is to create a continuous, full length Quicktime of the background layer. This would be a Quicktime or image sequence that covers the entire length of the project. This method is simple at the compositing end of the project. Just insert it into a timeline or exposure sheet and check the registration before outputting. The down side to this approach is that it can take a long time to render the 3D, and can generate a large file if you're working on a long project or are short on memory or hard drive space. The second approach is to create a Quicktime or image sequence to be edited, based on the information in the exposure sheets showing the locations of the held frames and the zooming frames. This exercise is explained first in an exposure sheet mode, then in a timeline mode.

In this exercise, the entire length of the scene is 295 frames. The first frame is held. The zoom lasts for 10 frames. The last frame of the zoom out is held. Since only 10 frames are actually zooming, why render 280 static frames. You aren't capturing any film grain at this point, so why not render a really nice-looking, high-resolution, high-quality, 13 frame Quicktime or image sequence? The held frames can easily be stretched to cover the needed length. This is the method we will use.

When the 3D is rendered, frames can be printed out, punched, or in some way registered to your animation drawing set-up and field guide, and used as the background layout. Methods of registering have been covered in the Layout and Animation chapters.

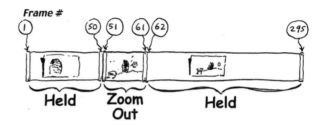

The 2D cavebear animation can be created using this print out as a guide. The guide is scanned along with the animation. The digital sheets for the animation layers are set up as before. The animation is output as a Quicktime and inserted into the compositing program's timeline as it was in the previous exercise. Setting up the background for output is different.

To add the 3D to our exposure sheets:

Step 1. Make note of the frames of the Quicktime that needs to be held and the frames that contain the zoom.

Step 2. Insert the rendered Quicktime into the background layer and turn off or remove the animating layers. You only want the background layer displayed. You may need to save a copy of this version of your animation document as something specific, '3D Background Output,' or something like that.

Step 3. Render the first frame of the Quicktime.

Step 4. Reposition/push/slide/adjust the Quicktime down to frame 49.

Step 5. Insert the rendered first frame into the sheets and extend it down to meet the Quicktime at frame 49. You have frame 50 of the sheets/timeline = frame 1 of the Quicktime. Frame 51= frame 2 of the Quicktime, (the first frame of the zoom out).

Step 6. Leave the Quicktime inserted so the last frame of the Quicktime = the first frame of the background held at the end.

Step 7. Render the last frame of the Quicktime.

Step 8. Insert the rendered frame and extend it to the end of the scene.

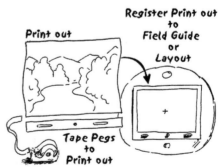

COMPOSITOR'S NOTE:

If you're working in After Effects or a timeline/layers type program, these elements will need to be entered on separate adjacent layers instead of sequentially in the same exposure sheet layer as illustrated above. In a program that requires individual frames instead of Quicktimes, you may need to render the zoom out frames and re-enter them in the sheets. An alternative to rendering your 3D as a Quicktime is to render your 3D as

a sequence of image files. If that option isn't available in your 3D program, you can render a Quicktime and 'Export' it as a sequence of images from Quicktime Player or Movie Player. Whichever method applies. The sheets have background, animation, and foreground elements and are ready to be output. Select your output options, click OK, and render.

Animating Over Live Action

Digital video or live action shot on film and transferred to a digital format can be digitized to your hard drive and combined with your animation.

Unlike animating over 3D, a medium you can completely control every parameter of, live action can require more effort in the early set-up stages. You will be matching the angles that the camera gives you, so you will more than likely have to make a few compromises

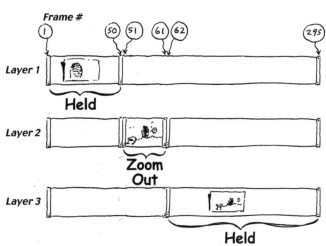

in the angles and positions of the animated character. The procedure of printing out significant frames, printing them out, and using them as guides for the animation is similar to animating over 3D. For example:

- From your storyboard, layouts, or exposure sheets, choose the frames that are important: Start of scene, points of character interaction with the live action, end of scene, etc.

- Check the live action for camera movement. Locked off footage is easier to work with; there is no movement in the background to alter any areas that the animation is registering to. If there *is* motion, you will need to render individual frames and make print outs of the beginning and end of the moves in order to make sure that the character is moving along with or *tracking* with the live action.

- Enter the digital live action into the project's timeline.

- Print out the significant frames, register them and animate away, using them as a guide.

An Alternate Approach

Instead of printing out each and every start and stop frame of the live action's motion, you could use the 'Tracking' feature in the After Effects Production bundle or similar program with that type of control. This allows you to 'pin' the animated layer to a specific position or location on the background live action footage, allowing you to move and 'track' it along with the motion of the live action.

Animator's Note:

Though animation is usually done at the film rate of speed, 24 fps, when animating something that will be used over live action, it is usually better to animate at 30 fps. Especially if there is going to be any registration or interaction between the live action and animation. Even though animating at 30 fps requires additional drawings per second, it's worth it for the direct relationship between the live and animation. Otherwise, you're calculating between 24 fps and 30 fps and inaccuracies can occur that can prove to be costly.

CHAPTER 10

EXPERIMENTAL ANIMATION

We open the chapter on a WIDE SHOT of a stage. The curtains are closed.

The curtains open to reveal an author, disguised as a fat bear, sitting at his desk contemplating the question: *What is experimental animation?*

Back in the animation chapter the question was 'what is animation?' The dictionary definition was a big help. Maybe that might work again. According to the dictionary, an experiment is a procedure adopted on the chance of it succeeding, for testing a hypothesis, or to demonstrate a known fact.

The first part of the defintion, adopting a procedure on the chance that it might work...trying something new is what we're talking about.

If you normally draw with a pencil on paper and you decide to try a ball point pen or rollerball or crayon or stick of chalk or paste, aren't you experimenting?

If you normally animate on paper then scan it into your computer system for ink & paint, but for a particular job, decide to do traditional ink & paint on cel, then scan those cels into your computer system for further manipulation, you are experimenting.

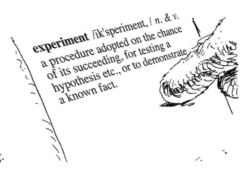

experiment /ik'speriment, / n. & v. a procedure adopted on the chance of its succeeding, for testing a hypothesis etc., or to demonstrate a known fact.

If you're a drawing person, someone who draws their animation in a traditional manner using extremes and inbetweens, then sit down at a computer and map your drawn animation onto 3D shapes and render, the results would be experimental to you. The opposite, a 3D person drawing the action, would also apply.

As the owner and operator of a small studio with a definite approach and style, our experiments tend to lean toward enhancements, improvements, variations, and

'speed-ups' of what we normally do. Things that may add additional time or cost to the production schedule and budget, things that may jeopardize the delivery of the job and therefore affect our reputation, and (no matter how noble we may feel about working primarily in the educational realm) the payment. Painting on glass on the scanner may be intriguing or fun, but if the job doesn't get delivered on time, we may not get work from this particular client again.

When you're dealing with the realities of deadlines, you tend to think that the experimental stuff is best done in the carefree days of youth.

The bulk of this book has been an exploration and explanation of how we, one particular studio, go about creating traditional animation. There's been a lot of "how we think" and "how we do it" and very little re-hashing, re-writing, or re-presenting in different words existing information that can be found in other books.

Experimental animation is a bit different. There are experimental animation techniques that have been around for a while that can serve as inspiration and guidance. Most animators know about experimental animation techniques but not all have done it.

So, What is Experimental Animation?

Four basic traditionally known experimental animation techniques are going to be explored. Each technique will be explained in its original, traditional animation context. We will then explore how to convert them to a desktop computer animation set-up. We will also keep it quite simple. The experimental animation techniques that we'll take a look at are:

- **Cutout and Collage** animation: Animating flat shapes.
- **Sand and Paint on Glass** animation: Animating 'fluid' medium.
- **Object, Clay, and Puppet** animation: Animating solid objects.

Input Devices

The most important part of any animation shooting set-up is the device used to record the image onto film, video, or your hard drive—the camera. To shoot animation, you'll need a camera capable of taking single frame shots. There are a

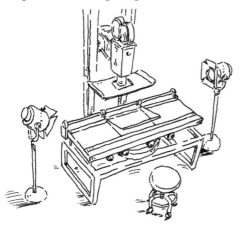

few choices available if you're producing digitally. Two of the most popular choices are the Connectix Quickcam and the iBot camera from Orange Micro. The Connectix Quickcam is a USB connected camera used primarily for video conferencing and webcasts. Though it comes with its own holder designed to enable the camera to sit on top of your monitor, CPU, or the edge of a shelf or desk, it also has a mount on the bottom of it that enables you to mount it to a tripod.

The iBot camera delivers a higher quality picture at a larger size than the Quickcam. This can come in handy if you happen to produce something you want to output to 640 x 480 NTSC video later. The iBot camera has a stand attached to it that enables it to stand on the desktop and other places like the Quickcam. Unlike the Quickcam, unfortunately, the iBot does not have a tripod mount on it, so if you want to be able to use a tripod, you'll need to do a little arts and crafts work to make a platform for the camera. There is a step-by-step project in the Appendix of the book to show you how to make a platform for the iBot digital Camera.

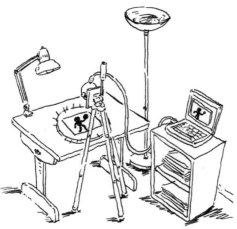

USB Connection

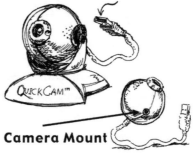

Camera Mount

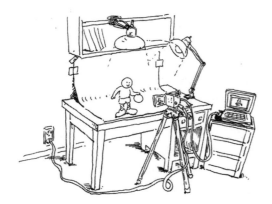

Firewire Connection

Using a Digital Video Camera

IBots and Quickcams are fun and cute and not terribly expensive in relation to other digital accessories you could yearn for, but their image quality won't be as crystal clear and sharp as the sample pictures on the box and certainly not good enough for an actual production requiring broadcast quality visuals (which is why they weren't

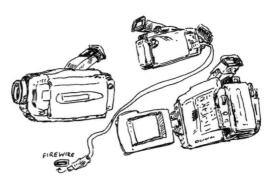

mentioned earlier in the Camera, Compositing, and Output chapter). Even though this is experimental animation, you still want as decent an image as possible just in case you get lucky and produce something wonderful. My personal dilemma is producing images that can be reproduced in this book. With all of that in mind, I am moving on to Digital Video (DV) cameras in the Pro-sumer range.

These cameras have features similar to *Professional* level cameras but are priced for the general *Consumer* market. The tests and projects shown in this book will be done using one of these as the Camera/Input Device. The model I'm setting up and using in this chapter is a Sony TRV 18 NTSC Digital Video camera. This model has a Firewire connection so it transfers data very fast. This model also has a frame-by-frame recording feature, so stop motion can be done directly to tape without a computer or software program. This single framing feature has a drawback, however, there is no variation in the frame rate. It records in six frame chunks, so your animation will have a jerky, 'clicking' quality, the equivalent of shooting on 6s at 30 frames per second, or 5s at 24 frames per second. If that doesn't bother you and you can make use of the action by marrying it to a music track with a heavy beat, enjoy.

There is another drawback to using digital video cameras as input devices. DV cameras have three main modes:

- **OFF:** In this mode...oh, for crying out loud. In this mode, the camera is off.
- **CAMERA or RECORD mode:** This mode allows you to shoot video to the inserted tape or non-tape storage media (memory cards, for instance) or use the camera as an input device. For our animation purposes, the image seen through the lens is recorded onto your hard drive by the software program. You're digitizing through the camera instead of a scanner.

- **VCR or PLAYBACK mode:** In this mode, you are able to see or playback what has been recorded onto the tape or non-tape media, using the DV camera as a VCR deck.

When a DV camera is in the CAMERA or RECORD mode, being used to input video to your program, but not recording directly to its inserted tape or media, the camera is in STANDBY mode. It is essentially 'waiting' to be told to record. When cameras are in STANDBY mode, they have a feature that automatically turns them off after a few minutes of what the camera senses to be inactivity. This saves battery life and wear an tear on the camera. But it makes it difficult to do the kind of single frame recording we want to do, because as soon as you enter CAMERA mode, you are starting a countdown; the clock is ticking while you set up your shots. The camera turns off in about five minutes, depending on the model of camera, and will have to be manually turned off then back on to reset the clock. This doesn't sound like a really big deal, but it means you have to touch the camera rather firmly to operate the camera's ON/OFF switches and can mess up the camera's focus and position on the tripod and the scene's framing. Luckily, the solution to this problem is simple—record a few frames of video to the camera's tape every few minutes. This will reset the STANDBY mode clock. After every few shots of digitizing, press the START/STOP button on your camera's remote control unit. Your camera, untouched by human hands, will record six frames of video to tape and reset the STANDBY clock. This bit of extra effort will result in higher quality images for you to work or play with.

ANIMATOR'S NOTE:

There is a question, though: if the images are composed and entered into a timeline where you have absolute control over the timing and motion of the images, is it still experimental?

Cutout Animation

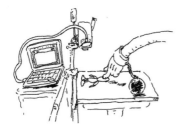

Cutout Animation is a technique that uses drawn or photographic images that are cut out of paper, positioned under the animation camera, moved incrementally and shot, single frame, onto film or video. It is similar to traditional cel animation because of the incremental moves and single frame recording method, but different in other ways. For one thing, if you're working in the traditional animation camera mode or shooting under a digital camera hooked up to a computer, you have less control over the action and less fluidity in the characters than drawn characters.

The size of a character's animating parts are fixed, so squash and squeeze isn't available.

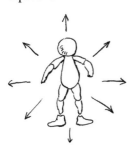

Because you're working with actual 2D pieces of a fixed size, you can't animate a character in perspective without additional difficulty when working in the traditional animation or rostrum camera set-up. The technique works well for ideas and projects that can be designed for a simple, flat plane.

If you're using the technique digitally, however— scanning the elements into the computer system—then using a program like After Effects to arrange, animate, and output the animation, you have a lot more options. Some techniques of traditional animation, like squash and squeeze and animating into perspective, are available to you because of the total control you have over the digital images.

Characters can be separate, free-moving pieces or they can be jointed—connected at the areas that would be hinged or jointed in the human body; elbows, knees, wrists, neck. There are a few ways to joint a character.

Brass Fasteners: Remember them from elementary school?

Paper Buttons: A circle punched out of the joint area of one of the pieces to be joined (A), is glued onto the joint area of the piece it will be joined to (B). The pieces are joined at the 'button hole' (C), and a piece of paper is glued over the joint, careful to avoid gluing the attached circle (D).

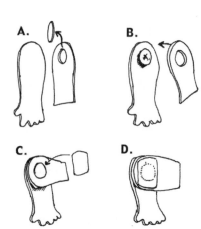

Thread and Tape: The pieces to be connected are joined by a short length of thread and taped to the area of the piece to be joined.

Making the Images:

The paper that you use for the cutout images should be a bit on the thick side to save them from the wear and tear that comes from the constant handling they'll get while being repositioned. If you're using laser or ink jet printed images, try printing them on card stock. A good way to protect the artwork is to laminate it using thin transparent adhesive laminate. The nice thing about cutout animation is that there is no ink & paint phase of production if you render your cutout images in color.

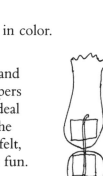

You will need:

- Paper. Preferably a heavier stock. Strathmore, Canson, and Arches are good quality brands of paper. Watercolor papers or cover stocks can be used for a textured look or the ideal surface for inks and uhh...watercolors. A quick trip to the craft store at the mall revealed the wonderful world of felt, foam, and a variety of doilies. 3" x 5" note cards are also fun.

- You'll also need cutting tools: X-acto knives, scissors, a scalpel...years of repressed anger.

When the character has been designed, drawn on the paper, colored, and cut out, the parts are assembled to check them out, test the sizes, and do sort of a dry run. At this stage, the pieces can be hinged or jointed to make it easier to handle and control them.

Timing:

You can work with an exposure sheet like traditional animation, but you're not in complete control of every possible animated expression like traditional cel. The sheets are sort of an overall suggestion, not a frame-by-frame guide. You need to know the boundaries of your scene, the 'stage' area that is being seen and recorded by the camera, in order to accurately time out your animation moves. Knowing the distance to be traveled and the number of frames you want the action to occur in will give you increments your character or object needs to travel per camera exposure.

If Producing Traditionally:

- Your stage is the camera set-up's tabletop. The glass platen is used to hold the pieces in place. The lights are aimed similar to a traditional cel animation shoot; you want to avoid a lot of shadows. Lift glass, move pieces, lower glass, take the picture, repeat until completed.

- Keeping the pieces of lightweight paper in place when they're not under the glass can be a problem. Breezes and sneezes. Bits of double-sided tape can be adhered to the back of the pieces. If the tape is too and you feel your pieces may be damaged or may stick to the background, the adhesive can be lessened a bit by repeatedly rolling your fingertip over it. The natural oils from your skin tend to 'dull' the adhesive.

- If the animation is being lit from above, a magnetic board can be placed under the background and a bits of metal (not aluminum) foil or magnetic recording tape can be adhered to the back of the cutout pieces.

- If your paper is opaque enough, a silhouette effect can be done by shooting the cutouts over a bottom light.

If Producing Digitally:

A digital video camera can be mounted to a tripod, hooked up to your computer, and a set up like the traditional one described earlier. Single frame shooting can be done by using the Stop Motion feature in Adobe Premiere or your camera's built-in single frame feature. Because you have a lot of near instant image manipulation options available in digital production, you don't need to fuss with your lights quite as much as with traditional. Eliminating shadows will probably still be your main concern, therefore you may need multiple lights. This can cause some exposure problems, so be familiar with your camera's range of exposure options.

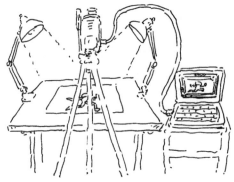

An alternate method for executing this type of animation, one that will give you a lot more control over the elements, is to digitize the elements by scanning them or shooting the images with a digital camera, then arranging, combining, and outputting them from a program like After Effects. Since you're making tweened animation, action that has been calculated by the computer, the motion will be very smooth. There are also a lot of image manipulation effects available.

The Project:

I'm going to set make a simple character bounce a basketball and move across the screen. Setting up the project:

- I'm using an animation desk as the stage/tabletop. As described in earlier chapters, this is an art table with a large hole cut out of the middle into which a florescent lighting unit has been attached. The disk sits in the hole. It's a pretty basic animation set-up that's been available for a long time. The disk has been removed and a half inch thick piece of foam core has been placed on the tabletop to cover the hole. The foam core is covered with a sheet of flat green paper.

- I'm using a tripod with the Sony TRV-18 digital video camera mounted to it as the input device. A Macintosh iBook loaded with Premiere and After Effects is sitting off to the side, my digitizing target.

- I have an overhead incandescent ceiling fixture and a florescent shop light hanging over a drafting table in one of the rooms of the studio. Sitting on a table in front of the desk is a halogen lamp. This particular dandy has two settings; bright, yet cozy and blinding. I'm using bright, yet cozy.

- I set the tripod and camera in the area I usually sit in behind the desk.

- I hook up the camera to the laptop, fire up Premiere, and open the Stop Motion window (File > Capture > Stop Motion) to figure out where the shooting area will be.

- Still looking at the screen, I place objects on the paper and move them towards the edges until they disappear from the screen. This gives me the stage area. I mark off this area and remove the objects.

The Character:

I made a simple, feature-less character and basketball prop for this bit of cutout animation. The character was drawn on a piece of Strathmore board with a Sharpie, then cut out with an X-Acto knife. The character is set in an initial pose on the stage area and the composition is checked in the Stop Motion Preview window. The character looks fine. The software, camera, and lighting is set, so it's time to begin.

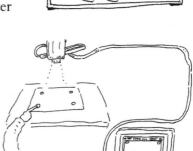

The Action:

I drew a quick and dirty storyboard of an action to animate. If, however, it becomes too difficult (with my limited experience in this sort of animation) or too boring, I'm going to abandon the board and in favor of a freewheeling experimental approach. Some notes on the experiments:

- The character is bouncing a ball, so I'm going to move the ball first on each move, because it's the focus of the action and it will also serve as a reminder. If I'm called away and return to a set-up where the ball is too far from the hand,

---

I'll know I need to pose the character and shoot the frame.

This is a straight ahead piece of animation, but choosing and being familiar with a frame rate, I can estimate the timings of the character's actions. I can also decide on how many frames I want to shoot per move.

- By shooting at 24 frames per second on 2s, it may be easier to figure timings out because I'm accustomed to working at that rate.

- If I shoot at a lower frame rate like 12 or 15 frames per second on 1s, I will have a shorter shoot. The Quicktime can be stretched out to a longer length in Premiere or After Effects.

If you're following along, try to make the character act a bit. Try overlapping some actions. Try having the character bend over and dribble closer to the ground, therefore, faster. Have the character move around a bit. Shoot at least two or three seconds of action. It's not a lot, but enough to get a feel for the process. Experiment and have fun.

The Results:

1. The character starts in a relaxed, initial position.
2. The character glances off screen. A basketball rolls into the scene.
3. The character sticks his foot out...
4. ...scoops up the ball and flips it up into the air.
5. The character puts his foot back on the ground, reaches forward...
6. ...and begins to dribble the ball.

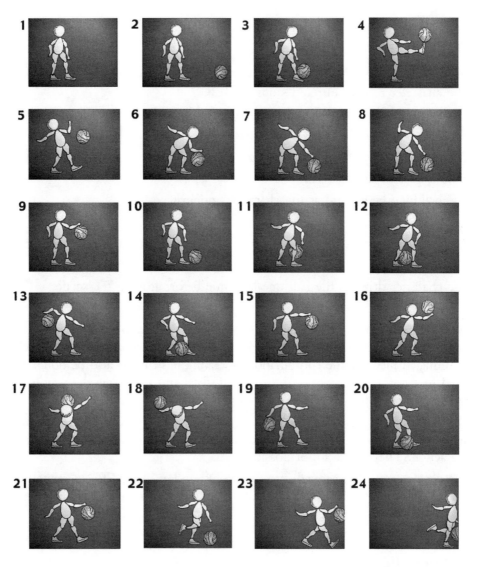

7. The character continues to rapidly dribble the ball...

8. ...close to the ground.

9. The character stands, gains control of the ball...

10. ...bounces it again...

11. ...and leans forward as the ball bounces behind his back.

12. The ball hits the ground behind the character.

13. The character stops the ball...

14. ...and bounces it between his legs.

15. The character reaches out and stops the ball.

16. The ball rolls over the character's left hand...

17. ...and over his shoulders.

18. The character stops the ball in his right hand...

19. ...and begins to dribble again.

20. The ball hits the ground as the character anticipates...

21. ...and begins to walk out of the scene.

22. As the character exits the scene...

23. ...he dribbles the ball.

24. The character dribbles the ball one last time before leaving the scene.

One of the interesting things about experimental animation is a certain element of imperfection. The fact that the action is a bit jerky or odd can add life and charm to the animated piece. Some combination of techniques can be also be done. This animated footage can be imported into After Effects and may pave the way for further experimental play. A couple of thoughts that come to mind are:

- The green background that the character was shot against can be keyed out and the animation placed over a different background. Drawn and animated or 3D or live action. There are a lot of possibilities.

- The character can be scanned into the system and an After Effects version can be produced, perhaps a character 'defending' against the traditionally shot character. When completed, the two versions can be combined.

Sand Animation

Sand animation is another straight ahead (no inbetweens) technique of animation done under camera like cutout animation. Instead of having solid elements to arrange and shoot, you are drawing with, pushing around, or otherwise manipulating a dry, fluid medium—sand. The sand is enclosed in a well-sealed container or area to protect your camera's tabletop and general work area. The image is altered (animated) and another shot is taken, continuing this process until the sequence is completed. Because the medium is fluid, you have to be careful with the thickness and amount of sand that you're drawing in. Too much, too thick and it will flow back into and cover up the areas you've drawn and cleared out.

Sand animation is often shot over a bottom light, producing a high contrast effect. Areas filled with sand are black. Clean, clear areas show up as white. Areas with a thin layer of sand will photograph as shades of gray. If the image is over exposed a bit, the effect can have a glowing, eerie look. If you shoot with a top light, you will see the grain and texture of the medium you're using.

Making the Images:

Images are created by moving the sand around with your fingers or with brushes. Small, fine detail can be done by using fine-pointed brushes or even skewers (save those kebob sticks). You can use your fingers, brushes, sticks, skewers, or maybe try a comb, a fork, a spoon, knitting or crochet needles.

You will need:

- Typically, a fine grain variety of sand, but for experimental purposes, whatever you can get your hands on. If you live near the beach, you're lucky for obvious reasons. If you don't, a trip to a building supply store may be in order. Sometimes a toy store might have sand that is intended for children's sandboxes. These can be problematic if they are premixed with a urine absorption agent. Just kidding. A gardening supply place might also be a good place to find the needed material.

- Sand isn't the only material that can be used. Beads, beans, assorted grain...or any dry, fluidic, granular substance can work. Keep in mind that you are making 'drawings' instead of moving solid shapes, so you actually can have a character animate in perspective. Of course, that's just from seeing examples on film, video, and in books. Once I actually set up and give it a try, I'll probably crawl back to these pages whimpering like a puppy and hit the 'delete' key.

- Extra sand to use as additional filler material.

- A salt shaker can be used to sprinkle sand to fill in thin areas. A kitchen strainer or sifter could be helpful for the same purpose.

Timing:

Timing is best approached with the knowledge that since it is a straight ahead form of animation, it's a good idea to take some time and plan out the animation a bit. Notes on a storyboard can be useful or even reference drawings, little sketches on stick notes. If a character has to cover a specific distance in the frame, the distance can be measured off and the increments that need to be covered for each shot can be calculated.

If Producing Traditionally:

If you're producing in the traditional mode, using an animation or rostrum camera, you'll be working on the camera's tabletop over the light box area since that's where the camera is pointing. You will not, however, be working directly on the tabletop. You will need a contained, glass bottomed area to work in over the light box. A homemade tray or box, a glass dish...something with a transparent bottom and sides to contain the material being animated.

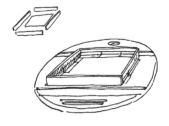

If Producing Digitally:

If you're producing digitally, you'll need to put together a set-up that is similar to a traditional animation camera set-up. A camera pointed downward over the area where you will be playing with the sand is needed. A sturdy tripod of some sort is also important. You'll need to set up your work area to make sure you have access not only to the material you're animating but the mouse button as well, assuming you're taking the digital camera shots with the mouse. If you're working at a frame rate that allows you to use the built-in stop motion feature of your digital camera, then you'll need to have access to your camera, too. Pressing the button on the digital camera can cause it to move slightly, so if your camera has a remote control unit, use it.

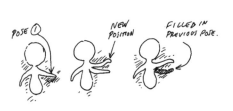

The Project:

Another ball bouncer, using a bottom light technique.

Setting Up:

Since a bottom light set-up was needed, this sand painting exercise was set up on my animation table, the same one described and used in the cutout animation project.

- A glass (Pyrex) baking dish was the first container used. It is actually a bit deeper in the middle, so any attempt to get an opaque thickness near the edges resulted in too much sand in the center of the dish. Any drawing attempted in the center area filled in.

- The next set-up tried, the one that worked, required a bit of building. Since the animation disk fits over the bottom light unit perfectly, I decided to try to use it as the sand holder.

- Tracing paper was taped to the Plexiglas to protect it and to diffuse the light.

- Four sides, about an inch high, were measured and cut, then taped around the edges of the Plexiglas.

- The Plexiglas was placed back in the disk, the disk was placed back in the hole in the animation table, and BOOYAH! A Bottom Light Sand Corral. It worked.

The Action:

- The drawings were all done with a fat, soft, watercolor brush, a thinner slightly stiffer nylon watercolor brush, and a stiff oil painting brush.

- Each new pose was done by drawing the new position of each moving part and filling in the previous pose.

- The filling in was done by gently brushing sand into the clear area left by the previous drawing, or by sprinkling sand, by hand or with a salt shaker filled with sand, into the necessary area.

- Brushing leaves thin, translucent strokes in the sand, so additional sand can be sprinkled on the thin areas or graded over with a stiff flat edged object. I used an old business card.

The Results:

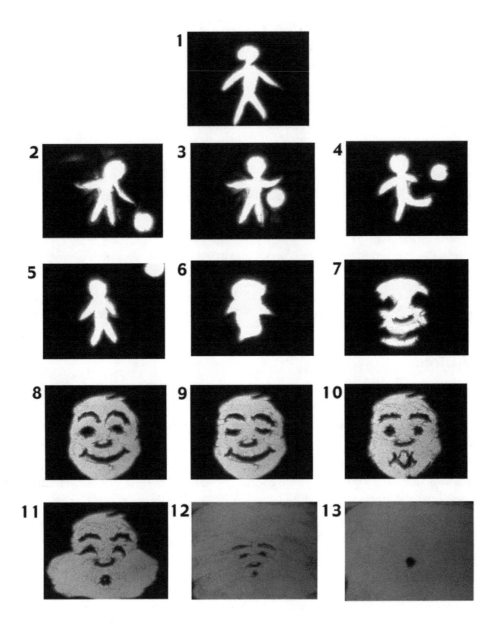

1. The character was drawn in an initial pose.
2. The character leans over as a ball 'rolls' into the scene.
3. The character dribbles the ball a couple of times...
4. ...then kicks the ball...
5. ...sending the ball out of the scene.
6. The character expands...
7. ...begins to morph...
8. ...into a face.
9. The character blinks...
10. ...inhales...
11. ...puffs its cheeks and blows.
12. The character animates into the distance...
13. ...becoming a small dot and before disappearing.

Straight ahead animation tends to take on a life of its own. You start out in one direction and something will inspire a whole different direction. Inspiration, usually, but fatigue or disinterest can also lead to a change of direction.

Paint on Glass Animation

Paint on Glass animation is a technique where designs are executed by using a fluid medium (inks, watercolors, oil paints, etc.) on glass or other non-porous surfaces. The designs are altered and shot on film or video, creating the animation. The technique sounds like and is, in fact, very similar to sand animation. Paint on glass animation can produce very beautiful results, but is very time-consuming and requires a lot of concentrated effort. An animation artist who is more accustomed to the immediacy of drawn animation may have a difficult time with the focus, time, and effort required to produce the animation. But then again, you never know until you try. With that in mind, here goes.

Making the Images:

Having an idea of how the media you're painting with needs to be manipulated in order to create the animation can be helpful when you're setting up the overall design of your project. The fact that the image is 'moved' by adding and removing paint can help you set up your scene.

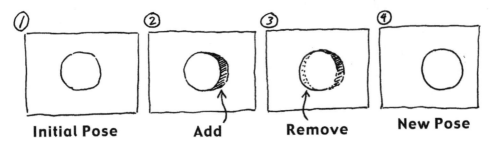

Initial Pose   Add   Remove   New Pose

- Drawing number 1 shows the initial pose.
- Drawing number 2 shows that the painted image is 'moved' by adding or expanding an area of the image into the direction of the action. If the image was shot at this stage of the process, it would appear to be expanding or growing.
- Drawing number 3 shows the area of the image to be wiped away, absorbed, or otherwise removed from the image, creating a new position of the entire image.
- Drawing number 4 shows the new pose. This procedure is repeated to create the animation. Knowing the animating technique can help you decide how many characters you need, how complex an environment to use, or the placement of objects and props in the environment.

You will need:

Water-based inks or acrylic paints can be used if something is added to slow down or prevent drying. Glycerin, available from a pharmacy, or products called 'acrylic retarders,' available from art supply stores, can be used. There are probably other possibilities. The paint can be applied with brushes, your fingers, or any tool that can spread paint or ink. You will also need something to remove your paint media; cotton swabs, a soft, absorbent brush, tissues, sponges, or small furry animals are items that could come in handy.

Timing:

Timing is approached like any other straight ahead animation technique.

If Producing Traditionally:

Like sand animation, paint on glass projects can be done over a bottom light set-up or a top light set-up. A bottom light will give you a more high contrast effect with shades of gray in the watery translucent areas of the painting. A top light set-up will give you the full color and textures of the painting.

If Producing Digitally:

If you're producing digitally, the same things apply.

The Project:

A ball bouncing character shot with a top light technique.

Setting Up:

- This project was shot on the same set-up as the one used for the cutout animation project. The overhead light was turned off, though, because it reflected off on the glass.

- The glass from a 10" x 14" inch picture frame was used as the paint surface.

- A small, inexpensive set of oil paints were used as the paint media, applied with a fairly narrow oil paint brush, to give it a nice amount of texture. The paint was used straight from the tube; no extenders or thinners were added. To move and remove paint from the image, cotton swabs, tissues, a clean stiff brush, and a can of odorless thinner were kept at the ready.

- The glass was secured to the tabletop with small pieces of duct tape, the camera was aimed at the glass and connected to a laptop running Premiere.

- Premiere was set to record at 15 frames per second. I shot on 1s. Before beginning to actually shoot, the camera was set to record single frames. During the actual shoot, after each 'mouse click' to record to Premiere was done, the 'record' button on the camera's remote was pushed in order to record onto tape. Though the camera records on 6s, it is still good to have as a back-up copy of the animation. The camera copy can be digitized and time compressed in order to play back at a faster frame rate.

The Results:

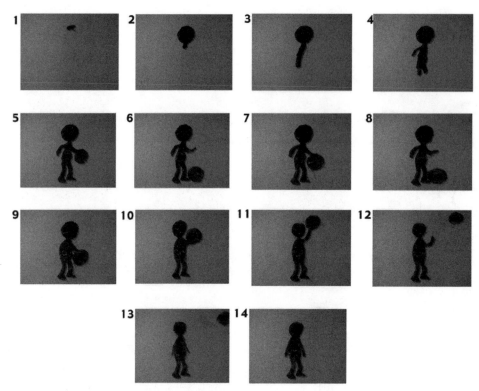

1.   An initial area is painted on the glass.

2-4.   The first four panels show the character animating.

5.   The character's initial pose.

6.   The character bounces the ball.

7.   The ball bounces up...

8.   ...and is bounced again.

9.   The character grasps the ball...

10.   ...lifts the ball...

11.   ...takes aim at an offscreen hoop...

12.   ...and shoots the ball.

13.   The ball heads out of the scene as...

14.   ...the character settles into a final pose.

Object, Clay, and Puppet Animation

Before computers hit mainstream, back when a wireframe on your desktop was a wire frame on your desk top, there were three main forms of 3D animating: Object animation, Clay animation, and Puppet animation.

In each case, like traditionally drawn animation, cutout animation, or any other kind of animation, you

place an object or pose a character on a stage (or background), take shots of this animatable item with a camera capable of shooting single frames, move the animatable item, take another shot, and continue this action until the scene is completed.

These three techniques share a similar set-up and have some common elements. The basic set-up is:

- **Camera:** A camera capable of shooting single frames of film or video.

- **Stage or background:** Depending on the complexity of your story, your setting can range from a simple paper diorama to a fully furnished set.

- **Lighting:** The lighting system is also variable depending upon the complexity of your production, ranging from expensive professional lights to simple household lights including flexible armed desk lamps and clip-on fixtures.

If you're working in a traditional mode the set-up looks like this:

If you're working in a digital mode, you use many of the same elements in the traditional set-up with a camera

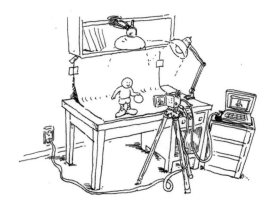

hooked up to your computer. For a set-up on or near your animation table or desktop, you can put together a simple set-up like this:

Each of the three varieties of stop motion animation has its own unique qualities.

Object Animation

Object animation is the simple basic entry level of stop motion type animation:

- Place an object on a stage or background in front of a camera.
- Shoot the exposures of the object onto film or video.
- Repeat the preceding action, reposition the object, and shoot it.

Any type of object on any type of background will work. This type of animation is good to start with and learn with. By doing this type of animation, you can develop an eye for movement and incremental distances, and even though you're working with inanimate objects, you can practice anticipation and overlap.

Clay and Puppet Animation

Clay animation and Puppet animation go a step further than Object animation. In these two techniques, you are making characters that can be made to act. Using a soft pliable clay, you can make characters and make them act. Clay animation is the medium used to make one character or object 'morph' into another. One of the problems of animating characters, in clay or puppet, is balancing them, especially when you animate a walk. Models will balance better with heavier and larger 'cartoony' feet. Another thing that can help balance is to imbed magnets into the feet of the character and use a metal board under a thin ground material. A reverse of the items will also work; placing metal in the feet of the character and working over a magnetic sheet placed under a thin ground material. The option most often used is to work over a thicker ground material and stick pins in the feet to stabilize them when the character is standing on one foot. To use this technique, the 'ground' should have a texture that will hide the pin holes. If you're using a clay medium that is heat sensitive, beware of the heat from your lights.

Object animation is relatively simple to execute, since common everyday objects that already exist are usually the items put to use. Clay and puppet animation can require a lot more time and effort because you are making the characters, stages, and objects. Depending on the complexity of your ideas and goals, the whole set-up phase can get complicated and time-consuming. With that in mind the project for these techniques is quite simple.

The Project:

Back to the basketball bouncing guy, this time as a combination clay and puppet character.

Making the Images:

In a lot of puppet animation, models are built around articulated skeletons, armatures that can be put into and hold a pose. Armatures can be wire and wood or ball and joint. These armatures can be covered by clay, molded foam or latex, or little custom-made articles of clothing. The character used in this example was made from a widely available sculpting medium called Sculpey. The head and torso were molded over a styrofoam shape to keep them light in weight. The feet were made of solid Sculpey so they would be heavier and help to keep the character stabile.

Timing:

Frame rates, anticipation, squash and stretch, overlapping action—the things that make 2D animation interesting—make Object, Clay, or Puppet animation interesting. It's similar to Cutout animation in its 'physically move the object and take a picture' approach.

The character was placed on a green background stage, bent into an initial posed, and animated frame by frame.

The Results:

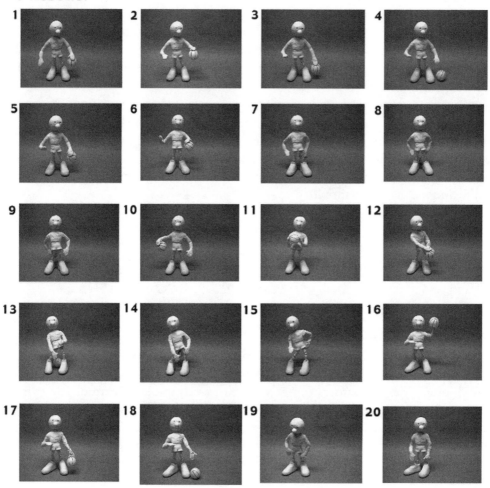

1. The character's initial pose, palming the ball.

2. The character lifts its arm slightly, in anticipation...

3. ...then lowers the arm to dribble the ball.

4. The ball is removed from the character's hand and placed on the 'floor.' The character's hand is posed to receive the ball when it bounces back up.

5. The ball is placed back in the character's hand.

6. The character lifts its arm in anticipation of the next bounce.

7-10. The character bounces the ball behind his back. The ball is on the floor in frame 8.

11-15. The character bounces the ball between his legs. The ball is on the floor in frame 13.

16. The character brings the ball up...

17. ...then lowers it down...

18. ...and drops it.

19. The ball rolls out of the scene...

20. And the character comes to a final pose.

Conclusion

Well, there it is. Experimental animation. Not every single experimental technique was explored, but enough to become aware of the category as a whole and maybe even enough to be curious and...experimental. As a professional, there is a tendency to only be concerned with things as they relate to production. New styles, new tools, and new programs are all viewed in that light. Experimental animation can be a way of expanding your animation experience in a creative and interesting way, returning you to an earlier, student-like frame of mind where it was all new and it was natural to want to experiment with new and different techniques. It's good, on occasion, to take a bit of time to try something out of the ordinary. It could add a bit of inspiration and freshness to your creative life.

APPENDIX

Exercise 1:

Traditional Track Reading

In the Audio chapter a soundtrack was read digitally. This is the same audio track being read but in a traditional film mode, which requires different equipment and preparation.

Like the digital version, this exercise will show you how to read voice over track (where you only need to know the location and timing of individual words or phrases) and lip sync track (where you need to know the phoenetic location and timing of the words and syllables in order to make a character appear to speak).

This exercise uses the same script, storyboard, and audio track as the digital version.

In order to show how to read track for film on mag stripe (film stock), the audio track needs to be transferred to mag stripe. To do this I would:

- Re-open the file in SoundEdit16, version2 (or whatever audio program was used).

- Make sure that the 'levels' window is open (in another program, whatever the name of the window is called that shows you the output level of your audio file).

- Play the audio file and note the output level. If the level is low (-16dB or lower), the file needs to have its level boosted (increased). 'Amplifying' the file will increase the volume. 'Normalizing' the file

will also increase the volume and even out the highs and lows of the file. Experiment and try to get as clean and clear a file as possible that plays back and outputs at between -4dB to 0dB. No matter the program you use, it is always best to start with a clean, clear, strong audio track.

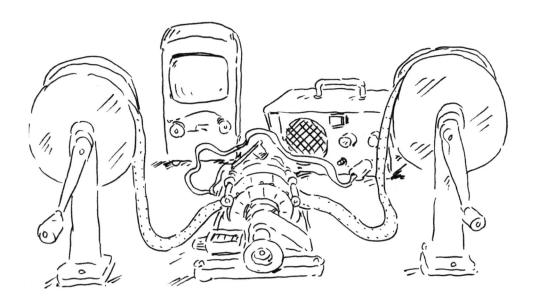

- The audio file will need to be sent to an audio facility that can transfer it to mag stripe. Generally, it's a good idea to contact the audio facility and find out what file formats they can work from and what type of storage media they want you to send the file on (Jaz, Zip, CD, DVD). Some facilities have a website that allows you to post your files. If the file isn't too large, you may even be able to send your files as email attachments.

OK, you sent the file, it's been transferred, and sent back to you. In fact, here's a picture of it.

Here we go.

How To Read a Track

Equipment Needed:

- Synchronizer
- Amplifier
- A cinema scope if you're lining up or viewing a visual film track along with the audio mag stripe.
- A film winder set-up.
- A frame of beep tone.
- Plenty of leader to label the head of the track. In a crunch, you can write your labeling information on tape and adhere it to the leader at the head of the film.
- A permanent marker ('Sharpies' are the brand most often used) for writing labeling information and other permanent info on the film stock.
- A china marker (also known as 'grease pencils') for marking temporary information, like the location of audio information or proposed edit marks on film stock. If you make a mistake or change your mind, you can easily wipe the china markered marks off of the film stock.
- A regular pencil with an eraser for writing on your exposure sheets.
- Your exposure sheets.
- Your script, in order to know exactly what words are being said.

Bare Essential Set-up

The bare essential set-up is essentially the same as the ideal set-up but with a couple of exclusions.

- The cinema scope can be eliminated if you are only reading track or working with audio elements.
- The film winder can be eliminated from the set-up if you work carefully in a clean, roomy environment. Since you're generally working on short sections of track, you can unwind and rewind the track as needed. Be careful not to let the mag track dangle down to the floor. It can get scratched or even stepped on and creased.

Next, you'll need to prepare the track elements. When you prepare the track you are setting it up for eventual transfer to video or use as an element in a sound mix. Your track needs to be set up so it will be in sync with any other elements it will be combined with later on in the production.

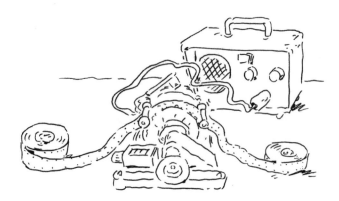

Step 1. Place your mag stripe in the synchronizer, lock it down, place the head on the mag stripe, and advance the mag stripe to the first audio sound. Mark this frame with the china marker. Based on your script or storyboard, you can decide where your audio needs to begin. For this exercise, the first sound will start at frame 5. Roll the mag stripe back 5 frames and make a mark. To the left of the mark, label the frame '1st frame audio' or something like that.

Step 2. Remove the mag stripe from the synchronizer. Insert and lock down your leader stock.

Step 3. Label the head of the leader. You'll need the name of the production and its production number, if there is one, the production company (you), length of production, and the date is nice to include. Shoe size optional.

Step 4. Count off at least 10 feet of leader. This might seem like a lot of leader, especially if you're on a tight budget, but it doesn't have to be the expensive, plastic, or light struck stuff. It can be plain old cheap 'fill' leader. This length of leader is useful to the technicians at the audio or video transfer house when they place the elements on the transfer equipment. It gives a very secure hold, and in case the leader snaps, they don't have to remove the elements from the machine. They can just splice it right there, keeping it in sync and saving...time and money.

Step 5. Somewhere after the 10 foot mark, lock down the synchronizer and draw a pair of lines connected by an 'X' at this frame. This is your start mark. Reset the counter to '0.' Advance 8 feet and lock down the synchronizer again. Draw a pair of lines to indicate a frame again. This frame corresponds to the '2' on a piece of academy leader and is the spot where the 'beep' tone will be placed. Beep tone can be cut from the little adhesive strips that are available or an inexpensive solution

is to use a frame of the tone that is recorded onto the head of your audio track. It works just as well.

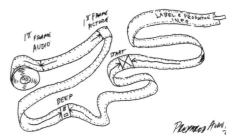

Step 6. Advance 2 more feet, to the 10 foot mark. This is your first frame of film and audio, the beginning of your film. Mark this frame and reset the counter to zero.

Step 7. Splice in your mag stripe here at the first frame of the production, using the '1st frame of audio' mark as your guide.

Step 8. Advance the mag to the first frame of audio again to make sure that it's all lined up correctly. Congratulate yourself. Your track is prepared.

Preparing Your Exposure Sheets

Step 1. Using the basic exposure sheet that has been used throughout this book, take enough sheets to cover the length of the audio track.

Step 2. Number the sheets sequentially.

Step 3. Starting on the first sheet, indicate the seconds on all sheets.

Step 4. Returning to the first sheet, indicate frame numbers. You do this, marking off every 10 frames, by simply adding the correct sequential number in front of the 0 in the far left column.

Step 5. When you're done, the exposure sheets should look like the samples.

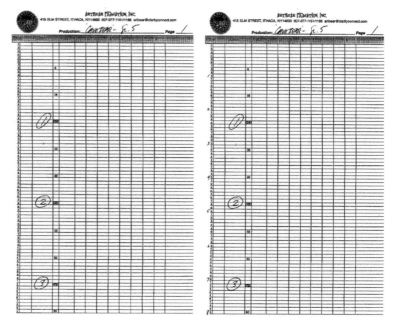

The Technique Used for Track Reading

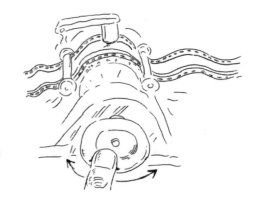

Step 1. Place your thumb on the wheel of the synchronizer and roll it back and forth. You'll hear the audio from your soundtrack being played on the amplifier. Continue to play your track like this until you become accustomed to the way it sounds and you find the speed that gives you the clearest and cleanest audio playback. This is called 'scrubbing' the audio track.

Step 2. At this beginning point, the first frame where the sound appears, write the word on the frame line in the 'dialogue' column of the exposure sheet.

Step 3. Scrub forward to the end of the word and draw a horizontal line representing the last frame of the word or phrase.

Step 4. Draw a vertical line from the written word to the horizontal line.

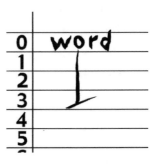

You have just indicated the length of the word or phrase. If you are reading a phrase, you can scrub backwards to the beginning of the phrase and advance through the phrase, indicating the frame that each word or significant word appears. For example, if we were reading a track and came upon the word "word" at frame 10 and it was 4 frames in length, it would be indicated like this:

To read track phoenetically for lip sync or music and effects sync, you follow the same procedure, but with a narrower focus. Instead of finding the first frame of sound for a word and writing down the entire word, you will be finding the first sound of the word and indicating each syllable, breaking the word down into its basic components in order to draw the appropriate mouth movements later. You need not indicate the breakdown of the word with correct spelling. It is better to actually spell things out phoenetically because it makes it a lot easier to read and understand when you

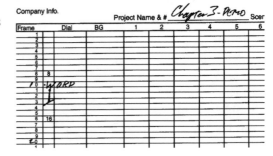

---

are in the throes of animation ecstacy, acting out the mouth movements in front of a mirror when nobody is looking. Or even when they ARE looking. For example, the word 'phoenetics' would be written: F-eh-net-iks or something like that.

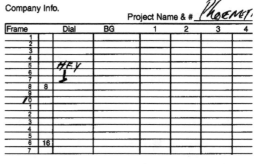

As you roll and scrub through the track, make note of the location of each word or phrase that you need to read. You can make note of these word locations on your script, storyboard, or even on the exposure sheets, but the best place is on the clear part of the mag stripe itself. Use a china marker/grease pencil for this. A simple line or mark of some sort across the clear part of the mag where the words are recorded will act as a guide later when you are doing the actual reading. You don't have to be absolutely accurate because you are doing a preliminary search for the words and phrases.

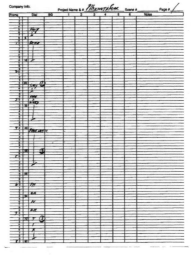

Your absolutely accurate notation will be done when you scrub through and commit the locations to the exposure sheets. You can be as accurate as you like, though, even giving yourself the length of each word or phrase. Using these marks as a visual aid, you won't be working completely in the dark later.

Once you've gone through the entire track and marked your mag stripe or notated your script or storyboard, rewind to the first word at frame 5 and begin the actual track reading.

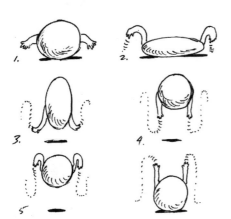

Exercise 2:

Overlapping Action

The animation principle of overlapping action was explained in the Animation chapter. The following exercise will demonstrate it.

ANIMATOR'S NOTE:

A registration trick: These drawings were originally done in a flipbook, so they're registered to each other. In order for you to use them in the upcoming exercise, you'll need them registered, too. If I had thought ahead, I would have placed some sort of registration mark near each drawing, making it easier to lay one drawing on top of the other and line them up. But I didn't, so another static, or at least steady, element in the drawings needs to be used—the shadow. If you Xerox or trace off the drawings, cut them out, position them on animation paper, set up your animation board in order to re-draw them, and line up the shadows to maintain registration.

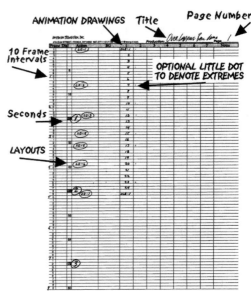

As explained in the Animation chapter, overlapping action occurs when the action of a part of an object or character causes other actions or reactions to follow. The reaction of the arms on the bouncing ball when it squashes is the overlapping action. When the winged/armed ball reaches the top of its jump, the arms trail behind it and arrive at the upper position after the

---

ball starts its descent (overlapping action). The little dotted lines coming from the fingertips of the ball's arms are indications of another principle of animation: 'follow through' and 'paths of action.' An object in motion follows a curving path of action based on its previous position.

This is going to be a 2 second **cycle** using the 6 layout/poses of the Overlapping Action Ball that you somehow managed to redraw in register on animation paper. The exercise is being animated at 24 frames per second.

A reminder: A cycle is a piece of animation that repeats. In this case, it hooks up to the first drawing.

Step 1. Prepare an exposure sheet.

Since the piece is being animated at 24 frames per second, an exposure sheet with 80 frames that has been broken down into 8 frame blocks (1/3 of a second) is being used.

- Number the sheet. Put a title at the top. "Overlapping Ball Exercise" will work just fine.

- Indicate the number of seconds on the sheet. The sheet contains 3 and 1/3 seconds. Even though the exercise is only two seconds, number the entire page, just in case you decide to add to the cycle.

- Indicate the frames. Number the frames on the sheet in blocks of 10 by placing the appropriate number in front of each zero in the column on the left side of the sheet.

Step 2. Timing.

Time the layouts/poses to give yourself a rough idea of how you want to time the animation, where you want the character or object to be, and when you want it to be there.

- Place the layouts on the animation pegs on your animation disk, sequentially, with the lowest number (LO-01) on the bottom, and the highest number (LO-06) on top.

- Using the rolling technique you just learned, roll through the drawings, see the action and imagine it moving through the action in 2 seconds.

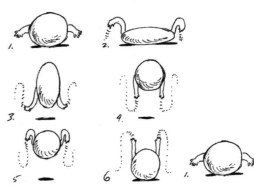

- Develop a little scenario or plan to define and explain the action that you are about to animate. It can help you personalize and enhance the action if you think of it as being a part of a little story.

The scenario for this little exercise is:

- The ball starts at a static pose (1)
- The ball lowers (squashes or, if I'm thinking in more anthropomorphic terms, squats) to gather energy (2)
- Leaps up into the air (3)
- Pauses, because what goes up must come down and in order to come down, you have to stop going up (4, 5)
- Falls back to earth and resumes its original position (6)

ANIMATOR'S NOTE:

An animator will often use a stop watch when flipping and rolling through the drawings, but a useful technique is to count off one second intervals in your head. If you have music training, it will probably be extremely easy. You could, in fact, use a metronome. If you don't have musical training, you need to develop your own internal one second metronome. You can do this by using a watch or other timepiece with a sweep hand that clicks off one second intervals (instead of one that sweeps past the numbers). Watch the sweep hand and count off the seconds with it until you are able to count off a one second interval without the aid of a timepiece. It may take a while to get so good at it that you can do it anytime and anywhere, but the ability does indeed develop.

GARDNER'S guide to Creating 2D Animation in a Small Studio

- Using a stop watch or your own internal metronome, roll through the drawings, imagine them moving through the action in two seconds, but this time, actually time them and indicate them on the appropriate frame in your exposure sheet. The timing that I personally arrived at is indicated on the exposure sheet below.

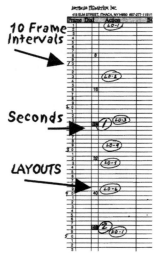

These poses were done in the style of the actual animation, so they don't need to be redrawn or cleaned up (in traditional cel animation production, these would be considered xerox ready). They are extremes; key positions of the animating character or object.

Step 3. Identification on the exposure sheets.

Indicate the name of the animation with initials and number the animation in the sheets.

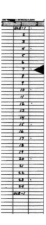

Numbering: This animation exercise is 2 seconds long at 24 frames per second, on 2s, so there will be 24 drawings.

Pre-numbering your sheets is a way of seeing where you are at any given point in relation to the overall amount of time of the piece. It also gives you a visual representation of the overall time of the piece and can help you visualize the timing.

Naming: I used OLB (for Over Lapping Ball), but there are other, less arbitrary and more helpful ways to name a series of animation files; ways that can help you identify it later. You can create an 'initialing system' using the numerical correspondences of the alphabet (A=1, B=2, C=3, etc.) that tells you:

- The scene number
- The layer the animation is intended for
- Which character is in the file

This is useful if you are looking for a particular scene on a hard drive with difficult to see or non-existent picture icons. It is also useful if you want to be able to just pick up a folder of animation and know what it contains without having to thumb through it. For example, the first drawing of a bear character in Scene **3** that works on Layer **1** would be BCA-01. Don't use too many initials, though. There is a limited amount of space in your exposure sheet.

Step 4. Identification on the artwork.

Remove the layout drawings from the pegs and number the layout poses with the number that corresponds to the frame they are on.

- Layout-01=OLB-01
- Layout-02=OLB-07
- Layout-03=OLB-12
- Layout-04=OLB-15
- Layout-05=OLB-17
- Layout-06=OLB-20

If you're using a pen to number the drawings, have a bottle of correction fluid handy or use a pencil, because you might change your mind. Sometimes, your ideas about the timing of a scene change or you have new ideas when you get further into it. **ALSO,** draw an arch or some sort of mark near, over, or around the extreme drawing's numeral. This mark will help you distinguish your extreme, key poses from your breakdowns and inbetweens. If you need or want to alter your animation in any way, you will more than likely be altering your extremes/key poses. Even if you're extending the amount of time that an action will take, you'll need to use your extremes/key poses to accurately add further breakdowns and inbetweens. A distinguishing mark of some kind will help you find the important drawings easier. Make sure the mark isn't too large so it doesn't show up in the field of view.

Step 5. Start animating.

This is where you do your actual animation timing on drawings called *extremes*. Remember: layouts are indicators of where the animation needs to be at a particular instance in time. How it arrives there is up to the animator.

Animator's Note:

In this section, while I'm setting up and drawing the breakdowns and inbetweens, I'm jotting down explanations for some of the choices I'm making. Some of the decisions are purely technical; a straight inbetween drawing that needs to be exactly in the middle of a pair of other drawings should be drawn as close to that position as possible. A lot of times, though, a breakdown or inbetween drawing can be drawn *favoring* one extreme or another, meaning that instead of being drawn as an exact representation of the middle position of an action, it is closer in appearance to one of the extremes. I'd better

insert a drawing to explain that a bit better so you don't have to go thumbing through the Animation chapter: *A straight breakdown would be a representation of the exact middle position between two extremes.*

A breakdown that favors an extreme is drawn closer to the position of the preceding or following extreme.

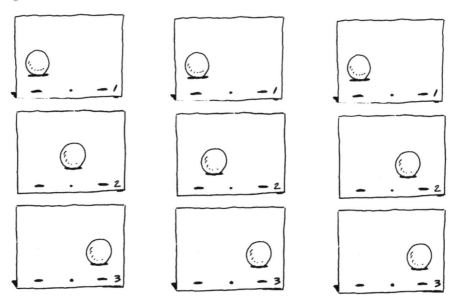

Drawing a breakdown or inbetween that is straight in the middle or favoring one side or the other affects the visual flow of the action. Straight inbetweens give the appearance of a straight and simple flowing action. Inbetweens that favor one side or the other help to create the illusion of 'slowing-out' of a position or 'slowing-in' to a position. When you need to slow-in using straight inbetweens, you simply add more drawings to one side or another of the breakdown. You would indicate that on your preceding extreme's timing chart like this:

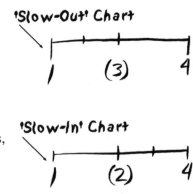

Note that you will be adding drawings to your animation and therefore extending the time of the entire animated piece that you're working on. Let's suppose, however, that you are working to a pre-recorded audio track and are restricted to the amount of time your animated piece can be and you cannot add additional frames. This is a situation where you would use the *favoring* technique. When you want to create the illusion of a drawing slowing-in or slowing-out, you simply draw the object or character physically closer to one extreme or the other in the breakdown.

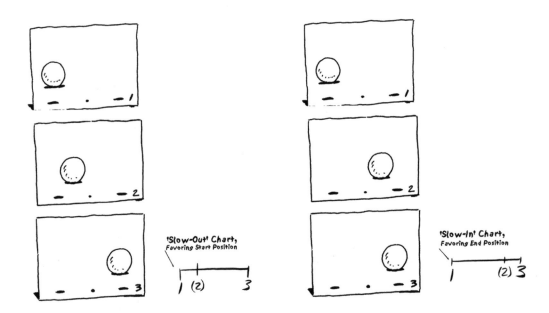

These techniques are not restricted to the situations that have been given as examples. Most breakdowns are not EXACTLY in the middle of two extremes and therefore are favoring one side or the other, anyway. When working as an animator, you make the choices of where and when you need to use the various approaches and techniques. As you explore, experiment and develop your own variations to different techniques; you'll wed them to your personal likes, dislikes, and opinions and develop your own personal style. Having said that, I will get back on track.

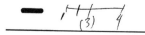

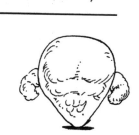

- Place the starting point drawing, OLB-01, on the pegs.

- Place the next drawing, the second key pose and destination position, OLB-07 on the pegs.

- Flip back and forth between OLB-01 and OLB-07 to check and analyze the action. Doing this can show you where to make additions, variations, or improvements to the animation.

Notice that the ball just sort of falls or lowers into the second position. It might make a livelier piece of animation if there was another pose between the two positions. An anticipation pose.

- Remove OLB-07 from the pegs and replace it with a blank piece of paper. (OLB-01) is still on the pegs on the bottom.

- Make the additional extreme drawing of the ball, standing a bit taller, sort of taking a deep breath before it squats to gather its energy for the leap into the air. The overall time of the entire animation exercise piece is pretty short, so this anticipation pose shouldn't be too elaborate. I've indicated a simple re-shaping of the character, since it's going to pass through the pose as opposed to actually striking the pose.

If it was a longer piece, a more fun or elaborate pose could have been something like this:

- Number the new extreme PLB-04, the midway point (time wise) between the starting pose and the destination pose.

- Flip back and forth between OLB-01 and OLB-04 to see the action. We need to 'ease-in' or 'slow-in' to the action because we're coming from a static pose to an action pose. This means there should be more drawings near or, favoring, OLB-01 than OLB-04. Make a chart on OLB-01 to indicate the timing.

The timing chart represents the two extremes, OLB-01 and OLB-04 with OLB-03 as the *breakdown* and OLB-02 as the *inbetween*.

ANIMATOR'S NOTE:

Charts are generally written at the bottom of the page, outside of the field of view, way down near the pegs. They can also be drawn in a vertical format near the outer edges on the page.

This keeps your animation area clear for later Xeroxing onto acetate for ink & paint. If you're working digitally, it's not such a huge problem because artwork is a lot easier to clean up. Also, charts are generally done on the extreme drawing that you are coming FROM. For example, the chart for a drawing between a Drawing-01 and a Drawing-03 would be written

on Drawing-01. While charts are very valuable as reminders of how you want to approach your timing, they are absolutely necessary if you are handing out your animation to an assistant who will be doing the breakdowns and inbetweens. They are the clearest indication of your timing desires.

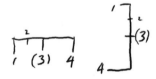

The animation drawings that are being referred to here in the text are all two digit numbers, meaning that even though the actual number may be within the 0-9 range, it is referred to as 00-09. The '0' at the front of the single digit numbers is a placeholder that helps keep your files in order when you're working *digitally*. The actual numbering that you do on your paper drawing can be done in a normal manner.

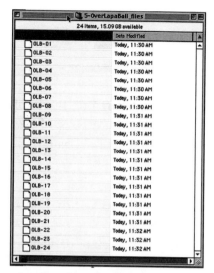
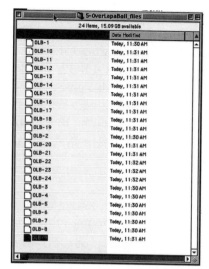

- Put the drawings back on the pegs in animation order and continue with the timing, animating, and breaking down. OLB-01 goes on the bottom, the new extreme, OLB-04, goes in the middle, and OLB-07 goes on top. Roll the three drawings to see the overall action.

- Flip back and forth between OLB-04 and OLB-07 to see and analyze the action. Since OLB-07 is a pose where the ball character is actually pausing to gather its energy for the big leap, I'd like to 'slow-in' to this pose and spend a bit more time with it. Make a chart on OLB-04 to indicate this timing decision.

The chart shows that OLB-04 is the extreme you're coming out of, OLB-07 is the extreme you're going in to, with OLB-05 as the breakdown (mid-point drawing), and OLB-06 as the inbetween drawing.

To continue:

- Place OLB-12 on top of the stack. OLB-12 is the pose where the top of the ball has pretty much reached its highest point, but the rest of it has just completed the process of freeing itself from the bonds of Mother Earth's 2D gravitational umbilicus.

- Place a blank page on top to draw the next breakdown.

- Flipping back and forth between OLB-07 and OLB-12, analyze the action and imagine where the breakdown should be drawn. I'm 'seeing' a breakdown that is stretching upward into the leap while the bottom of it is still resting on the ground. Since the ball has some inertia to overcome, getting off of the ground and getting up into the air, it should 'slow-in' to the breakdown pose, which means there should be more drawings favoring OLB-07, the drawing it's coming from than OLB-12, the drawing it's going in to. This should also give a nice bit of 'snap' to

the action occurring between OLB-10 and OLB-12. Therefore, the breakdown will be OLB-10. Indicate this timing on the chart that you make on OLB-07:

OLB-10 is the breakdown with OLB-08, OLB-09 and OLB-11 as the inbetweens.

- Draw OLB-10.
- Place OLB-10 in its correct order in the stack and make a chart on it as a reminder of the upcoming inbetween, OLB-11s position.
- Place OLB-12 on top of OLB-10 and roll through the stack of drawings to view the action so far.
- Place OLB-15 on top of OLB-12, followed by a blank sheet of paper to draw the next breakdown on.
- Flip back and forth between OLB-12 and OLB-15 to see and analyze the action.

I chose to do two things with this pose. First, knowing that the ball is reaching the high point of a motion and will be coming to a stop before coming down again, I want to 'slow-in' to the static pose, and later, 'slow-out' of that static pose when the ball falls into its downward motion. This will make an overall smoother bit of motion. The arms, however, are a different matter. The arms are going to pass through this pose, ending up in the pose in OLB-20, before hooking up to the starting point pose in OLB-01. I think it would be nice if the arms could move at an even pace from OLB-12 to OLB-15, which means that the drawings need to be broken down in *thirds* instead of in *halves* (mid-points). The chart for this kind of breakdown/inbetween action looks like this:

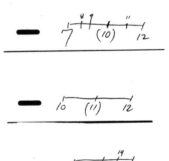

- Write the chart on OLB-12, place the drawings and the blank sheet of paper in order, and draw the breakdown drawing, OLB-13.
- Place OLB-13 in correct order, with OLB-15 next on the stack, followed by OLB-17 on top. Add a blank sheet of paper on top and you're ready to proceed.

- Flip back and forth between OLB-15 and OLB-17 and draw the inbetween OLB-16. The ball is starting back downward. I drew the top of the ball very close to OLB-15 while drawing the bottom of the ball directly inbetween the two extremes. The arms are drawn as a pretty straightforward mid-point/inbetween. Since this was a simple, single inbetween, I didn't mention anything about writing the chart on OLB-15. If the inbetween was going to favor one or the other of the extremes, however, it would have been a good idea to write out the chart.

- Place OLB-16 in correct order, place OLB-17 on top, followed by the next extreme, OLB-20 and a blank sheet of paper.

- View and analyze the action by flipping back and forth between OLB-17 and OLB-20.

Ha Ha! You thought I was going to say 'flip back and forth between OLB-17 and OLB-20 to view and analyze the action' didn't you?

- The ball is falling and therefore gathering speed in the area of space between OLB-17 and OLB-20 so the action would be 'slowing-out' of the OLB-17 pose into the OLB-20 pose. The breakdown drawing would be OLB-19. To illustrate the fact that you can be creative and flexible in your placement of breakdowns and inbetweens, I've drawn a breakdown where the bottom of the ball is drawn at the mid-point between OLB-17 and OLB-20 and the top of the ball favors (is drawn closer to) the previous pose, OLB-17 (it's going to be a bit elongated). The chart to write on OLB-17 looks like this:

Close up of OLB-20 chart.

- Draw the breakdown, OLB-19.

- Place OLB-19 in its correct order in the stack, place OLB-20 on top of it.

- Remove the entire stack from the pegs, take the starting point drawing, the drawing we will be hooking up to, OLB-01, from the bottom of the stack and place it on top of the stack, followed by a blank sheet of paper.

- Flip back and forth between OLB-20 and OLB-01. An object falling from this height (any height, really) can be squashed to some degree after it comes in contact with the ground. OLB-20 is touching the ground, and has regained its original shape as it begins its 'squashing phase.' So, we know that the breakdown drawing needs to be a squashed version of the ball similar in shape to OLB-07 (the extreme where the ball is squatty and gathering its energy earlier on). So there's the shape of the drawing, but what about the timing? I've decided upon a slow-in to the squashed pose and a straight inbetween and therefore a crisper, eager return to the original pose. The breakdown drawing will be OLB-23. Also, it should be mentioned that the new drawing, OLB-23, could also be considered a new extreme drawing since it is a significant new pose for the ball/character.

- Draw OLB-23 as the squashed pose and write a chart reflecting this timing on OLB-20.
- Place the completed OLB-23 in its correct order, on top of OLB-20. If you like, you can place OLB-01 on the very top and roll through the action to get an idea of the concluding action and hook up. If not...
- Place OLB-23 on top of OLB-20, followed by a piece of paper.
- Flip back and for the between OLB-20 and OLB-23 to analyze and view the action. Since it was decided that OLB-23 is a slow, squashy pose and needs to 'slowed-in' to, OLB-21 is the breakdown. OLB-22 will be the inbetween.
- Place OLB-23 in its correct order in the stack, place OLB-01 on the very top and roll through this upper portion of the stack to view the action. When you're done looking at the action, remove the drawings from the pegs, reverse the order of the drawings so that OLB-01 is on top and OLB-23 is on the bottom, in preparation for the final drawing phase, *inbetweening.*

INBETWEENING NOTE:

This is the last drawing phase in the animation chain of events. Since the technique for drawing one drawing between a pair of other drawings is the same for breaking down and inbetweening, I'll try not to be totally redundant and remedial in giving the steps involved.

- Place OLB-01 on the pegs. Note the chart to know which drawing you'll be doing and where it will be positioned.
- Place OLB-04 on top of OLB-01, followed by a blank sheet of paper.
- Flip back and forth and draw the breakdown, OLB-03.

GARDNER'S guide to Creating 2D Animation in a Small Studio

- Remove OLB-03, place it on top of OLB-01 followed by a blank sheet of paper.
- Flip back and forth and draw OLB-02.
- Place OLB-01, 02, 03, and 04 on the pegs in ascending order (OLB-01 on the bottom, OLB-04 on top) and roll through the drawings to see the action.
- Note the chart on OLB-04, then place OLB-07 on top of the stack followed by a blank sheet of paper.
- Flip back and forth between OLB-04 and OLB-07 and draw the breakdown, OLB-05.

Take a look at the arms as you flip back and forth. Notice that they are sort of rubbery and not stiff and jointed. Here's where the 'lines of action' that were mentioned earlier in the chapter come into play. The arms are sort of like a ribbon or rope being whipped through the air. The extremes set a path that the breakdowns and inbetweens follow. Also, remember that things animate in an arching motion. The hands are a subtle example of this type of action.

- When OLB-05 is done, place it in order on top of OLB-04 followed by OLB-07 and a blank sheet of paper.
- Flip back and forth between OLB-05 and OLB-07 to draw the inbetween, OLB-06. OLB-06 could actually be drawn favoring OLB-07 instead of a straight inbetween. Favoring the OLB-05 extreme may give a smoother action. This is an instance where you could experiment by doing the inbetween two different ways. It's a little more work, but it will give an additional bit of experience and an opportunity to see how variations in approach look.
- When OLB-06 is completed, put the drawings in order on the pegs. Place OLB-10 and a blank sheet on top of the stack. Note the chart on OLB-07 (you're slowing out of OLB-07, so the breakdown is OLB-09.
- Flip back and forth and draw the breakdown OLB-09. Note the arms again.

OLB-10 has a definite path/shape to follow on OLB-09.

- When OLB-09 is completed, remove OLB-10 from the stack, place OLB-09 on top of OLB-07, followed by a blank sheet of paper.
- Flip back and forth between OLB-07 and OLB-09 to draw the inbetween OLB-08.

When completed, place the drawings in order on the pegs and continue to draw the inbetweens. The inbetweens are all straightforward, single drawing inbetweens from OLB-10 to OLB-20, so I won't bother continuing the "place drawings in order, place a blank sheet of paper on top, flip back and forth and draw the inbetween" instructions. By now you've got the idea.

Assistant Animator's Note:

At some point the stack of drawings on the pegs will grow too tall. As you flip and roll the drawings, they will slip off of the pegs because they are too close to the top of the peg. Just take the stack of drawings off of the pegs and start fresh. When you remove the stack, take OLB-01 from the bottom of the stack and place it on the bottom of the undone stack because it is the drawing that you will end up hooking up to.

Some notes on the inbetweens:

- OLB-11 can be stretched a bit extra by leaving the bottom of the ball on, or very near, the ground and drawing the top of the ball at the mid-point.
- OLB-18 can be stretched a bit, too, with the top favoring OLB-17 and the remainder done as a straight inbetween.
- OLB-21. False alarm. I thought there might be something to note in this 'slow-in' situation, but it is actually very straight forward and un-noteworthy.

That's it. Two seconds of animation that made use of, or at least alluded to, some of the information in the chapter.

Working With the Animation Files

This animation exercise was done on 2s at a frame rate of 24 frames per second, therefore, 12 drawings equals one second. I just thought I'd mention that again to set up the next bit of stuff. In a program that allows you to enter single frames into your animation sheets like Animation Stand or Flash, you will enter your individual frames in their appropriate layer and frame, matching the paper exposure sheets. Check and refer to your frame numbers often as you build your sheets to make sure that your timing is correct and the correct files are being entered into the sheets. If you're working with a timeline in a program that is more of a video editing, effects, or compositing program like Premiere or After Effects, things are a bit different. In spite of the fact that the default medium that the programs are used for is Quicktime movies, you can still work with single frames of images like animation files. The single frame images are imported into the program as a 'Sequence of Images' into a layer of the timeline.

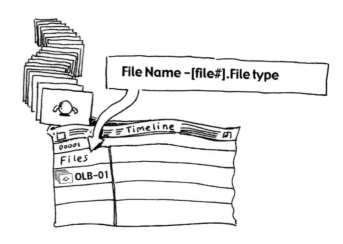

File Name -[file#].File type

If artwork is 'imported' into a timeline as a 'sequence of images,' it will be on 1s and therefore twice as fast as it should be. To view it at the correct speed, you will need to adjust your output frame rate. A couple of ways to do that are:

- Change the frame rate to 12 fps. 12 drawings played at 12 frames per second equals one second.

- Use time stretching. 12 drawings, or one half second of action, on 1s, stretched out to one second puts the animation on 2s.

Exercise 3:

Making a Platform for an iBot Platform

The stand attached to the iBot camera covers an area of about 3 and 3/4" by 3 and 3/4 quarter inches. I just happen to have a piece of foam core that is 6" wide by 4 1/4" tall and 1/2" thick so I'm going to use that as the platform to attach the camera to. I'm using a tripod with a detachable, interchangeable camera mount. To prevent any damage to my existing mount, I purchased a spare.

- The mount is placed in the center of the piece of foam core with the side that attaches to the tripod facing you (up).
- Apply pressure to the mount making it flush with the surface of the board and mark off the area around the mount.
- Scoop out the marked off area about a quarter inch deep.
- Place mounting squares to the side of the mount that will come in contact with the foam core.
- Secure the mount to the foam core with duct tape.
- Make sure the camera is facing forward and secure the iBot camera to the foam core with duct tape.

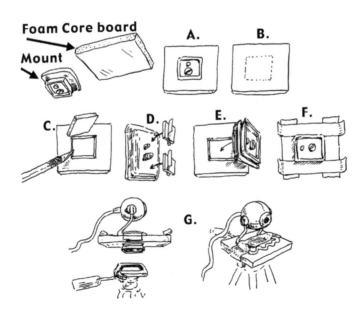

GARDNER'S guide to Creating 2D Animation in a Small Studio

GLOSSARY

Acetate
The clear plastic material from which animation cels are made.

Action safe
The area of an image that action takes place in that will fit safely within the frame of the TV screen when broadcasted.

Ambient sound
The natural background sounds in an environment. For example, the sound of waves crashing at the beach or the roar of traffic in the background in an urban environment.

Animatic
A very simply animated version of a storyboard. The artwork used to make the storyboard is animated by mechanical means (pans, zooms, and the like) instead of full animation.

Animation stand
The combined equipment used to shoot animation onto film or video; the camera, tabletop, compound, lights, etc.

Anti-aliasing
Smoothing the rough looking and 'blocky' edges of a curved bitmap line.

Audio recording
Sessions where audio track are recorded for a project.

Audio time code
The audio signal used to generate and enable sync.

Backgrounds
The layer of artwork that represents the environment in which a scene is taking place.

Bar sheets
Forms with lines representing frames of film or video with an adjacent music staff used for writing music notation in relation to film frames. Similar to exposure sheets.

Betacam
A popular, broadcast quality analog video tape format.

Billable
In animation production, a term that means you can invoice the client for an additional amount of money above and beyond the budget for any changes that they make after giving their written, 'signed off' approval.

Bitmap
Digital images composed of pixels that are resolution dependent and become rough and 'blocky' (aliased) when enlarged.

Bottom lights
The unit of lights used in a camera stand used to light artwork from underneath.

Breakdowns
Drawings placed between animation extremes used to further define and time the animation.

Bristol board
A variety of thick paper/thin board used for making background artwork.

Budget & administration phase
The phase of production dealing with the financial aspects of the project.

Camera person
The person that operates an animation camera stand; a camera operator.

Camera stand
The same as an animation stand.

Cast
In the context of this book, to audition and choose a person to perform audio work for a project.

Cel
Transparent acetate sheets used as the media for transferring animation drawings.

CGI (computer-generated images)
Animation that is drawn in a computer program; art that is totally generated by the computer like vector graphics or 3D graphics and animation.

Checker
In traditional production, the person who makes sure that all of the art elements exist and work together correctly before a job is shot onto film or video.

Composite
The combination of elements using transparency prior to digital output (the combined layers form a composite). Also the word for the phase of production where this is done.

Concept
The overriding and defining idea behind a project.

Contract
The written, protective, and binding agreement signed by the Supplier or Producer (you) and the Client (them).

Cycles
Segments of animation that can repeat like walk cycles, waving cycles.

Design
The graphic style of an animated piece.

Digital animation
Animation generated by a computer. Also commonly used to describe any animation manipulated digitally.

Disposables
Items used in a production that are consumed or disposed of.

Dry media
Any non-liquid art medium or coloring tool; pastels, crayons, color pencils, and charcoal are examples.

Drying rack
A rack with several narrowly spaced shelves used to hold animation cels during the ink & paint phase of production.

Dubbing
To duplicate an audio or videotape; to add audio to a film or video; or to add audio to a film or video in another language.

Exposure sheets
Forms that have lines representing frames of film or video used to direct and organize an animated scene.

Extremes
The primary action defining drawings done by an animator.

Field guide
Generally a plastic grid used to define the area the animation camera will film and show.

Film to tape transfer
A session where animation or any film element is transferred to videotape.

Final camera
The stage in traditional production where the completed project, in color, is sent to animation camera to be shot on film or video for final delivery.

Flipping
A technique for viewing drawn animation. You can flip a stack of animated drawings or flip back and forth between drawings as you draw.

Hand-out money
Working capital or money that will be used to acquire supplies, equipment, or retain the services of workers.

Inbetweens
The final drawings in a sequence of animation that fill in and smooth the action.

Ink & Paint
The phase of production where color is added to the animation drawings in an animation production.

Inking board
A Plexiglas or masonite board with animation pegs attached used when tracing animation artwork onto acetate cels (inking).

JPEG
A standard image compression mechanism. JPEG compression is "lossy," meaning that the compression scheme sacrifices some image quality in exchange for a reduction in the file's size.

Kill fee
A 10-20% payment that can be claimed if the client cancels the job at any point, usually before the storyboard is completed.

Laying back
Combining a mixed version of the audio elements with the video is called laying back the audio to the video. The session is called a layback session.

Layouts
Drawings based on the storyboard, that are used to guide the animator, showing character poses, background and prop information, and camera directions.

Leica reel
A storyboard shot onto film or video and synced to an audio track. In digital production, the storyboard can also be scanned.

Light box
A light unit generally used by photographers to view slides, but also used in animation as a light source for tracing.

Mag stripe
A variety of film stock with two stripes of audio tape applied to its surface used as an audio medium in film production. A variation is called 'full coat' where the entire surface is audio tape.

Music rights
Legal permission to use a piece of music in a production.

Output formats

The specific format that a project will be put in for viewing. For example, Quicktime, Video for Windows, animated GIF, and Flash (SWF), for video, and tape, CD, AIFF, etc. for audio.

Overage

Costs of changes that are above and beyond the original, contracted, agreed upon amount. Overages are 'billable.'

Overlay

The top, held layer of the artwork in a scene of animation.

Oxberry stand

The same as an animation stand or a camera stand. Oxberry refers to a specific brand of animation camera stand.

Pantone

A brand of printing ink, color paper, swatches, and other color-related items used in the graphics industry.

Path of action

The path that a character travels in a scene.

Peg strips

Punched strips of paper or card stock that can be taped onto paper or cel in order to register it.

Pencil test

An action test of the animation shot on film or video, usually in black and white.

Persistence of vision phenomenon

The blending of rapidly moving images that creates the illusion of motion.

PICT

Another type of image format. A PICT file can contain black and white, color, or grayscale information, as can a TIFF or EPS file. A PICT image uses a language called QuickDraw to render the graphic. QuickDraw is limited in precision and cannot contain complex curves or special text effects, making a PICT image a bad choice for imagesetting to film or plate. A PICT file is acceptable for laser printer or low resolution output.

Polycons

Small lidded plastic containers used to hold paint.

Pose or Leica Reel

The storyboard of an animated film that has been recorded onto film or video and synced with an audio track. Gives a nice general idea of a production's flow.

Protective cels

A cel placed on top of finished artwork to prevent damage.

Quicktime
A primary and popular digital video format.

Registration line
A line traced from a background or static object used to depict the point where a character comes into contact or interaction with it.

Resolution
The measurement of a digital image using pixels as the measuring unit.

Right of first refusal
An agreement with a client that states that should a project that you produced become lucrative leading to further productions, they are required to offer the production to you and your company first.

Rolling
A technique for viewing animation while it's on the pegs being drawn. Similar to flipping, but in sequence instead of back and forth.

Scratch track
A rough audio track used for reference or timing.

Script
Scripts are stories intended for film or video written in a way that describes the action and scenes and dialogue of the piece.

Scrubbing technique
Moving the play head back and forth through a video or audio track.

Signing off process
The protective procedure of having your client give their approval of the final versions of various production elements like design, script, and pencil test, in writing.

Sound editor
A person that edits, syncs, arranges elements, and otherwise works with audio elements.

Sound mix
Combining and blending the separate audio elements together before combining the audio with the visual element.

Speed lines
Lines drawn behind a character or object to denote speed or motion.

Still photo rights
The legal permission required in order to use photographs in a production.

Storyboard

The sequence of drawings that visualize a script or idea. The storyboard acts as a guide for the production.

Straight ahead animation

A simple form of animation that flows forward without extremes.

Supervised transfer

Video transfer that is attended, guided, and directed by you, the producer, and the client.

Syncing

Sync. Simultaneous occurrences. Things happening at the same time. In the case of film or animation, the correct lining up of the audio and the visual elements.

Thumbnail storyboard

A small-sized, rapidly and roughly drawn storyboard, generally used as a graphic shorthand visualization in the margins of a script.

TIFF

An industry standard file format developed for the purpose of storing high-resolution bit-mapped, gray-scale, and color images.

Timecode

A signal encoded onto videotape used for reference, time, and sync.

Timeline

A schedule that includes delivery dates for each stage and approval dates for each stage.

Title safe

The area of an image containing titles that will fit safely within the frame of the TV screen when broadcast.

Track reading

Breaking an audio track down into individual sentences, words, or phonetic sounds and writing the information onto exposure sheets.

Traditional animation

Animation that is drawn on paper in the original, traditional manner.

Traditional production

An animated production where the animation is drawn on paper, transferred to cel for ink & paint, then shot on film or video.

Triacetate

The technical name for the plastic material that cels are made from.

TV cutoff

The area of an image that is cropped by the frame of a TV screen when broadcasted.

Underlay
The bottom, held layer of the artwork in a scene of animation.

Unintentionals
Overages or additional work added to a project by a client oversight or subterfuge. "Oops, we accidentally added an additional amount of work that we don't want to pay for."

Vector art
Artwork based on vectors, that is independent of resolution, therefore, scalable without displaying a 'blocky,' bitmap appearance.

Vectors
The enclosed areas that contain the shape and color data that make up a piece of vector art.

Voice over
Narration or other vocal audio track without an onscreen actor or source.

Workstation
A computer and desk set-up.

Xeroxing
The general term for photocopying. Similar to Kleenex being used for any facial tissue. In animation terms, the process of transferring the drawn animation image onto an acetate cel.

GARDNER'S guide to Creating 2D Animation in a Small Studio

RESOURCES

Cartoon Colour Company

9024 Lindblade Street
Culver City, CA 90232-2584
800-523-3665
310-838-8467
310-838-2531 fax

Animation Supplies: paint, cels, paper, cel punches, pegbars, discs, and anything else you may need. They even have stopwatches for timing animation.

Cartoon Supplies.com

214-597-0968
801-751-2612 fax

Paper, tables, punches, discs, etc.

Alan Gordon Enterprises

1430 North Cahuenga Blvd.
Hollywood, CA 90028
213-466-3561
213-871-2193 fax
www.A-G-E.com

FAX brand animation discs, registration devices, production equipment, drawing tables. The big stuff.

Lightfoot Ltd.

36125 Trans Ct.
Temecula, CA 92592
909-693-5165
909-693-5166 fax
www.lightfootltd.com

Pencil test systems, workstations, punches, pegbars, equipment, and software.

MAC Edge

1 Washington Ctr.
Dover, NH 13820
603-750-5100
603-750-9998 fax
www.macedge.com
contact: Kent Kicza
(kent@macedge.com) Computer equipment, peripherals, VAR support.

BIBLIOGRAPHY

Blair, Preston. *Cartoon Animation*. Tustin, CA, Walter Foster Art Books, 1995.

Canemaker, John. *Winsor Mckay - His Life and Art*. New York, Abbeville Press, 1987.

Culhane, Shamus. *Animation from Script to Screen*. New York, St Martin's Press, 1988.

Finch, Christopher. *The Art of Walt Disney - From Mickey Mouse to the Magic Kingdoms*. New York, Harry N. Abrams, Inc., 1973.

Graphic Artists Guild. *Graphic Artists Guild Handbook: Pricing and Ethical Guidelines - 11th Edition*. Graphic Artists Guild, 2003.

Halas, John and Rider, David. *The Great Movie Cartoon Parade*. New York, Random House, 1988.

Katz, Steven D. *Film Directing Shot by Shot*. Studio City, CA, Michael Wiese Productions, 1991.

Laybourne, Kit. *The Animation Book: New Digital Edition*. New York, Three Rivers Press, 1998.

Newton, Dale and Gaspard, John. *Digital Filmmaking 101*. Studio City, CA, Michael Wiese Productions, 2001

Perisic, Zoran. *The Focal Guide to Shooting Animation*. London and New York, Focal Press, 1978.

Taylor, Richard. *The Encyclopedia of Animation Techniques*. Philadelphia and London, Running Press, 1996.

Index